BURNT OFFERINGS

International Contributions to Burnt Mound Archaeology

Compiled by Victor Buckley

Wordwell Ltd—Academic Publications
9 Herbert Lane
Dublin 2

Editor—Fmer Condit

First published 1990
Wordwell Ltd
9 Herbert Lane
Dublin 2
Republic of Ireland

ISBN 1 869857 07 0

Typesetting—Wordwell Ltd/The Type Bureau
Printed by Craftprint Ltd
Jamestown Rd
Inchicore
Dublin 8

The publisher acknowledges the generous financial contribution of the Office of Public Works, Dublin, and Historic Buildings and Monuments, Scotland, towards publication costs.

Contents

PART 1
Irish Contributions

PART 2
Scottish Contributions

List of Figures

List of Plates

ACKNOWLEDGEMENTS

The publication of this book on recent researches in burnt mound archaeology follows the holding of the first international Burnt Mound Conference at Trinity College, Dublin, in October 1988.

I wish to thank the participants in the conference not only for giving lectures on the day and contributing to constructive debate on this type of monument but also for the production of their papers for publication. I would also like to acknowledge the support of my colleagues in the Archaeological Survey, Office of Public Works, particularly David Sweetman, in fostering my interest and suffering my enthusiasm in this project. Special thanks are given to the ESB and in particular Larry Donald for generous financial support of the conference, and to National Irish Bank and in particular Jim O'Neill (Balbriggan) for their support in dealing with the financial affairs of both conference and publication.

This publication is entirely funded as a joint venture by the Office of Public Works and Historic Buildings and Monuments Scotland. Special mention must be given to John Mahoney, Chairman of the Commissioners of Public Works in Ireland, and Patrick Ashmore, (AOC) Historic Buildings and Monuments Scotland, who both had the foresight to recognise the importance of this work and its international implications and gave it their full support.

Initial text editing of the Scottish material was by John Barber and Chris Russell-White and final text editing by Emer Condit. The cover was designed by Catherine Mac Conville and Brenda McArdle. Redrawing of original drawings (Figs 8–10) by Brian Ronayne. I would like to thank Nicholas Maxwell, without whose continued efforts the arduous process of publication would have been much tougher, and lastly my wife Laureen, who has supported this project throughout.

FOREWORD

The study of burnt mounds or fulachta fiadh in Ireland has a long tradition (Hackett 1884–5) which led to the production of a major and 'definitive' publication (O'Kelly 1954). This encapsulated the results of survey, excavation, scientific dating, historical literary sources and their interpretation, coupled with a survey of British parallels for this type of monument. Since then, partly owing to the fact that 'definitive' and 'substantive' publications tend to detract from further research because 'it has all been said', little has been added to our overall knowledge of this enigmatic site type. This is also due to the nature of excavations of fulachta fiadh which, because they are mainly rescue excavations, tend to concentrate on the central area of the site, the trough or pit or hearth area. Similarly in Scotland the publication of the excavations of Orcadian burnt mounds at Liddle and Beaquoy (Hedges 1974–5) led to an increase in our knowledge of this type of site but also a consequent lack of interest in their place within a wider prehistoric settlement framework. Work on 'boiling mounds' had also been carried out in Wales (Cantrill and Jones 1911), England (Layard 1922) and the Isle of Man (Cubbon 1965), and on the Continent work in Scandinavia was being conducted on prehistoric 'skärvstenshögar' and in northern Germany on 'splittersteinhügel'.

Increased archaeological field survey in Ireland in the 1980s has shown that there are a minimum of 4000 fulachta fiadh in the country, with over 2000 examples in Country Cork alone, approximately 1 per 3.7 sq. km (Ó Drisceoil 1988). This would make fulachta fiadh the most common prehistoric site type in Ireland, almost outnumbering all other prehistoric sites. O'Kelly (*op. cit.*) had postulated, using the literary evidence, a long life-span for the use of this type of site, from the Bronze Age through to the sixteenth century AD. However, accurate scientific dating of a randomly excavated sample (Brindley and Lanting, this volume) has shown a predominance of second-millennium BC dates for their use.

Fulachta fiadh or burnt mounds, which carry no historical or mythical connotations in popular folklore as do 'fairy forts' in the case or ringforts or 'Diarmuid and Grainne's Beds' for megaliths, and which are small and tend to be amorphous in shape whilst situated in prime areas for land reclamation, are at the forefront of the destructive processes of that same land reclamation. Therefore their study takes on a renewed importance in the 1990s when increased work of this kind may wipe out these important pointers to our prehistoric settlement in north-west Europe.

In 1987 the idea of fulachta fiadh being used primarily as cooking sites was contested (Barfield and Hodder 1987) and the hypothesis of bathing and their use as a primitive sauna bath put forward. This paper was to lead indirectly to the holding of the first international conference on burnt mound archaeology, held in Dublin in 1988. At that conference the various results of the study of this site type in recent years were examined — surveys and distribution, excavation, dating and specialist analysis. These papers are presented here in an attempt to take the study one stage further and at least bring up to date the pioneering work carried out in Ireland, Scotland and elsewhere in the late nineteenth and early twentieth centuries. The book is divided geographically to allow researchers to retrieve the maximum information from within their own national boundaries, but must be seen as an overview of a site type which transcends those boundaries to form one of the crucial markers in our understanding of north-west European prehistory.

REFERENCES

BARFIELD, L. and HODDER, M. 1987 Burnt mounds as saunas, and the prehistory of bathing. *Antiquity* **61**, 370–9.

CANTRILL, T.C. and JONES, O.T. 1911 Prehistoric cooking in South Wales. *Archaeologia Cambrensis* **9**, 253–65.

CUBBON, A.M. 1965 Clay head cooking-place sites: excavation of a group of coins. *Proc. Man Hist. Antiq. Soc.* **91**, 40 51.

HACKETT, W. 1854–5 Proceedings and Transactions. *Jour. Roy. Soc. Antiq. Ir.* **3**, 59–61.

HEDGES, J.W. 1974–5 Excavations of two Orcadian burnt mounds at Liddle and Beaquoy. *Proc. Soci. Antiq. Scot.* **106**, 39–98.

LAYARD, N.F. 1922 Prehistoric cooking places in Norfolk. *Proc. Prehist. Soc. East Anglia* **3**, 483–98.

Ó DRISCEOIL, D.A. 1988 Burnt mounds: cooking or bathing? *Antiquity* **62**, 671–80.

O'KELLY, M.J. 1954 Excavations and experiments in ancient Irish cooking-places. *Jour. Roy. Soc. Antiq. Ir.* **84**, 105–55.

PART 1

IRISH CONTRIBUTIONS

1. SURVEYS

Fulachta fiadh in County Cork

D. Power

CORK ARCHAEOLOGICAL SURVEY
In September 1982 the Office of Public Works commissioned the Department of Archaeology, University College Cork, to carry out a rapid survey of all known and suspected archaeological sites in County Cork. This fieldwork has now been completed and a Sites and Monuments Record (SMR), detailing the nature and location of some 14,608 archaeological sites in the county, was launched in October 1988. Over the next few years a series of regional inventories will be published, giving brief descriptions of every known monument in the county, on the lines of those already published by the Office of Public Works for counties Louth, Monaghan and Meath.

FULACHTA FIADH
The most numerous single monument type listed in the SMR is the 'fulacht fiadh': 1914 of these sites were located and recorded in the field by the Cork Archaeological Survey, while a further 564 are listed in previous fieldwork reports but only located by townland (see below). The nature of this work did not allow for instrument surveying, but a written and photographic record was made of each site and measurements taken using hand-held tapes and measuring rods. In the case of the more numerous monument types which exhibited a degree of morphological conformity a pro forma sheet was designed on which specific information is recorded for each site. This information, easily collated by computer, allows us to examine the general physical perimeters of surviving features.

GENERAL FEATURES
Of the 1914 sheets filled out, 1100 (57%) recorded spreads of 'burnt material' and 814 (43%) recorded mounds of 'burnt material' of some shape or form. This 'burnt material' consisted of fragments of heat-shattered stones mixed with charcoal-enriched soil; the material is very

Fig. 1 — Percentages of shapes of mounds, Co. Cork.

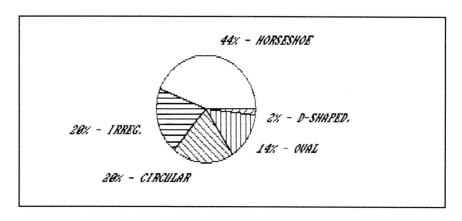

characteristic and immediately recognisable to an experienced fieldworker.

Nearly half of all surviving mounds (Fig. 1) were of the classic kidney or horseshoe shape (44%), with 20% circular, 14% oval and 2% D-shaped. In fact, it is likely that many of the latter are weathered profiles as nearly all mounds over a metre in height are kidney-shaped.

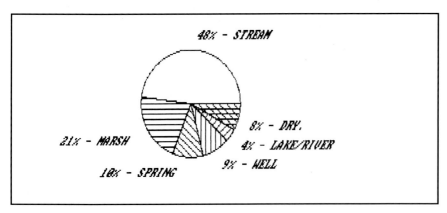

Fig. 2— Percentages of water sources, Co. Cork.

In terms of water source (Fig. 2) there is a clear preference for location beside a stream (48%). Marshy or poorly-drained areas (21%) were also popular, and often the sites were encountered as small dry islands in wet areas. Very few sites were recorded in bogland as such, and those that were are partially covered by the bog.

The measurements of the mounds themselves show a limit in range of heights, widths and lengths. No mounds had a height greater than 2m nor a length or width larger than 28m, with one exception: this was 3.38m high, 45m wide and 38.5m long. It therefore seems reasonable to conclude that fulachta fiadh in County Cork tend towards a kidney-shaped mound of a limited size range, and located beside a stream or in a wet, marshy area. (Plates 1 and 2).

DISTRIBUTION PATTERN

When we look at the overall distribution of fulachta fiadh in the county we immediately see a preferential distribution with noticeable concentrations in the East Muskerry and Duhallow areas, but we must first detail some factors which are clearly affecting the present known distribution.

In County Cork fulachta fiadh are marked only on the third edition of the Ordnance Survey (OS) 6" maps (published in the 1930s and 1940s). But this was only a partial cover and excludes a large section of the south-west of the county (see Fig. 3). These third edition OS maps depict 1023 fulachta fiadh, but a further 891 sites have been located by subsequent fieldwork (nearly all by CAS). However, the average number of new sites added to maps on which fulachta fiadh were already depicted was 10.3 per map, whereas only an average of 1.2 sites were added to maps on which no sites are depicted. Of the 153 OS 6" maps covering County Cork 65 (42%) depict fulachta fiadh, but sites are now recorded for 120 (77%). To what exact extent fieldwork has compensated for the partial coverage by third edition OS 6" maps is impossible to show, but our impression is that there are no heavy concentrations in the south-west in any case. A programme of sampled field-walking might prove this.

We must also allow for the bias of earlier fieldwork. Most notable in this context are two MA theses submitted in the 1930s to the Department of Archaeology, UCC. Both Michael Bowman's work on the barony of Duhallow (NW Cork) and P.J. Hartnett's in East Muskerry (mid Cork) list hundreds of fulachta fiadh not marked on the OS maps. Bowman mentions sites in nearly every townland in his area but gives no more precise information regarding their location. These two areas have the highest known concentrations in the county. Is this a coincidence?

A convenient way of examining the overall distribution pattern is to plot the number of sites known per 6" map, with an area adjustment along the

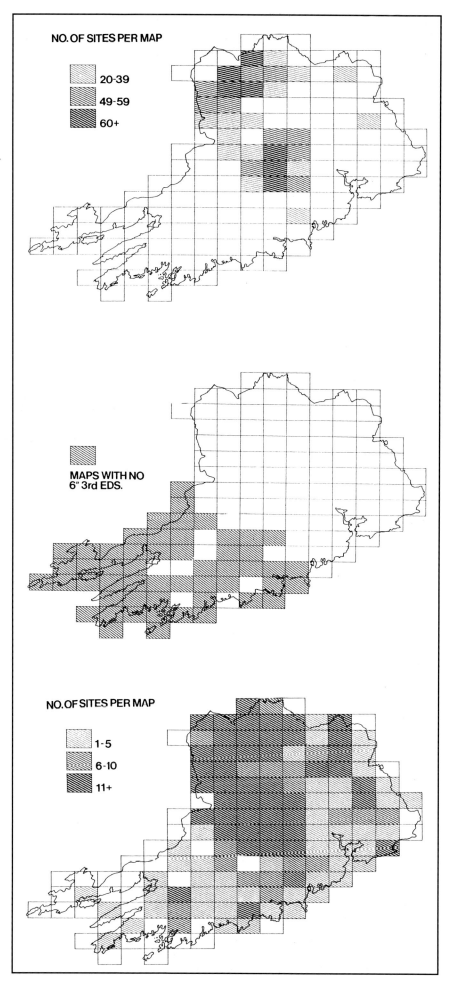

Fig. 3 —Distribution maps showing high and low density groupings, Co. Cork.

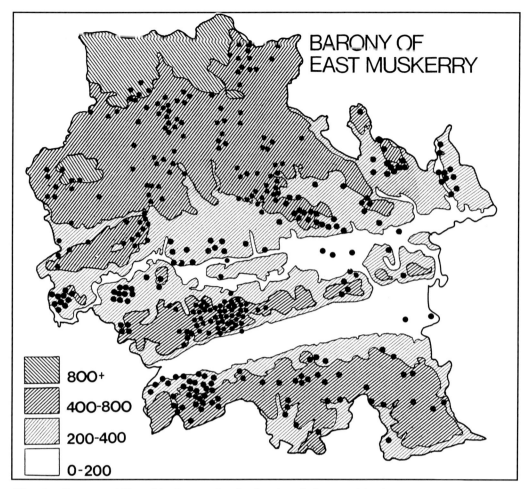

Fig. 4— Barony of East Muskerry, distribution in relation to altitude.

county boundaries and coastline where only part of the map is used. The picture becomes clearer if we plot the higher density maps (Fig. 3). This shows two areas of high concentration in the north-west (Duhallow) and in the middle (East Muskerry) of the county. If we plot the sites in East Muskerry (Fig. 4) on a relief map of that barony a number of interesting facts emerge. This is an area of east–west sandstone ridges (anticlines) with intervening limestone valleys (synclines) carrying the Lee and Bride rivers, while to the north the land rises towards the Boggera Mountains. There seems to be a clear avoidance of the river valleys with sites clustering along streams draining the sandstone ridges. There is also a noticeable falling-off of sites when the land rises above the 800ft contour. This preference is very evident if we plot all known sites against the altitude ranges at which they occur (Fig. 4).

Once again the fulacht fiadh is shown to be a creature of predictable habit, having a clear preference for some areas over others and preferences within areas for particular habitats.

It is not proposed to do more here than simply point out these facts. The Cork Archaeological Survey have created a large data base of information about fulachta fiadh which should be of use to anybody interested in examining these sites in more detail.

REFERENCES

BOWMAN, M. 1934 Placenames and antiquities of the barony of Duhallow. Unpublished MA thesis, National University of Ireland.

HARTNETT, P.J. 1939 Survey of the antiquities in the barony of East Muskerry, Co. Cork. Unpublished MA thesis, National University of Ireland.

Ó DRISCEOIL, D. 1980 Fulachta fiadha: a study. Unpublished MA thesis, National University of Ireland.

Plate 1 —Fulacht fiadh in Camerbirrane, West Muskerry, Co. Cork.

Plate 2— Fulacht fiadh in Gortnaglogh, Duhallow, Co. Cork. Ranging rods mark "horns" of mound.

Preliminary observations on the distribution of fulachta fiadh in County Kilkenny

T. Condit

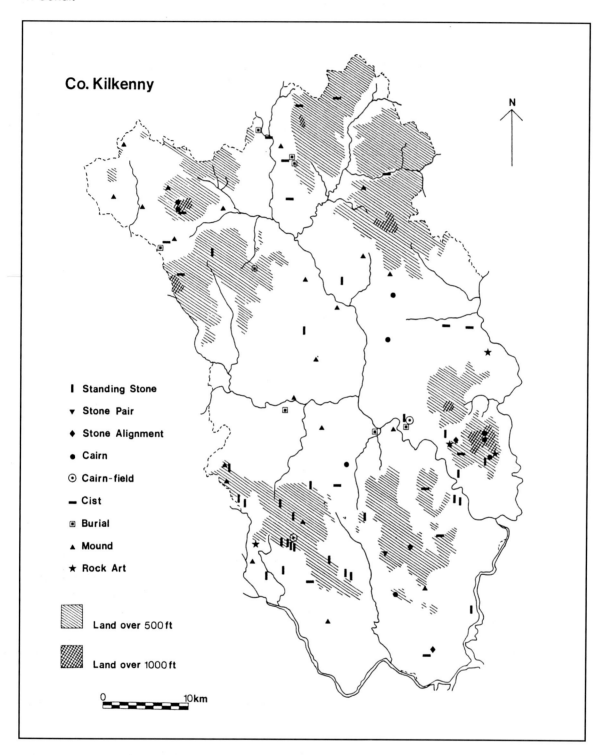

Fig. 5— Bronze Age monuments in Co. Kilkenny.

Speculation on the function of fulachta fiadh currently ranges from the traditional view that they are cooking sites (O'Kelly 1954), possibly only employed on a seasonal basis, to the most recent alternative theory that they may have been used as saunas or sweathouses (Barfield and Hodder 1987). While the primitive form of immersion heating associated with fulachta fiadh can be shown to have been used in the Early Bronze Age, and although documentary sources indicate the employment of

18

similar methods through the Early Christian and medieval periods, the majority of radiocarbon dates from sites sampled indicate a 'floruit' period in the Middle and Late Bronze Age (Brindley and Lanting, this volume). The following article aims to display the distribution of fulachta fiadh in County Kilkenny and compare it with the distribution of other Bronze Age monuments.

The Leinster county of Kilkenny is situated on the south-eastern fringes of Ireland's central plain and is considered one of the country's most prosperous agricultural areas. The principal rivers of the county are the Suir, the Nore and the Barrow, the Suir forming the southern boundary with County Waterford, the Barrow forming the eastern boundary with counties Wexford and Carlow, and the Nore dissecting the northern half of the county. Kilkenny comprises three distinct topographical units. The limestone uplands of the Slieveardagh hills and the coal-bearing Castlecomer Plateau lie on the north-west and the north-east respectively. To the south-west are the uplands of the Slievenamon range, complemented on the south-east by the granite mountain of Brandon Hill. Sandwiched between these two areas of upland is Kilkenny's rich lowland area or 'Golden Vein' (Conry 1974), renowned for its diverse agricultural potential.

Bronze Age monuments display a more or less even distribution across the county (Fig. 5), with particular concentrations on the uplands of Clomantagh Hill in the north-west, on the southern uplands around Garryduff on the west, and on Brandon Hill on the east overlooking the Barrow. Aerial photography, in particular the recording of more than eighty ring-ditches (most likely the remains of ploughed-out barrows), suggests that the central area of the county and the northern Nore valley were settled in the Bronze Age much more densely than conventional field survey would suggest (Fig. 6). A significant feature associated with at least six ring-ditch complexes is the appearance of parallel linear ditches (c. 70–100m apart) which are most likely the remains of prehistoric field systems.

FULACHT FIADH DISTRIBUTION

As early as 1853 William Hackett noted the existence of fulachta fiadh in County Kilkenny. He then postulated that the '-duff' suffix in place-names such as Garryduff and Ballyduff originated in 'the cinder era'. He goes on to say: 'This is so well known here [County Kilkenny], that if you ask a countryman why is Garryduff so called, he will answer — "Yerra then, I don't know, if it isn't by reason of the folach fia that's all over it" ' (Hackett 1853-4). While Hackett's etymological suggestions seem unlikely there seems no doubt that fulachta fiadh would have been recognised by at least some of the inhabitants of County Kilkenny in the last century.

Almost one hundred years later, with the introduction of more scientific approaches to archaeological sites, O'Kelly noted that the greatest numbers of fulachta fiadh occurred in counties Cork and Kilkenny (1954, 144). He noted over thirty examples in County Kilkenny from a list compiled by and subsequently published by Ms Ellen Prendergast (1955). Today there are over 250 known locations of fulachta fiadh in County Kilkenny. The distribution map (Fig. 7) shows the locations of individual sites and groups comprising anything between two and ten. The map is based on information collected by the Sites and Monuments Record Office (Gibbons et al. 1987) and on preliminary fieldwork carried out by Victor Buckley of the Archaeological Survey of Ireland.

As is customary, virtually all the sites are located close to streams and streamlets. At this stage, even allowing for the differential recognition of fulachta fiadh by fieldworkers and the different areas concentrated on by the various sources, a number of significant clusters can be recognised. In the north-west of the county the sites are located on the rich limestone grazing lands north of the Slieveardagh mountains. One group at Rathlogan, near Johnstown, can be shown to be composed almost

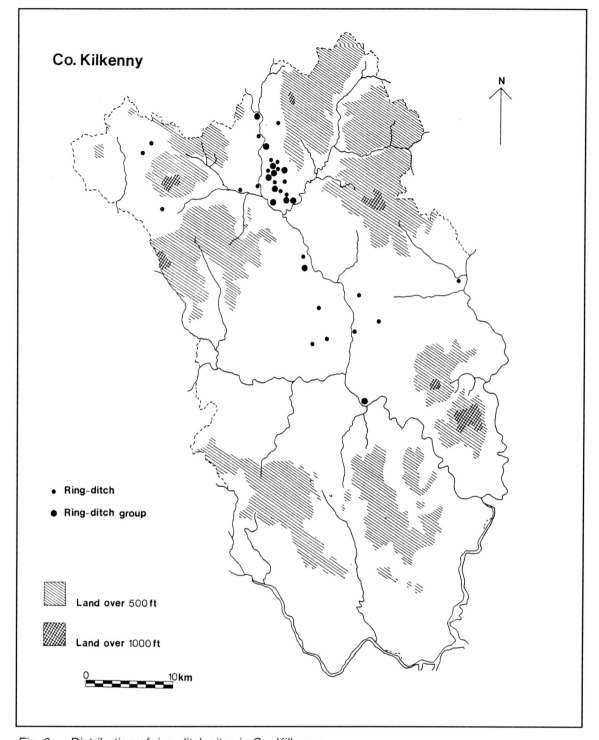

Fig. 6 — Distribution of ring-ditch sites in Co. Kilkenny.

entirely of burnt limestone, thus fitting into the growing recognition of the use in fulachta fiadh of limestone, a rock type initially thought unsuited for cooking purposes (O'Kelly 1954, 144–5).

In the north-east of the county a large number of sites can be seen in the vicinity of Castlecomer, an area in which no great number of other Bronze Age monument types has yet been found. The easternmost cluster of sites within this group is situated on the Coal Measures which form the Castlecomer Plateau. The glacial drift in this area is composed of a mixture of Carboniferous shales, sandstones and flagstones, considered to be favoured rock types in fulachta fiadh. However, the gley soils of the area contribute to poor natural drainage and are unsuitable for tillage. As regards modern land usage, it is only with artificial drainage and spreading of lime and fertiliser that these soils would have the potential for grass

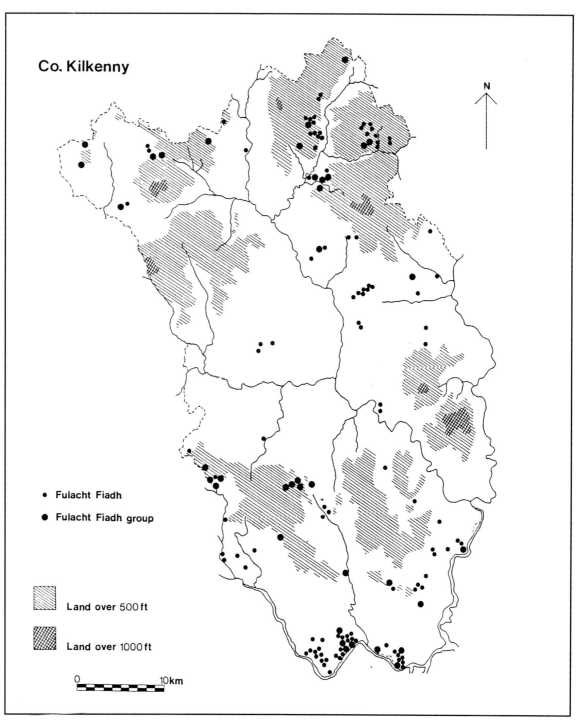

Fig. 7—Fulacht fiadh distribution in Co. Kilkenny.

production. Even then, poor drainage would contribute to rush infestation, leaving only the drier periods of the summer as the grazing season (Conry and Ryan 1968, 4). While poor agricultural conditions may explain the general absence of other Bronze Age monuments from this area, the presence of fulachta fiadh suggests, perhaps, the seasonal use of cooking sites as perceived by O'Kelly (1954, 132). More knowledge concerning the Bronze Age environment would be required before any more weight is attached to the transhumance or hunting associations of fulachta fiadh.

In the central area of Kilkenny, an area intensively cultivated from medieval times, a number of fulachta fiadh have been noted, mostly in isolated pockets of marginal land. Following recent aerial reconnaissance in the area by Michael Gibbons and the author, many amorphous soilmarks, most likely ploughed-out fulachta fiadh, were noted. This suggests that detailed recording from the air, followed by field survey, would be required before the number and locations of fulachta fiadh in this area could be more accurately established.

Another significant grouping of fulachta fiadh occurs on the lower slopes of the south-western uplands. This contrasts with the absence of fulachta fiadh in the area of Brandon Hill. However, this absence may have more to do with the non-friability of granite, the dominant rock type of the Brandon Hill area, and thus the non-recognition of sites in the locality (Buckley, this volume). The dense cluster of fulachta fiadh at the southernmost end of the county is concentrated in an area dominated by Old Red Sandstones. It partly reflects intense fieldwork carried out in this particular locality by the teachers' group in the 1970s (National Museum of Ireland Topographical files). However, like the concentration of sites on the Castlecomer Plateau this cluster of fulachta fiadh is conspicuous in that it occurs in an area where virtually no other Bronze Age monuments are recorded. This, in turn, also raises the question of how many more fulachta fiadh would turn up if a survey of the same intensity were carried out throughout the county.

A number of fulachta fiadh have been excavated in County Kilkenny, at Muckalee and Webbsborough (Prendergast 1955), at Ballyhimmin (Prendergast 1977), at Catstown (Ryan, this volume) and Clohoge (O'Flaherty 1987). The only sites with radiocarbon-dated material are those from Catstown. However the dates cannot be considered to reflect the date of construction and/or period of use of the site (Ryan, this volume). As with most other excavated fulachta fiadh, artifactual evidence is very scarce. The Webbsborough site threw up some interesting artifacts: two virtually identical 'spheres or marbles' (diam. 2.3cm) of baked fire-clay were found at the bottom of the cooking pit (Prendergast 1955, 6–7; Cherry, this volume). The similarity of these to balls found mainly in passage grave contexts led the excavator to consider the possibility of Early Bronze Age origins for fulachta fiadh. Whether or not the Webbsborough marbles are good parallels for passage grave balls, we should always be cautious of dense objects which may have sunk to the bottom through the soft organic fill of a cooking trough.

Overall the fulacht fiadh is the predominant Bronze Age site type in County Kilkenny and it could be said that our knowledge of the sites themselves and how they fitted into Bronze Age society is inversely proportional to their numbers. Indeed, if the results of this preliminary survey are anything to go by, we could be looking only at the tip of the iceberg in terms of numbers of sites. More palaeoenvironmental evidence would go a long way towards helping our appreciation of fulachta fiadh. In the meantime, the common occurrence and apparent simplicity of these sites present a very intriguing mystery for archaeologists to unravel.

ACKNOWLEDGEMENTS

I wish to thank the Commissioners of Public Works for permission to use the data from the Sites and Monuments Record for Co. Kilkenny. Thanks also to my colleagues in the SMR office (Michael Gibbons, co-director, Mary Tunney and Olive Alcock) and finally to Victor Buckley who introduced me to fulachta fiadh and provided me with strange fare from the wooden bath in his garden.

REFERENCES

BARFIELD, L. and HODDER, M. 1987 Burnt mounds as saunas and the prehistory of bathing. *Antiquity* **61**, 370–9.

CONRY, M. 1977 Kilkenny's 'Golden Vein': its soils, land-use and agriculture *Irish Geog.* **7**, 19–28.

CONRY, M. and RYAN, P. 1968 *Soils of Co. Carlow.* Soil Survey Bulletin no 17, National Soil Survey of Ireland. Dublin. An Foras Talúntais.

GIBBONS, M., MURPHY, M., ALCOCK, O. and CONDIT, T. 1987 *Sites and Monuments Record for Co. Kilkenny.* Dublin. OPW.

HACKETT, W. 1854–5 Proceedings of the Royal Society of Antiquaries. . *J. Roy. Soc. Antiq. Ir* . **3** 59–61

O'FLAHERTY, B. 1987 Fulacht fiadh, Clohoge, Co. Kilkenny. In R.M. Cleary, M.F. Hurley and E.A. Twohig (eds), *Archaeological excavations on the Cork – Dublin gas pipeline.* Cork Archaeological Studies No. 1.

O'KELLY, M.J. 1954 Excavations and experiments in ancient Irish cooking-places. *J. Roy. Soc. Antiq. Ir.* **84**, 105–55.

PRENDERGAST, E. 1955 Pre-historic cooking places in the Webbsborough district. *Old Kilkenn Review* **8,** 1–10.

PRENDERGAST, E. 1977 A fulacht fiadh at Ballyhimmin, near Castlecomer. *Old Kilkenny Review*, new ser., **1**, no. 4, 264–7.

Early Bronze Age fulachts on Valencia Island

Frank Mitchell

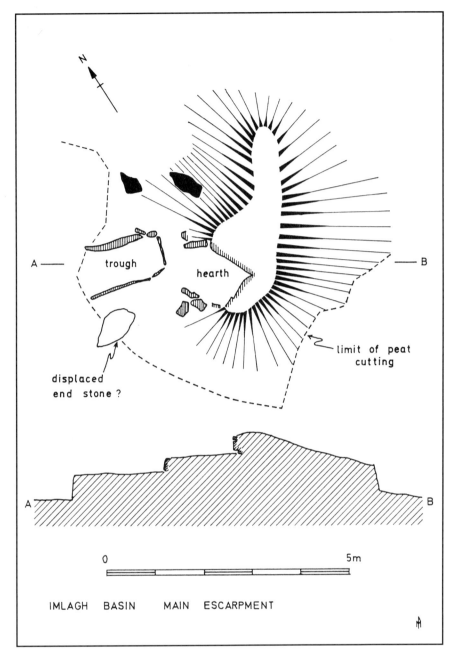

Fig. 8—Plan of Early Bronze Age Fulacht fiadh, Imlagh Basin.

Valencia Island, in south-west Kerry, is a small island, 11km long and 3km wide, lying north-east/south-west, with high ground at each end. On its north-west side there is a low-lying peat-filled basin, the Imlagh Basin.

The high ground at the north-west end of the island has two tops, Geokaun (270m) and Kilbeg Mountain (175m). Each has a wedge tomb at about 130m on its southern slope.

About midway along the south side of the island and 1km east of the bridge to Portmagee there is a low rise in ground, ending in Reenarea Point. I call the rise the Reenarea Rise; it was an attractive site for early settlement, with several antiquities, though it is now buried by peat. A drainage trench in an area where some peat had been cut away showed 30cm of highly humified peat, then 15cm of charcoal and burnt stones — the margin of a fulacht — and then 40cm of woody *Phragmites*-peat on mineral soil. The charcoal was of various woods, oak, willow/poplar and hawthorn, and a sample of small-vesselled wood gave a ^{14}C age of 3800 ±

24

100 years BP (I/15100).

In the central part of the Imlagh Basin there is an elongated rock rise, formerly completely buried by peat but now partly re-exposed by peat-cutting; I call it the Main Escarpment. On its south slope, towards its eastern end, the cutting has revealed a fulacht (Fig. 8). Here a muddy peat formed first, then *Phragmites*-peat, and then brown humified peat. After 200cm of peat had formed, a stone fulacht, with slab-lined trough and fireplace of smaller stones, was erected on the bog surface. Burnt stone and charcoal accumulated around to a thickness of 25cm. There were some flecks of vivianite. The charcoal was of stems of ling (*Calluna vulgaris*) only, which suggests that there was no large firewood available in the locality; it was dated to 3250 ± 100 BP (I/14083). Further peat

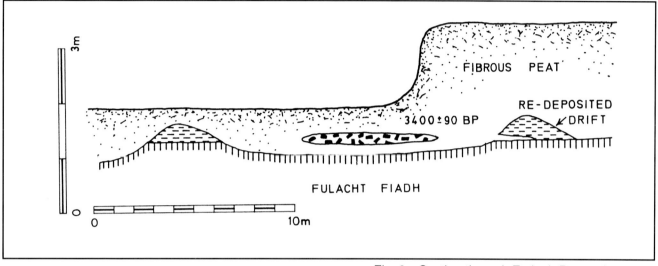

Fig. 9—Section through Emlagh Bog embayment

growth then swallowed up the structure; recent peat-cutting has now exhumed it. As a result the fulacht stands up on a pedestal of uncut peat surrounded by cut-away bog. It deserves protection as a national monument.

A short distance across the Basin to the east there was in pre-peat times a low-lying area with springs; this has now been filled with peat in what I call the Emlagh Bog Embayment. This was a favoured locality for early settlement, and peat cuttings show various antiquities. These include a wall dated to 4760 ± 100 BP (I/14206), presumably Neolithic, a cobble trackway dated to 3930 ± 90 BP (I/14208), an Early Bronze Age date, and a stone hearth at the same level.

A short distance to the east of the springs a bank of peat, still 2m high (Fig. 9), formed the boundary of a field from which peat had been removed. In 1984 a trench had been dug along the base of the bank, and this revealed a small area of charcoal. After a thin layer of peat had formed on the mineral soil, two small pits or trenches, about 5m across, had been dug. Low piles of upcast, about 3m across, rested on the basal peat. In the northern trench there was a thin layer of stones and charcoal; the charcoal, which had a ^{14}C date of 3400 ± 90 BP (I/13912), was composed exclusively of twigs of ling, again suggesting the absence of large firewood in the locality.

At the west end of the Imlagh Basin, under the north slope of Bray Head, which forms the western extremity of the island, there is thin bog, in what I call the Bray West Bog Embayment. There are springs at the base of the slope, and in 1984 a drainage trench was cut north through the peat. At three points in the trench small lenses of stone and charcoal, the remains of hearths (Fig. 10), were intersected. One lens (No. 1) was covered by about 130cm of humified peat; it was about 3m across and 50cm thick. A sample, again of ling charcoal, from its base had a ^{14}C date of 3160 ± 90 BP. Below the lens there was 60cm of *Phragmites*-peat and then 50cm of amorphous peat on mineral soil. Pollen of plants of cultivation were associated with the hearth

There are no finds of Early Bronze Age objects from Valencia itself, but there is an old record of a hoard of flat copper axes from the vicinity of

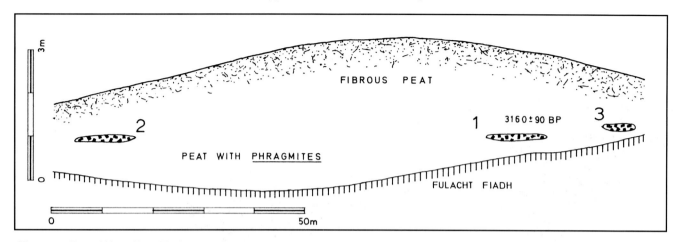

Fig. 10—Bray West Bog Embayment.

Cahersiveen on the mainland nearby. The island has two wedge tombs, a trackway dated to 3900 BP, a hearth, and four cooking sites with stone and charcoal, ranging in date from 3800 to 3200 BP. The sites are widely distributed over the island, and vary in elevation from sea-level to 140m.

These features are described in detail in my recent publication *Man and environment in Valencia Island* (Royal Irish Academy, 1989). The radiocarbon dates by Teledyne Isotopes have not been calibrated. I am indebted to Phelim Manning for the drawing of the plan of the fulacht on the Main Escarpment.

2. EXCAVATION

The excavation of a fulacht fiadh at Coarhamore, Valentia Island, Co. Kerry

John Sheehan

INTRODUCTION

While large numbers of fulachta fiadh have been recorded in Munster in recent years it has also become increasingly apparent that the distribution of this monument type is both sparse and sporadic on the peninsulas of south and west Kerry. Just over a dozen such sites were recorded during the field survey of the Dingle Peninsula (Cuppage 1986, 73), while just over twenty examples have been noted to date during an on-going programme of field survey on the somewhat larger Iveragh Peninsula. A significant number of the latter occur on Valentia Island (Mitchell, this volume), one of which — under threat from drainage operations — was excavated by the author in the spring of 1988.

Valentia Island lies just off the north-western coast of the Iveragh Peninsula (Fig. 11). One of the larger offshore Kerry islands, it measures 11km in length and 3km in width, its longer axis lying NE–SW. The Coarhamore fulacht fiadh is situated approximately midway along the southern shore of the island, overlooking Portmagee Channel. It is located on the 'Reenarea Rise', a small but distinctive physiographical unit described and discussed by Mitchell in his study of Valentia (Mitchell 1989, 82–84). Comprising a broad promontory delineated on the north by a gully, this slightly elevated, peat-covered area breaks the uniform seaward slope that characterises most of the southern side of the island. The peat on the Rise has been cut over in places and survives to a maximum depth of 2m. The area is now largely used for rough grazing.

The slight elevation of the Rise together with its coastal location probably enhanced its attractiveness to potential settlers. Before the initiation of blanket-peat growth here, dated by Mitchell to 5630 ± 100 BP, it contained oak woods (Mitchell 1989, 82). The prehistoric settlement of the Rise is at present evidenced by an intra-peat fulacht fiadh dated to 3800 ± 100 BP (Mitchell, this volume), and by traces of an undated but pre-peat stone wall nearby (Fig. 11, c and d). A ringfort at Reenarea Point represents an element of the Rise's Early Historic settlement (Fig. 11), as does a now-levelled circular stone hut site with an associated souterrain (Fig. 11). With the exception of the site which forms the subject of this paper (Fig.11a), and of its apparently associated hut site (Fig.11b), the remaining indications of settlement on the Rise — such as several areas of cultivation ridges and a number of rectangular house sites (Fig. 11f) — appear on surface evidence to be post-medieval or early modern in date.

THE EXCAVATION

Before excavation the Coarhamore site was seen to consist of a slab-lined trough, rectangular in plan, which was located immediately beside a broad, low, turf-covered mound (Fig. 12).[1] A modern drain ran close to the site on the south, while a few metres to the north rose a fairly prominent rock knoll. A poorly preserved and partly peat-buried hut site, circular in plan, occurred 17m north-east of the fulacht fiadh. This structure was not investigated.

Initially an area centred on the stone trough, 20 sq. m in extent, and a 1m-wide trench through the mound were de-turfed for excavation. The latter was positioned where the mound material appeared to be deepest. As the nature of the site was revealed, the area to be investigated south of the trough was extended. The excavated areas totalled 38 sq. m.

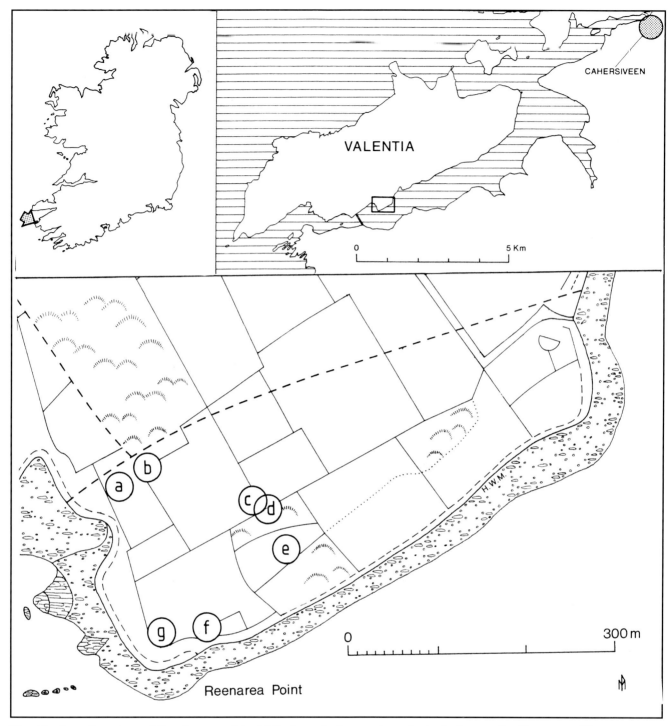

Fig. 11—Location map of Coarhamore fulacht fiadh and other archaeological sites on the Reenarea Rise.

The trough (Fig. 13, profiles C–D, E–F)

The trough was accommodated in a pit excavated into a somewhat uneven surface composed of very fibrous brown peat (layer 11) which underlay all the archaeological deposits noted on the site. The pit was somewhat irregular in plan, measuring 2.74m x 2.32m, and was of uneven depth, shallowing out towards the north-east. Its precise limits on the east were not determined, but elsewhere it featured rather steeply-cut sides.

The trough was constructed towards the S end of the pit and was formed of regular sandstone slabs. Its internal dimensions averaged 1.40m NW–SE x 0.95m NE–SW. Single slabs laid on edge formed its ends and NE side, while the unequal length of the SW side stone required a small, vertically-disposed slab to be positioned at its S corner. The slabs averaged 0.65m in height and 0.12m in thickness and, with the exception

28

of the NW end stone, rested directly on the bottom of the excavated pit. The stability of the trough was strengthened by the inclusion of a number of stones in the pit fill (layer 6), particularly a slab which inclined against its S corner and a number of stones positioned against the external bases of its NE side stone and NW end stone. A large rectangular slab (1.30m x 0.85m) formed a floor to the trough. Part of its N corner had become detached and lay embedded in layer 6 alongside. Above the level of the slab floor the trough averaged 0.60m in height.

Apart from the stones that served to stabilise the slabs, the fill of the pit largely consisted of a deposit of firm but loosely packed dark

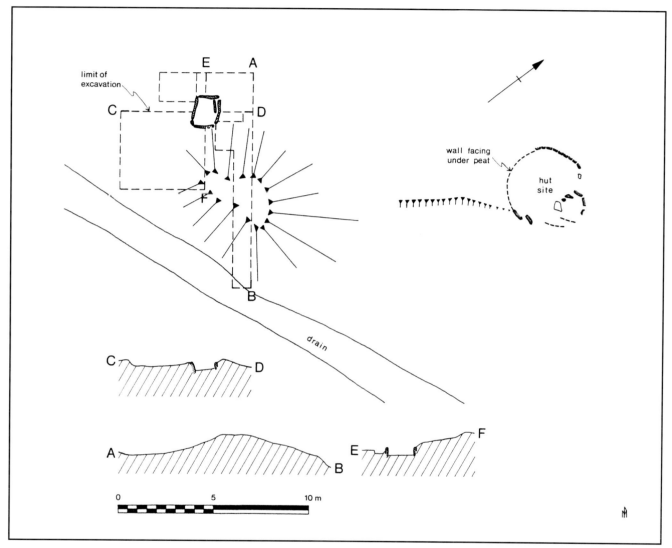

Fig. 12—Plan of the site and adjacent hut site.

brown/blackish peat with some charcoal content (layer 6), largely composed of material excavated from the pit. This deposit also underlay the floor slab. It was capped by a deposit of sticky gleyed clay of varying colour and consistency which averaged 0.08m in thickness (layer 8). This capping did not extend beyond the limits of the pit and was identified *in situ* as a redeposited series of horizon B and A2 soil types of immediate local provenance.[2] While the purpose of this deposit remains conjectural, its primary stratigraphical position is attested by the almost ubiquitous layer of fire-shattered stone (layer 5), associated with the firings carried out at the site, which directly overlay it.

Excavation of the trough's interior revealed only a thin deposit of very fibrous brown peat overlying the flooring slab. This did not exceed 0.10m in thickness, and was identifiable as A-horizon material similar to that overlying most of the site (layer 2). It became apparent that the trough's fill

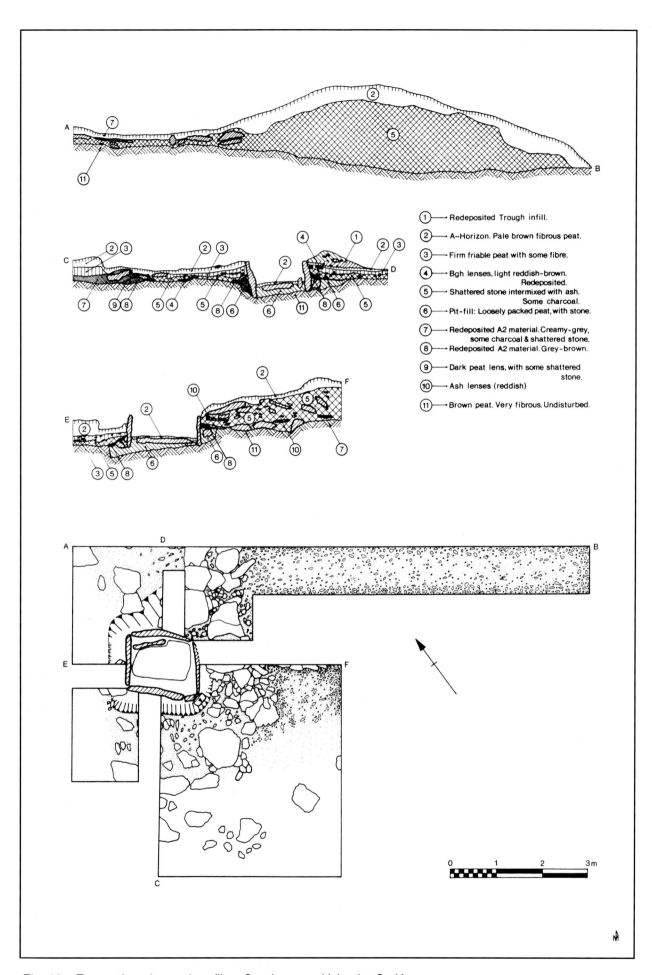

The following key accompanies the figure:

1 → Redeposited Trough infill.

2 → A-Horizon. Pale brown fibrous peat.

3 → Firm friable peat with some fibre.

4 → Bgh lenses, light reddish-brown. Redeposited.

5 → Shattered stone intermixed with ash. Some charcoal.

6 → Pit-fill: Loosely packed peat, with stone.

7 → Redeposited A2 material. Creamy-grey, some charcoal & shattered stone.

8 → Redeposited A2 material. Grey-brown.

9 → Dark peat lens, with some shattered stone.

10 → Ash lenses (reddish)

11 → Brown peat. Very fibrous. Undisturbed.

Fig. 13—Excavation plan and profiles, Coarhamore, Valentia, Co.Kerry.

had been removed in the past and was represented by a small mound of material immediately outside the NE side stone (layer 1). This deposit, which measured 1.40m x 1m in extent and 0.30m in maximum depth, was composed mainly of burnt and fire-shattered stone chips. It overlay the A-horizon material which forms the present ground level around the site, indicating that it was of relatively recent deposition.

The trough surrounds (Fig. 13, profiles C–D, E–F)

The excavated areas around the trough at the N and W revealed that a peaty deposit containing varying quantities of fire-shattered stone chips (layer 5) rested directly on both the pre-fulacht fiadh ground surface and on the layers capping the trough's pit (layers 11 and 8 respectively). This deposit, which occurred to a maximum depth of 0.10m, represented overspill from the mound and the casual detritus associated with the use of the site. It was in turn overlain by a layer of firm friable peat (layer 3) with some stone and fibre content, including modern roots.

The area excavated on the SW side of the trough revealed a somewhat different sequence. Here a number of sizeable slab-like stones interspersed with irregularly disposed deposits of gleyed clayey material were laid directly on layer 11 prior to the accumulation of layer 5. These horizon A2 and B soils (layers 4, 7 and 8) occurred up to 0.25m in thickness, though they generally averaged considerably less than this It appears reasonable to suppose that, in conjunction with the stone slabs, they were deposited here to form a more suitable working surface for the trough's attendants than that provided by the underlying brown peat.

The mound (Fig. 13, profile A–B)

Before excavation the mound appeared as a turf-covered area, roughly oval in plan, with overall dimensions of 10m NE–SW by 7m NW–SE. It averaged 1.35m in height above the surrounding ground level. The excavation of a 1m-wide trench through it revealed that the mound material rested on the brown peat (layer 11) noted elsewhere on the site. A sample of this peat obtained from directly underneath the mound yielded a radiocarbon determination of 2950 ± 80 BP (I-15470). The mound material (layer 5) consisted of burnt and fire-shattered sandstone intermixed with deep brown/dark reddish peat ash and nodules of peat charcoal.[3] Wood charcoal, while present, did not occur in any significant quantity. No turf- or dip-lines were evident in the mound's profile.

On the downward NW slope of the mound, excavation revealed a loose tumble of large stones and slabs. This feature appears to have served to retain the mound material, preventing its accumulation around the sides of the trough. None of the stones were set in or rested on the pre-mound surface (layer 11) and a number were separated from their fellows below by deposits of ash and burnt stone, suggesting that this loose bank was not a primary feature of the site and that the stages of its development were initiated only after the accumulation of mound material had commenced.

THE FINDS

Spindle-whorl (Fig. 14; NMI reg. no. E478:1)

This object is well finished though not truly circular. It is made of grey-green siltstone of sedimentary origin, and possesses a cleavage stripe. Its colour, lithology and cleavage suggest a local indigenous origin.[4] Its diameter varies from 30mm to 32mm. It is 7mm thick and features a central perforation of hourglass form 2.5mm in diameter at the centre, widening to 5.5mm on the faces. Both faces are decorated with a single incised circle. The object was found outside the W corner of the stone trough in the sticky gleyed clay deposit (layer 8) which capped the backfill of the pit.

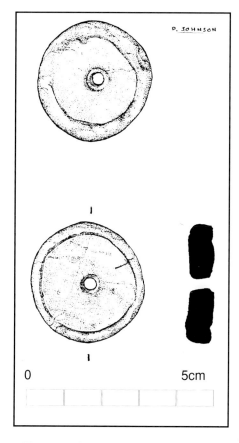

Fig. 14—Spindle-whorl from Coarhamore

P. JOHNSON

0   5cm

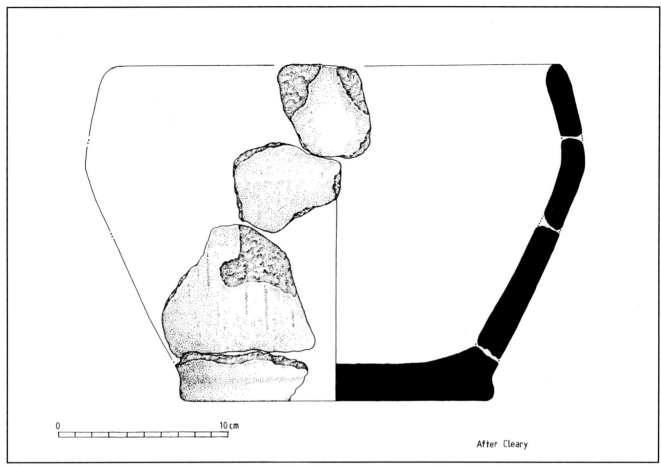

Fig. 15—Suggested reconstruction of the form of the Coarhamore pottery (after Cleary).

Pottery (Fig. 15; NMI reg. no. E478: 2–27) *(Report by Rose M. Cleary)*
The twenty-six sherds of pottery, weighing 416g in total, comprise two rim
fragments, five basal sherds and nineteen body sherds. Sherd thickness
varies from 9.3mm to 14.8mm, the upper range being accounted for by
the base. Conjectural reconstruction of the form of the vessel (Fig. 15)
indicates that it was a squat globular bowl approximately 19cm in height
and 18.5cm in basal diameter. It featured a rounded rim, a gently angled
shoulder and a flat base with a slight foot. It was slab-built, slab fracture
joints being visible on the basal sherds. The colour varies but is in general
red (Munsell 2.5YR5/6) with dark grey cores (Munsell 5YR4/1).

A thermal colour test (Hulthen 1976) gives a firing temperature of
800–900° C (Fig. 16). The presence of black/grey cores indicates that the
vessel was rapidly fired at a relatively high temperature. The sintering
interval is 1100–1200° C, which indicates the use of a Quaternary deposit
of clay. Impressions on the basal sherds and on some of the body sherds
indicate that the vessel was scraped smooth before firing.

One thin section was cut from the basal area of the vessel for
petrological examination. This was 14mm in thickness and is
representative of the vessel fabric. The clay structure is sandy in texture
with rounded quartz grains visible in the clay matrix. The distribution of
iron oxides is even with minor concentrations of limonite. The accessory
(or primary) minerals in the clay are fresh plagioclase feldspars. The
temper type is an igneous rock which is gabbroic in composition. It is
porphyritic in texture with large feldspar crystals and contains the mineral
olivine. The vessel is richly tempered with maximum grain size of 5.5mm
and the crushed gabbro inclusions comprise 45% of the vessel fabric.

The high proportion of plagioclase feldspars in the clay shows that it is
residual and derived from a volcanic region (Grimshaw 1971, 272). The
olivine gabbro is also volcanic in origin. Consequently both clay and

temper are exotic for the County Kerry region and this strongly suggests that the vessel was imported into the area. The source for the temper could be a glacial erratic in the area, but because the clay is also derived from volcanic bedrock it is likely that the vessel was not produced in the environs of the site. The source for the temper may be the Newry ring-dyke complex in County Armagh. Olivine gabbro was used in the Late Neolithic/Beaker period ceramic assemblage from Newgrange (Cleary 1980). In that instance, the boulders had been transported onto the site

Fig. 16—Tabulated results of the thermal colour test on the Coarhamore pottery (after Cleary).

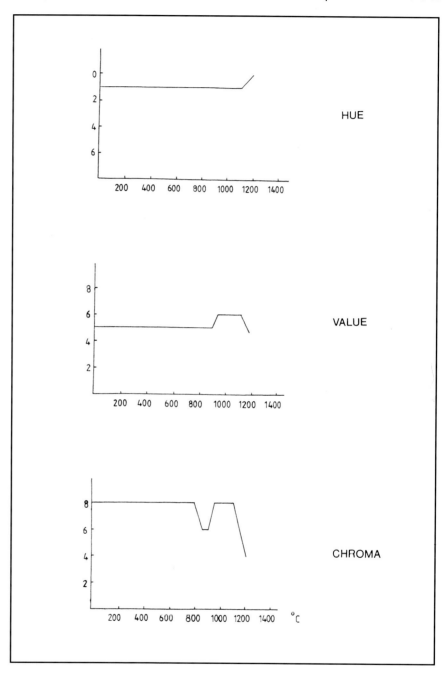

during the construction of the megalithic tomb.

Traces of soot are visible on the inner faces of the basal sherds, indicating that the vessel was used for cooking. The vessel is 'fresh' in appearance, suggesting that it was buried soon after it was discarded.

The pottery sherds were found together in the upper levels of the NW slope of the mound material (layer 5).

DISCUSSION

A number of the features revealed at the Coarhamore site are paralleled at other fulachta fiadh. The occurrence of hut sites in the immediate environs of such sites, for instance, is not uncommon. Occurring in both stone and timber and variously interpreted as meat-stores, sleeping-huts or occasionally as more permanent domestic structures — examples have been excavated at Drombeg, Co. Cork (Fahy 1960), Ballycroghan, Co. Down (Hodges 1955), and at both Ballyvourney sites in Co. Cork (O'Kelly 1954). Though the Coarhamore example was not excavated on this occasion, and remains undated, it would not appear unreasonable to suggest that it may have shared more than a merely spatial relationship with the adjacent fulacht fiadh. Its general plan and dimensions are not at variance with those of numerous stone-built circular huts in the south Kerry region to which a general Early Historic date is often tenuously applied (Henry 1957, 152–3). If coeval with the fulacht fiadh, the apparently permanent nature of its construction may evidence prolonged rather than periodic use of the overall site and may indicate a model of use at variance with the temporary hunter-encampment-type interpretations normally proposed for such sites. In this regard also the nature of the finds at Coarhamore do not readily support the conventionally proposed model. A spindle-whorl, for instance, would seem a rather incongruous item to be included amongst the equipment of a roving hunter!

The trough revealed at Coarhamore is best paralleled by the somewhat smaller example excavated at Drombeg, Co. Cork (Fahy 1960, 7–8). Both were of stone slab construction and were floored by a large slab, though the latter element was more carefully chosen and installed at the Drombeg site. The side and end stones of both examples rose somewhat above the surrounding ground level, more appreciably so at Coarhamore, and were presumably so designed to prevent site debris from falling into the trough.

While no evidence for a hearth was revealed in the areas excavated at Coarhamore it is probable that an example exists adjacent to the site. Given the location of the proposed 'working surface' revealed to the SW of the trough, it would appear likely that it lies in this area. The occurrence of the former feature is of interest. Formed of clays and stone, it cannot be readily paralleled on Irish sites, though it should be noted that a meaningful analogy is possibly provided by the short stone-laid causeway which linked hut 2 to the fulacht fiadh at Drombeg, particularly as the grey layer noted by the excavator underlying this feature could plausibly be interpreted as a primary earthen causeway (Fahy 1960, 6–7).

The identification of peat as the dominant fuel type in use at the Coarhamore fulacht fiadh is of some interest. Given that wood was in all likelihood the fuel of first preference when available, it suggests a dearth of suitable resources of firewood in the vicinity of the site during its period of use. This contrasts sharply with the availability of oak, hawthorn and willow/poplar as fuel for the earlier Reenarea fulacht fiadh (Fig. 11c), which has yielded an Early Bronze Age radiocarbon date (Mitchell, this volume), but finds parallel in three other Valentia sites where the only charcoal represented was that of Calluna vulgaris (Mitchell, this volume).

The antiquity and extent of the practice of using peat for fuel in Ireland have not yet been adequately investigated. The presence of quantities of peat ash in fulachta fiadh and certain prehistoric sites in Scotland and the Northern Isles effectively belies the legend that Torf-Einar Rognavaldsson, one of the early Norse earls of Orkney, introduced the practice of harvesting peat for fuel to these islands (Fenton 1984, 140). Indeed, early Irish law tracts — most notably the Senchas Mar — show that by the eighth century at least, when this text was compiled (Kelly 1988, 245), the use of peat for fuel in Ireland was common enough to merit legal discussion (Lucas 1970, 172). In addition, the identification of peat ash and charcoal in both industrial and domestic archaeological contexts at the Early Historic settlement at Reask (Fanning 1981) evidences the exploitation of bogs in Kerry as sources of fuel by this time. No evidence for prehistoric instances of this practice in Ireland is known to the author.

The volume of burnt stone material which formed the mound at

Coarhamore was calculated in order to achieve an approximate indication of the level of activity at the site during its period of use. An estimated volume of just 32 cubic metres was arrived at, based on surface indications of the extent and depth of the mound and on the depth of material encountered in the trench excavated through it. Using a Cu. M/Kg ratio of 1:1287 (established by weighing a sizeable sample) it was concluded that the estimated volume of the mound weighed just in excess of 41 tons. Based on Fahy's deduction that a single use of such a site would require the firing of a volume of stone equivalent to approximately half that of its trough (1960, 15), the Coarhamore mound would represent some hundred such firings. Allowing for reuse of the sandstone boilers, on the scale suggested by Buckley, this estimate may be multiplied by a factor of five.[5]

DATE

While the majority of excavated fulachta fiadh from Ireland have been dated to the Bronze Age it would nevertheless appear appropriate on the balance of the evidence to tentatively assign the Coarhamore example to the Early Historic period. This conclusion is reached largely through a consideration of the finds from the site, in particular that of the distinctive spindle-whorl.

The stone spindle-whorl (Fig.14) is of special interest in that it can be closely paralleled amongst local material assemblages of Early Historic date. It was found sealed in the clay capping of the pit fill (layer 8), clearly indicating that its loss was contemporary with the initial period of use of the only trough attested to on the site. Its disc form, and more particularly its decoration, indicates that a tacit general assumption that it is of Early Historic date would not go amiss (Laing 1975, 285). The occurrence of a pair of closely comparable decorated whorls from two early ecclesiastical sites elsewhere in peninsular Kerry — Church Island and Reask — strongly reinforces such an assumption. Both share a characteristic of the Coarhamore example in that they are unevenly shaped rather than truly circular in form and, more significantly, feature irregularly incised circles (and concentric circles) as their sole decorative elements (O'Kelly 1958, 101, fig. 14.7; Fanning 1981, 125, fig. 22.31). Elsewhere in Ireland a small number of similarly decorated flat spindle-whorls have been recorded from domestic sites of Early Historic date.[6]

The pottery from Coarhamore is rather more difficult to parallel. R.M. Cleary has suggested that while it is of poorer quality than the vessels from Carrigillihy, Co. Cork, it is comparable to them in general morphology (pers. comm.). The Carrigillihy assemblage is of Bronze Age date (O'Kelly 1951, 78–81, figs 7–8). The Coarhamore pottery (e.g. sherds no. 310 and 282), however, appears to be equally comparable to some sherds of the coarse ware excavated at Reask, Co. Kerry (Fanning 1981, 112–13, fig. 16),[7] most of which occurred in a layer that yielded a radiocarbon determination of AD 385 ± 90 (*ibid.*, 104). It should be pointed out, however, that neither the Coarhamore nor the Reask material is comparable to any of the recognised groups of native Early Historic wares (see Ryan 1973).

The radiocarbon date of 2950 ± 80 BP obtained from the brown peat which underlay the mound material does not necessarily militate against a late date for the site. Deriving from a context which, if originally undisturbed, could conceivably antedate the build-up of the mound by a considerable period, it may only be regarded as a very general *terminus post quem* to the mound's development. A second hazard concerning the interpretation of this determination involves the possibility that the boggy surface around the site underwent extensive trampling before and during the early stages of the build-up of the mound material — an activity which has been evidenced at a number of Welsh sites where the absence of recognisable pre-mound soil horizons has been noted (Williams 1985, 987). Given the location of the Coarhamore site in a bog, such a process would easily have resulted in the churning up and blending of the subcurface and surface peat horizons.

While present evidence indicates that Irish fulachta fiadh may be regarded as a predominantly prehistoric monument type, it would nonetheless seem unwise to view examples for which Early Historic dates have been proposed as aberrations. Several recently excavated examples in Scotland and Wales have yielded radiocarbon dates which demonstrate the currency of such sites in these regions during this period (Williams 1985), and there is no reason to believe that a different situation should have prevailed in Ireland. The date suggested here for the Coarhamore site should perhaps be viewed, in conjunction with the series of Bronze Age fulachta fiadh on Valentia Island, as an indicator of the longevity of a basic and very widely distributed method of generating heat transfer.

ACKNOWLEDGEMENTS
In addition to those mentioned in the footnotes the author wishes to record his thanks to the following: Professor G.F. Mitchell for his valuable assistance and advice during the excavation and for generously sharing his extensive knowledge of Valentia Island; Rose M. Cleary, Dept. of Archaeology, University College, Cork, for kindly examining and commenting on the pottery; Joanna Nolan, Eugene O'Sullivan and Michael Connolly for their assistance on the site; Ann O'Connor for typing the manuscript; Phelim Manning for preparing Figs 11, 12 and 13; Patricia Johnson for preparing Fig. 14; Joseph Dunne, Manager, Fás (Tralee), and the South-West Kerry Development Organisation for facilitating and funding the excavation.

1   The National Grid reference for the site is V 377 737.
2   The soil types revealed at the site were examined in situ by Dr Michael Conry, Oak Park Research Institute, Carlow.
3   Samples of the peat charcoal from Coarhamore were examined and identified by Dr Donal Synnot, National Botanic Gardens, Dublin.
4   The spindle-whorl was kindly examined by Michael O'Sullivan, Resource Environmental Management Unit, University College, Cork.
5   Mr Victor Buckley has concluded on the basis of experiment that some sandstone did not shatter until after five firings. I am grateful to Mr Buckley for informing me of these findings.
6   I am grateful to Mr Mick Monk, Dept. of Archaeology, University College, Cork, who discussed the Coarhamore spindle-whorl and its analogies with me.
7   Sherd nos 310 and 282 from Reask appear, from visual inspection, to be practically identical to the Coarhamore pottery. I am grateful to Mr Conleth Manning for drawing my attention to these sherds (which are not illustrated in Fanning 1981).

REFERENCES
CLEARY, R.M. 1980 The Late Neolithic Beaker Period ceramic assemblage from Newgrange, Co. Meath, Ireland. Unpublished M.A. thesis, National University of Ireland.

CUPPAGE, J. 1986 Archaeological survey of the Dingle Peninsula. Ballyferriter.

FAHY, E.M. 1960 A hut and cooking places at Drombeg, Co. Cork. J. Cork Hist. Archaeol. Soc. 65 (201), 1–17.

FANNING, T. 1981 Excavation of an Early Christian cemetery and settlement at Reask, Co. Kerry. Proc. R. Ir. Acad. 81C, 67–172.

FENTON, A. 1984 Northern links: continuity and change. In Fenton and Palsson (eds), The Northern and Western Isles in the Viking world, 129–45. Edinburgh.

GRIMSHAW, R.W. 1971 The chemistry and physics of clays and allied ceramic materials. London.

HENRY, F. 1957 Early monasteries, beehive huts, and dry-stone houses in the neighbourhood of Cahersiveen and Waterville (Co. Kerry). *Proc. R. Ir. Acad.* **38C**, 45–166.

HODGES, H.M.W. 1955 The excavation of a group of cooking-places at Ballycroghan, Co. Down. *Ulster J. Archaeol.* **18**, 17–28.

HULTHEN, B. 1976 On thermal colour test. *Norwegian Archaeol. Rev.* **9**, pt 1.

KELLY, F. 1988 *A guide to early Irish law.* Dublin.

LAING, L. 1975 *The archaeology of late Celtic Britain and Ireland c. 400–1200 AD.* London.

LUCAS, A.T. 1970 Notes on the history of turf as fuel in Ireland to 1700 AD. *Ulster Folklife* **15/16**, 172–202.

MITCHELL, G.F. 1989 *Man and environment in Valencia Island.* Dublin.

O'KELLY, M.J. 1951 An Early Bronze Age ringfort at Carrigillihy, Co. Cork. *J. Cork Hist. Archaeol. Soc.* **56** (184), 69–86.

O'KELLY, M.J. 1954 Excavations and experiments in ancient Irish cooking-places. *J. R. Soc. Antiq. Ir.* **84,** 105–55.

O'KELLY, M.J. 1958 Church Island near Valencia, Co. Kerry. *Proc. R. Ir. Acad.* **59C**, 2–136.

RYAN, M. 1973 Native pottery in Early Historic Ireland. *Proc. R. Ir. Acad.* **73C**, 619–45.

WILLIAMS, G. 1985 A group of burnt mounds at Morfa Mawr, Aberaeron. *J. Ceredigion Antiq. Soc.* **10** (2), 181–7.

Two fulachta fiadh in County Cork

M.F. Hurley

Detailed reports on the two fulachta fiadh under discussion have been published (Hurley 1987a, b); consequently only a brief summary of the results is offered here. Kilcor South IV was excavated during the construction of the Cork – Dublin gas pipeline, and was one of thirty fulachta fiadh recorded in the course of that project. It is noteworthy that not one of these thirty sites had any recognisable surface features such as crescent-shaped mounds. When the topsoil was removed, the sites were apparent as spreads of burnt shattered stone and charcoal. The sites were recorded in counties Carlow, Kilkenny and Tipperary, but by far the greatest concentration occurred in County Cork. Four sites were excavated; two of these — Clohogue, Co. Kilkenny (O'Flaherty 1987), and Brommfield East II, Co. Cork — produced evidence for nothing other than spreads of burnt material. It is possible that other features remain unexcavated as work was strictly confined to the extent of the pipeline corridor. In the case of two other sites, Kilcor South IV and Castleredmond (Doody 1987), both in County Cork, troughs were found beneath the burnt spreads. At Castleredmond a well-preserved cooking pit and two further possible cooking pits were recorded. One pit contained evidence for substantial posts at each of the four corners, and at three of the corners the remains of earth-cut slots into which horizontal planks would have fitted were apparent.

At Kilcor South IV , the principal features uncovered were a pit containing the remains of a wooden plank trough, a hearth site and a low spread of burnt shattered stones and charcoal. The rectangular pit was much larger than was necessary to accommodate the trough. A platform made from a large flat stone and an oak (*Quercus* sp.) plank facilitated access to the trough. This arrangement may have been a response to the need to have the trough at a sufficiently low level to fill naturally from groundwater seepage. The trough was made from a combination of horizontally laid planks and brushwood supported by stakes. It measured 1.40m x 1.45m. A radiocarbon date of 3185 ± 30 BP has been obtained for the wood from the trough. A hearth was revealed as a spread of oxidised clay with a small stone revetment *c.* 6m south-east of the trough. No diagnostic small finds were recovered from any of the Cork – Dublin gas pipeline fulachta fiadh.

At Clashroe, Meelin, Co. Cork, a fulacht fiadh was excavated in 1985. The site at Clashroe is one of a group of at least six fulachta fiadh located by the Cork Archaeological Survey in this area. The principal features uncovered were a mound of burnt shattered stones; a wooden trough surrounded by an area of stones trampled into the clay; and a buried turf horizon, covered by redeposited clay probably resulting from the excavation of the pit in which the trough was placed. A hearth occupied a shallow pit on the eastern side of the trough and 11 stake-holes occurred on the south and west sides of the hearth. The trough was set in a pit which was no deeper than was necessary to accommodate it.

The trough consisted of two individual pieces of timber and may originally have been comprised of three pieces. The greater part was hollowed from a single oak trunk. On the eastern side a groove had been chiselled or axed out to accommodate a plank which blocked one end. It seems possible that a similar plank may have blocked the western end. The tree trunk had been hollowed out with an axe or adze, evidenced by elongated scallop-shaped depressions. The maximum length of the trough was 1.8m by 0.6m wide. A ^{14}C determination from the wood of the trough produced a ^{14}C date of 3490 ± 35 BP (GrN-13.877).

A hearth was set in a shallow depression or pit on the north-eastern side of the trough. The pit was filled with black soil, ash and lumps of charcoal. The majority of identifiable charcoal fragments were birch

(*Betula*), hazel (*Corylus*) and holly (*Ilex*). A ^{14}C sample from the charcoal gave a date of 3370 ± 35 BP (GrN-13.878). (The ^{14}C dates are given in conventional uncalibrated radiocarbon years.) Dr Lanting (Hurley 1987b, appendix I) states that 'comparing the dates with the new Belfast calibration curve it is apparent that the dates do not necessarily indicate a long period of use for the fulacht fiadh. Both dates can be placed in the period 1790 – 1730 BC (solar years).'

The trough at Clashroe is one of the best-preserved dug-out wooden troughs discovered to date in an archaeological excavation. Originally it would have contained upwards of 264 litres (58 gallons) of water, and would have required manual filling from a stream *c.* 10m away. No diagnostic small finds were recovered from the site. One small fragment of flint was struck, but it is not characteristic of any particular period.

The results from the gas pipeline greatly increased our awareness of the possibility of discovering fulachta fiadh in large numbers in areas where agriculture has obliterated all surface traces of the monuments. The existence of troughs in two out of four excavated sites would indicate that most of the thirty or so recorded spreads of burnt material were in fact fulachta fiadh. The well-preserved site at Clashroe is indicative of the type of results obtainable from the excavation of relatively undisturbed sites that are threatened by increasingly mechanised agriculture.

REFERENCES

DOODY, M.G. 1987 A *fulacht fiadh* at Castleredmond, Co. Cork. In R.M. Cleary, M.F. Hurley and E.A. Twohig (eds), *Archaeological excavations on the Cork – Dublin gas pipeline (1981 – 1982)*, (49–50). Cork Archaeological Studies no. 1.

HURLEY, M.F. 1987a A *fulacht fiadh* at Kilcor South IV, Co. Cork. In R.M. Cleary, M.F. Hurley and E.A. Twohig (eds), *Archaeological excavations on the Cork–Dublin gas pipeline (1981–1982)*, 46–8. Cork Archaeological Studies no. 1.

HURLEY, M.F.1987b A *fulacht fiadh* at Clashroe, Meelin, Co. Cork. J. Cork Hist. Archaeol. Soc. **92**, 95–105.

O'FLAHERTY, B. 1987 A fulacht fiadh at Clohogue, Co. Kilkenny. In R.M.Cleary, M.F. Hurley and E.A. Twohig (eds), *Archaeological excavations on the Cork–Dublin gas pipeline (1981–1982)*, 45–6. Cork Archaeological Studies no.1.

Ancient cooking places at Catstown, near Hugginstown, Co. Kilkenny

Michael Ryan

INTRODUCTION

In August 1973, drainage works exposed typical fulachta fiadh deposits at Catstown, Co. Kilkenny, and as they were under threat the National Museum investigated them in area excavations in the summer of 1974.

SITING

The sites lie almost at 600' OD on a southward-facing slope at the E end of the ridge forming the watershed between streams flowing northwards to the River Nore and those flowing southwards to join the Suir. Bedrock at the site is Old Red Sandstone of the main series — it is, locally, extremely coarse and friable and especially large pieces of quartz are frequent in it. The immediate area of the sites is marshy but no natural watercourses are evident, their place having been taken by modern drainage channels following field banks.

The fulachta fiadh were disposed along a NNW–SSE line: 19m separated sites 1 and 2 and 70m sites 2 and 3. Subsequently, what may have been a fourth site was identified S of site 1. There is no particular feature in the field which suggests itself as influencing the placing of each mound. All were on approximately the same level, in similar conditions of marshiness.

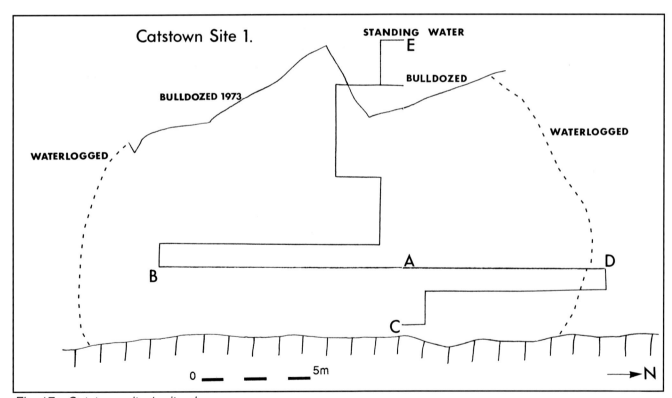

Fig. 17—Catstown site 1, site plan.

SITE 1 (Figs. 17 and 18)

Before excavation, site 1 presented the classic fulacht fiadh appearance — it was horseshoe-shaped, open to the west. In the centre was a rush-grown depression filled with stagnant water. Originally covered by furze and other scrub, its topsoil was partly skimmed off by bulldozing — the ends of the arms of the mound being carried away in the process. The field bank ran close to the E side of the site and the modern drainage ditch bordering it had been dug through part of the fulacht fiadh. The mound measured 21m N–S, 13.70m E–W, and rose to a height of 1m above the level of the field. Excavation of the site was rendered difficult by continuous seepage of water which took place even in dry weather and which necessitated constant use of a motor pump.

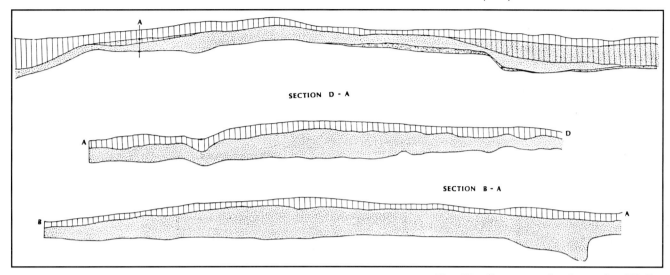

SECTION D - A

SECTION B - A

Fig. 18—Catstown site 1, section W–E.

The body of the mound was composed almost entirely of burnt stone and grit derived from the decay of the stone (Fig. 18, section B–D). Mixed with this was comminuted charcoal staining much of the deposit black. The stratigraphy of the mound was simple, as one would expect of a structure built almost entirely by dumping. It was not generally possible to see individual tip-lines because, presumably, of the sorting which one supposes took place when discarded stones were later retrieved for re-use and the percolation of rainwater which would have distributed the charcoal. It was impossible to establish the original edge of the mound since its method of construction was stratigraphically indistinguishable from slumping. No structures were buried under the deposit, which proved to be 64cm in maximum thickness. The topsoil was 16cm in maximum depth; the mound, therefore, was 80cm in maximum height above OGL. The difference of 20cm in the measurement of height above field level estimated at the commencement of excavation is accounted for by a slight rise in OGL. The original surface was irregular and contained occasional pockets of less compact soil, including one 1.64m wide and 42cm in maximum depth. This was entirely filled with the material forming the mound with no intervening layers of silt. It may have been natural or it might have been associated with the operation of the cooking place. It is possible that the depression was formed by the removal of a particularly large stone.

The site of the trough was identified in the area between the arms of the mound. A step had been cut in the marl subsoil (Fig. 18, section E–C), and immediately to the W was a slight depression scarcely differentiated from the surrounding ground level and filled in the main with the rubble of the mound; the bottom was, however, covered by a layer of finer gritty material with a greater concentration of comminuted charcoal intermixed with it and which was presumably washed down from higher levels. A scatter of twigs and portions of charred oak bough (E151:22) and a few fragments of what may have been oak(?) planking (E151:21) and a stick of alder were found in this depression and these, presumably, represent the remains of the lining of the cooking pit. (A sample of this material was submitted for ^{14}C assay; see below.) The maximum width of the depression was 2.40m and its maximum depth — taking the height of the step as an indication — was 42cm. Above the rubble filling of the pit there was a thick deposit (up to 44cm in depth) of disturbed mixed rubble and

41

topsoil from which came some fragments of modern material. From the main deposit of the mound came a notched stone disc (E151:2), possible whetstones (E151:11, 14) and crude stone 'discs' (E151:8–10, 15) (see S. Cherry, this volume).

Most of the wood from the pit area was readily identifiable — oak (*Quercus*) predominated, with smaller quantities of alder (*Alnus*); there was one fragment of willow (*Salix*). Charcoal from the lowermost deposit at the site of the pit was entirely oak. Charcoal — finely comminuted and partly incorporated in a concretion of soil — from OGL and the NW side of the mound proved unidentifiable.

The finds from the site were few and disappointing in that they provided little evidence for dating its period of use.

Stone

E151:2, notched stone disc, circular in plan with irregular edges, somewhat flattened on each face. A large, slightly off-centre perforation has been crudely reamed from each face. For a distance of about a quarter of its circumference, where the ring is thickest, the edge is notched in an irregular fashion. Both faces are striated. D. of ring 3.4cm; max. D. of central perforation 2cm; max. T. of ring 7mm. Found in rubble deposit.

E151:8, irregular stone disc, D. 8.8cm, max. T. 3.7cm.

E151:9, irregular stone 'disc', probably split from a heating stone. D. 8.4cm; max. T. 3.1cm. Found at the base of the main rubble deposit.

E151:10, irregular stone lamina, roughly rectangular in cross-section. The edges are concave in outline and in places have the appearance of being chipped — this may, however, have resulted from sudden cooling after heating. Both faces are flat — slightly uneven in places. Possibly an artifact. Made of sandstone. L.15.5cm; max. T. 3.9cm. Found in the main deposit of burned stone.

E151:15, irregular stone 'disc', irregular in outline, roughly rectangular in cross-section. Made of extremely friable stone. No indisputable evidence of deliberate manufacture. Max. L. 16.5cm; max. W. 11.2cm; max. T. 3cm. Unstratified.

E151:11, whetstone, irregular in outline, roughly oval in cross-section. Both long sides are curved and almost parallel. The short sides are irregular. One broad face bears a long bevel along one edge. All surfaces are worn, perhaps as a result of use, and all bear fine, probably accidental striations. L. 7.8cm; max. T. 2cm; max. W. 2.8cm. Found in upper level of main rubble deposit.

E151:14, whetstone, roughly rectangular in outline, square in cross-section. Both ends were formed by breakage. Two long sides are smooth and even and appear to have been rubbed. A third side is for the most part flat but slightly uneven in places. The remaining side is irregular and abraded. L. 9.6cm; W. 3.35cm; T. 3.5cm. Found lying in OGL.

Modern material

E151:3, rim sherd of china, probably from a small plate or saucer. The glaze is white with a brown inlaid line along the rim on one face. Found at base of the topsoil overlying disturbed material sealing the site of the cooking pit.

E151:12, body sherd of white china with crazed white glaze. The outer surface bears two close-set, horizontal grooves. Find circumstances as for E151:3.

E151:4a and b, two small fragments of modern, clear bottle-glass . Find circumstances as for E151:3.

E151:7a and b, two fragments of the bowl of a clay pipe, one of which bears a stamped Gothic letter 't'. The sherds join to suggest that the body was globular. The rim is flat. Max. T. of rim 2.8mm; max. T. of body 4.5mm. Found in disturbed layer overlying the site of the cooking pit.

Wood
E151:20, large irregular piece of wood found in fragments. From cooking pit.

E151:21, irregular fragments of oak(?) planking. Average T. 2.5cm. From cooking pit.

E151:22, irregular, charred portion of bough or small tree trunk displaying a large knot-hole. Estimated original D. 25–30cm. From cooking pit.

E151:23, piece of charcoal now in two fragments, possibly originally worked to a point. Max. L. 6.4cm; max. W. 2.3cm; max. T. 1.5cm. Found on OGL beside cooking pit.

Fig. 19—Catstown Site 2, Site plan.

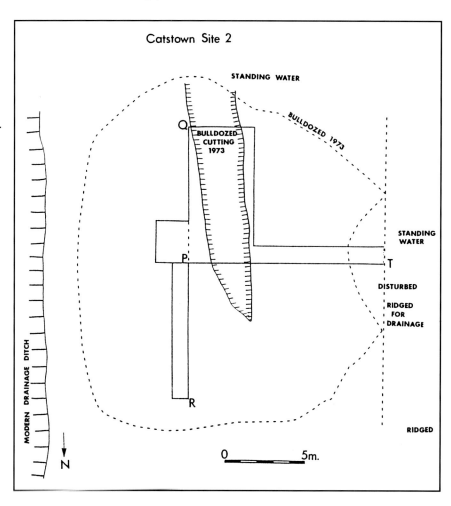

Miscellaneous
E151:5, amorphous fragment of vitreous matter, unstratified.

SITE 2 (Figs 19 and 20)
Before excavation site 2 appeared as a large, roughly oval mound with a slight indentation on its W side. It was originally covered by furze (*Ulex*), scrub hawthorn (*Crataegus*) and holly (*Ilex*) which had been stripped and

burned. A S–N bulldozer-cut, 9m long, was made in the mound in 1973. This disturbed only superficial deposits since the maximum depth of the cutting was 30cm and for most of its length was considerably less. In the bulldozed area, what appeared to have been a small setting of flat slabs was exposed and these were examined by the writer in August 1973. They were buried for safe-keeping and re-excavated in 1974 when the stones were all found to be lying loose on disturbed humus. It was clear that they had been shifted into position by the bulldozer although they could have derived from an ancient feature. Additional severe disturbance of the W side of the mound was caused by drainage works. Before excavation the mound measured 20m N–S, 16m E–W and 1.50m in maximum height above the surrounding field.

The structure of the mound was similar to that of site 1, being composed in the main of a rubble of burnt sandstone but, unlike the neighbouring site, a certain amount of differentiation was observable in the sectional profiles. This was to be seen as a greater or lesser quantity of charcoal staining in the rubble — the fine charcoal dust being washed through the stone and coming to rest in the lower part of the deposit. In addition to a greater intensity of charcoal staining, the lower levels tended to contain fewer pieces of rock and to be composed largely of a grit of decayed sandstone, a good proportion of which may also have percolated from the upper part of the mound. The absence of a large proportion of rock may in part be explained by the retrieval of stones for re-use, these when discarded again coming to rest on a higher level. Some patches of rubble with a higher charcoal content than in the surrounding deposit may have represented individual dumps of used stone. (This cannot be stated with any confidence, however, because of (i) the loose porous nature of the material of which the mound is composed (it is unstable), (ii) the sorting process to which it may have been subjected when the site was in

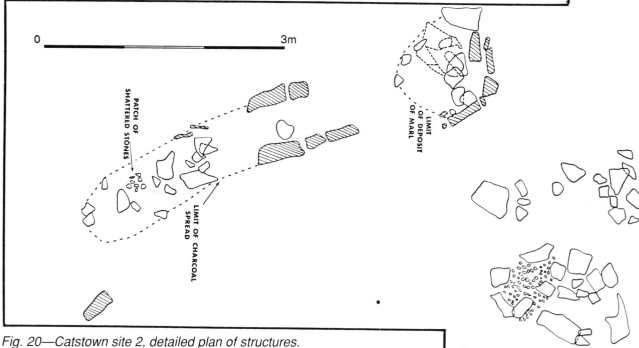

Fig. 20—Catstown site 2, detailed plan of structures.

use, and finally (iii) the inconsiderable size of the contents of the cooking pit in relation to the totality of burned stone present.) Slight differences in colour might have been due instead to small changes in relative porosity of compaction at different points in the mound. As with site 1, it was not possible to establish the original perimeter of the site since this had evidently not been deliberately defined. As was observed at the other site, OGL rose slightly towards the centre of the mound. Its maximum height above OGL was 84cm; the topsoil averaged 10–15cm in depth with

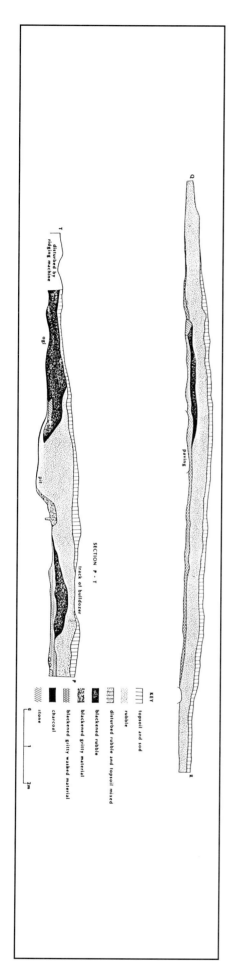

Fig. 21—Catstown site 2, section
P–Q–R.

occasional deeper pockets, and the main rubble layer was 56cm in maximum thickness.

Under the mound, in the SE quadrant, was a stone setting. It consisted of a pair of roughly parallel rows of small stones 50cm apart, five of which were set on edge into the marl of OGL. These ran SSE–NNE and terminated in an arc of smaller stones similarly bedded. Of the latter, four larger and three smaller stood and eleven others lay disturbed inside the area defined by the arc. The stones of the arc were set in, and the area enclosed was covered with, clean redeposited marl clearly differentiated from the underlying OGL. The space between parallel settings was partly filled with charcoal, predominantly of oak (*Quercus*) with some holly (*Ilex*), hazel (*Corylus*) and willow or poplar (*Salix – Populus*) present. The charcoal had been raked out at the S end of the structure and spread widely over OGL — a marked deposit of heat-shattered stones occurred in this area.

A marked circular patch of charcoal-stained soil (1m in diameter) occurred on OGL almost at the centre of the mound. Identifiable lumps of charcoal from it proved to be hazel (*Corylus*; 7 pieces), willow–poplar (*Salix–Populus*; 3 pieces), oak (*Quercus*; 1 piece) and ivy (*Hedera*; 1 piece). The feature may represent the base of an individual tip not subsequently disturbed. To the E of this was an area of irregular paving, the stones being set in clean redeposited marl on OGL. This area was not fully explored but a substantial part of it was opened. The stones were sealed by the blackened gritty material which formed the lowest level of the mound at that point. No post-holes, traces of intense burning or other features were associated with the paving.

On the W edge of the mound, on the site of the indentation apparent before excavation, a pit had been dug into OGL. Approximately half the area of the pit was examined — further work was rendered extremely difficult by severe and continuous flooding of the trench. The pit was shallower on its W side, and deeper, with a less inclined edge, on the E. The base of the pit sloped downwards slightly from E to W. On the sides and base of the pit patches of reddish marl and charcoal concretions occurred, suggesting severe burning at some stage. This pit was filled mainly with the coarse rubble of the mound; on its E side was a deposit of gritty sandstone. The bottom of the pit was covered by a thin layer of charcoal — eleven identifiable pieces were recovered, all of alder (*Alnus*). No traces of uncarbonised wood were noted. Immediately E of the pit a stake-hole occurred; it was 18cm deep and 6cm in diameter. The area of the pit explored was 2.36m long and 36cm deep.

A further, smaller pit occurred to the SW of that just described. The greater part of it was apparent in the trench. It was irregular in outline, 1.54m in maximum length, and 50cm of its width was showing in the trench. Its depth varied somewhat, 20cm being the average. The fill consisted entirely of rubble from the mound.

Just W of the smaller pit the mound and OGL are disturbed for a considerable depth by drainage operations. Excavation was extended into this area but no trace of any structure was identified.

There were no objects indisputably of human manufacture from the site.

SITE 3

Site 3 was horseshoe-shaped, open to the NW. It was originally covered with coarse grasses. At the time of inspection in 1973 the topsoil and sod had been stripped over most of the area of the mound, exposing the mass of burned stones of which it was composed. The area between the arms of the mound was waterlogged and overgrown with rushes. The site measured 14.50m N–S, 16m E–W, and was 50cm in maximum surviving height above the level of the field. This mound was destroyed during the winter of 1973–4 and no excavation of it was undertaken.

45

Finds

An amorphous fragment of vitreous matter (E151:1) came from the site. A stone 'disc' (E151:13) was found on the surface of the field in a scatter of burnt stone, to the N of site 3. It is irregular in outline and approximately rectangular in cross-section; L.16cm; max. W. 17.5cm; max. T. 3.5cm. It is just conceivable that the specimen is a manufactured object — it may, however, have been formed by heat-fracture.

SITE 4

During the excavations in 1974, an area of burnt stone came to notice in the SE corner of the field. It appeared to have been scattered by ploughing and it may have derived from the mound of a fulacht fiadh destroyed before the archaeological interest of the area was recognised. No traces of such a mound were evident when the sites were inspected in 1973. There were no finds from this area.

THE RADIOCARBON DATES

These were analysed in the Harwell laboratory. From site 2, charcoal from the hearth yielded a date of 760±60 BP (AD 1190) (Har-1369), and from site 1 wood from the disturbed pit area was assayed at 2440 ± 70 BP (490 BC) (Har-1367). While the latter may be taken as general confirmation of the prehistoric date of fulachta fiadh it is a surprising result as excavation indicated extensive recent disturbance of the area. The charcoal from site 2 was in a sealed context, although interpenetrated by some rootlets. As an isolated date it cannot be cited as evidence for the medieval survival of the practice of using cooking places although, given Geoffrey Keating's account, this is by no means entirely out of the question.

ACKNOWLEDGEMENTS

The writer is deeply grateful to the late Edward Walsh of Ballygriffin, Waterford, and to Mr John Maher whose fulachta fiadh survey was lodged in the National Museum. Thanks are also due to Roseanne Meenan, the late Frank Hickey, Stella Cherry and Sadhbh Moddel.

A medieval cooking trough from Peter Street, Waterford

Claire Walsh

A wooden trough was uncovered during excavation of the medieval properties at Peter Street, Waterford, in 1987. The trough was located 0.20m to the rear of a stone-footed house of early thirteenth-century date (Fig. 22).

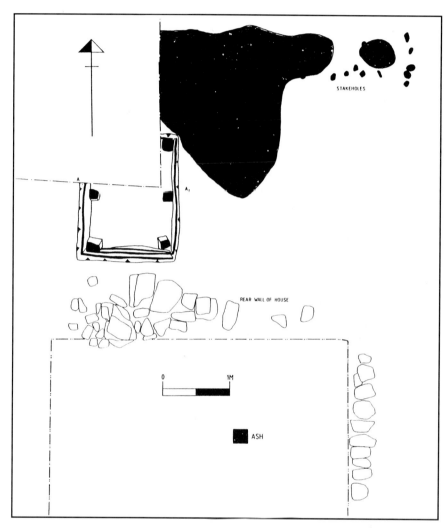

Fig. 22—Location of trough and contemporary features, Peter St. Waterford.

The trough was placed in a pit which was dug through earlier pits to a depth of 1.1m down to the natural boulder clay forming the floor of the trough. The trough measured 1.3m by 1.7m and was constructed of horizontally laid planks, retained at the corners and in the centre of the long side by upright posts (Fig. 23). These had pointed bases driven into the boulder clay. The uprights and planks were of oak (*Quercus* sp.) and were trimmed with an axe. The planks measured on average 0.24m in breadth and 0.04m in width. The sides of the trough stood to a maximum height of 0.62m.

The trough was filled with charcoal-enriched silt, fire-shattered stones (shale), twigs and burnt timbers (Fig. 24). Fragments of three stone mortars (Dundry stone, polished limestone, and granite) were recovered from the fill, as were several sherds of Saintonge green-glazed ceramic mortars. No formal hearth setting was found, although a spread of grey ash and charcoal filled a hollow *c.* 0.20m in depth adjacent to the trough. Several large shale blocks (the common local building stone at this period) were present in the ash spread, and may have been collected for heating.

47

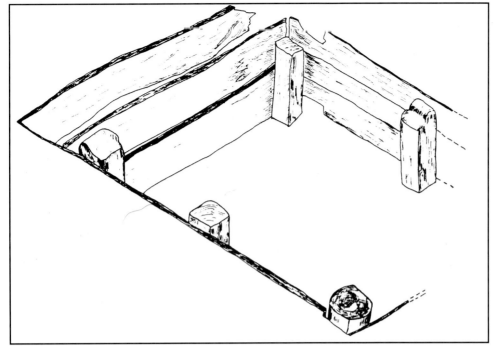

Fig. 23—Isometric view of trough.

A scattering of stake-holes at one end of the hearth may have supported a spit. Food debris — burnt animal bone, fish bones and oyster shell — littered the area around the trough.

There were no wells in the vicinity contemporary with the trough, and despite evident drainage problems in the immediate area in a later period the trough does not appear to have been self-filling. The contemporary dwelling on the plot was a large stone-footed timber-framed structure, with no evidence for specialised activities or industrial usage.

While several uses, e.g. bathing, brewing, textile-processing and leather-working, have been suggested as functions for fulachta fiadh (O'Driscoll 1988) the trough at Waterford appears to have been used for cooking. The presence of at least four mortars in the backfill suggests that the area was used for the preparation of food. While no further troughs have been located, the method of heating water with stones is evidenced by the presence of two groups of lime-coated 'pot-boilers', found adjacent to hearths in the vicinity in an earlier period.

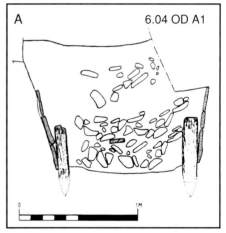

Fig. 24—Section across trough.

While the characteristic mound of a fulacht fiadh is considered to be the by-product of several hundred usages (Ó Drisceoil 1987, 52), the usage of the cooking trough at Waterford is related to the occupancy of one structure. The trough went out of use when the dwelling was dismantled with its stone footings partially levelled over the trough.

Dating for the trough is based on a preliminary stratigraphic and pottery assessment. An upright from the trough was submitted for dendrochronological dating (QUB - 7481), but proved problematical.

ACKNOWLEDGEMENTS

A full report on the trough and associated features will appear in the forthcoming excavation report. Microfloral analysis of the trough fill may elucidate its function. I am grateful to Maurice F. Hurley for advice on the text and permission to publish in advance of publication of full report.

REFERENCES

Ó DRISCEOIL, D. 1987 Discussion of fulachta fiadh. In R.M. Cleary, M.F. Hurley and E.A. Twohig (eds), *Archaeological excavations on the Cork–Dublin gas pipeline* 51–2. Cork Archaeological Studies No. 1.

Ó DRISCEOIL, D. 1988 Burnt mounds: cooking or bathing? *Antiquity* **62,** no. 237, 671–80.

3. OVERVIEWS

The finds from fulachta fiadh

Stella Cherry

Fulachta fiadh have yielded very few artifacts and the value of these for dating purposes is limited. Of the stratified finds recovered from scientific excavation most are of a nature which gives a broad range of dates. A large number of the recorded finds were recovered from destroyed fulachta fiadh or were surface finds in the general area of such sites and because direct association cannot be proved are useless for dating purposes.

Of the twenty-two sites which produced artifacts only seven have been excavated. Except for the gold ring fragment from Killeens, Co. Cork (no. 9), all are of stone. Of the unexcavated finds only one is reliably stratified; this is the bronze axehead from Ballynatona, Co. Cork (no. 5). The remainder of the finds include flints (nos 4, 12, 15 and 19), various stone artifacts (nos 1, 3, 7, 14, 20 and 21), pot sherds (nos 16 and 22) and a gold dress-fastener from Dooros, Co. Mayo (no. 18).

A Neolithic date has been suggested for some fulachta fiadh (Quinlan 1885–6), but the evidence for this is not conclusive. It is uncertain whether the three axeheads recovered by Quinlan at Clonkerdon, Co. Waterford (no. 20), were made of stone or bronze. The clay balls from Webbsborough, Co. Kilkenny (no. 17) (Prendergast 1955), though similar to those recovered from many megalithic structures, may be of a later date. Evidence from finds such as the barbed and tanged arrowheads from Fahee South, Co. Clare (no. 2), and the bronze axehead from Ballynatona, Co. Cork (no. 5), seem to indicate a Bronze Age date. Use of fulachta fiadh beyond the Bronze Age cannot be established on artifactual evidence because the finds of a later date are unstratified.

The finds are listed alphabetically in county order and the following abbreviations are used in the text.
NMI: National Museum of Ireland
Reg. no.: registered number
L.: length, W.: width, max.T.: maximum thickness
Diam.: diameter

1. CARRICKSLANEY, CO. CARLOW
SPHERICAL STONE
NMI reg. no. 1979:33
Sandstone: no evidence of use-wear or abrasion; diam. 6.4cm. Recovered from a field in which ploughing had exposed areas of blackened soil with concentrations of broken sandstone indicative of a fulacht fiadh.

2. FAHEE SOUTH, CO. CLARE
AMBER BEAD FRAGMENTS, SIDE-SCRAPER FLINT, SIDE/END-SCRAPER FLINT, TWO BARBED AND TANGED ARROWHEADS (ONE FLINT, ONE CHERT)
Amber: several fragments, once constituted a small bead.

Side-scraper, chert: broken at the distal end, rectangular in outline with retouch along the edge of one side. L. 3.2cm, W. 2.46cm, max.T. 0.16cm.

Side/end-scraper, chert: irregular in outline, broken at the distal end where retouch occurs; it is therefore difficult to distinguish it as either a side- or an end-scraper. L. 2.2cm, W. 1.53cm, max.T. 0.4cm.

Barbed and tanged arrowhead, flint: roughly triangular in outline, oval in cross-section, the tang is much longer than the one remaining barb;

49

retouch on both faces with slight traces of patination evident. L. 2.40cm, W. 1.81cm, max.T. 0.74 cm.

Barbed and tanged arrowhead, chert: triangular in outline, D-shaped in cross-section, with well-defined thin barbs (the extreme tip of one is broken); retouch on both faces and especially concentrated towards the edges. L. 1.72cm, W. 1.43cm, max.T. 0.45cm.

These finds were recovered during excavation of the site in 1981–2 (Unpublished: information from D. Ó Drisceoil.).

3. ADRIVALE, CO. CORK
THREE QUERNSTONES
I have been unable to find a description of, or context for, these quernstones, although a reference to them indicates that they came from fulachta fiadh sites near Millstreet, Co. Cork (Ó Drisceoil 1980, 181–2).

4. BALLYCRENANE, CO. CORK
BUTT-TRIMMED FLAKE, FLINT
NMI reg. no. 1972:354
Leaf-shaped flake, triangular in cross-section and slightly concave on its ventral face. Heavily worked at the butt end to produce a slight tang. The dorsal face of the flake shows traces of retouch, especially on the edges where it is crudely applied producing a denticulated outline. L. 7.7cm, W. 3.4cm, max.T. 1.3cm. In the late 1960s a fulacht fiadh situated in a marshy area close to Garryvoe beach in Cork was levelled; the flake was recovered from the spread of this material.

5. BALLYNATONA, CO. CORK
FLANGED AXEHEAD WITH STOP-RIDGE, BRONZE (Pl. 3)
NMI reg. no. 1936:1780
This has long, pronounced lozenge-shaped flanges and a stop-ridge which is almost straight horizontally. The septum, almost rectangular in shape, measures 2.25cm in width at the stop-ridge where it is 1.53cm thick, and 2.47cm in width at the butt end where it is 0.62cm thick. The butt end and the edge of one of the flanges have been slightly misshapen and flattened by hammering in modern times. Below the stop-ridge, on one side only, a slightly raised shield pattern is evident. The cutting edge is widely splayed with a width of 6cm. W. of flanges 3cm, overall L. 13cm. It seems to belong to the vaguely defined group of axeheads referred to by Smith (1959) as haft-flanged axes. This is the only well-stratified find from an unexcavated fulacht fiadh: it was recovered from a depth of about 122cm in the mound of burnt stones, resting on 15cm of similar material.

6. BALLYVOURNEY, CO. CORK
FIVE STONE DISCS, HAMMERSTONE, SPINDLE-WHORL, STONE
Five crude discs of local shale, showing little evidence of deliberate manufacture; may have formed as a result of heat fracture. Diams. range from 6.7cm to 12.5cm.

Roughly circular stone with traces of abrasion on its surface indicating its use as a hammerstone; diam. 9.5cm.

Spindle-whorl, shale, undecorated; the perforation, which is slightly off-centre, measures 9mm in diam. Diam. of spindle-whorl 3cm, max.T. 4mm.

The five stone discs and the hammerstone were recovered during excavation of the site. The spindle-whorl was a surface find from the area of the site a year before the excavation (O'Kelly 1954, 115–17).

Plate 3—Flanged axe head with stop-ridge, Ballynatona, Co. Cork (Copyright National Museum of Ireland).

7. CURRAGHCROWLEY WEST, CO. CORK
STONE CHOPPER
Made of shale, this implement, possibly a club or chopper consists of a rough handle with a trapezoidal head which narrows to a working edge. Traces of its manufacture can be seen on the surface of the handle. L. 24.7cm. It was recovered during ploughing in the vicinity of the site (Ó Ríordáin 1938).

8. DROMBEG, CO. CORK
SADDLE QUERN, PERFORATED STONE, STONE DISC
The saddle quern is roughly trapezoidal in outline with a slightly depressed working surface. Overall L. 53cm, W. 32cm, T. 5cm.

Stone slab, rectangular in outline and cross-section with a central perforation 6cm wide; overall L. 48cm, W. 25cm, max.T. 4cm.

Crudely shaped stone disc, diam. 36cm, max. T. 4cm.

These finds were recovered during excavation of the fulacht fiadh; the saddle quern was used as a covering slab on the primary drain of the site (Fahy 1960).

9. KILLEENS, CO. CORK
GOLD RING FRAGMENT
This consisted of a much-decayed metallic core covered by a thin layer of gold foil. Analysis of the core revealed the presence of tin but as the sample was badly eroded it is possible that other metals such as copper were originally present. The inner surface of the gold showed traces of pitting which may have resulted from its contact with the base metals of the core under acidic conditions similar to those from which the ring was recovered. Estimated external diam. 22mm, estimated internal diam. 15mm. This was the only artifact recovered during excavation of the site (O'Kelly 1954, 131).

10. BALLYCROGHAN, CO. DOWN
SHALE BRACELET FRAGMENT
This fragment has a polished surface and is oval in cross-section; internal diam. 6.6cm, diam. of cross-section 1.1cm.

In 1954 and 1955 a series of fulachta fiadh were excavated here. The shale bracelet fragment was the only find recovered during these investigations. It was found in the upper fill of a field drain which cut across the eastern side of site 3. Though no direct association between it and the site can be substantiated, the excavator suggests that it may have been discarded during utilisation of the site (Hodges 1955).

11. COARHAMORE, CO. KERRY
A number of artifacts were recovered during excavation of this site; these are discussed at length elsewhere (Sheehan, this volume).

12. BALLYGRIFFIN, CO. KILKENNY
CORTICAL FLINT FLAKE
NMI reg. no. 1970:188
Oval in outline with a D-shaped cross-section and traces of cortex covering its dorsal face. Struck from a rolled flint pebble. No traces of retouch; it is unlikely that this flake was ever used as an implement. L. 3.4cm, W. 1.5cm, max.T. 6mm. Recovered from a fulacht fiadh during ploughing.

13. CATSTOWN, CO. KILKENNY
NOTCHED STEATITE DISC, FIVE STONE DISCS, TWO WHETSTONES
NMI reg. nos E151:2, 8–11, 13–15 and 18

The notched steatite disc (NMI reg. no. E151:2) has a perforation which is slightly off-centre. Along the external edge of the disc nearest the perforation is a series of thirteen uneven linear incisions producing a notched effect. Diam. 3.4cm, max.T. 7mm, diam. of perforation 2cm.

Five crude stone discs (NMI reg. nos E151:8–10, 13 and 15), showing little evidence of deliberate manufacture; may have formed as a result of heat fracture. Range of diams. 8.4cm to 18cm.

Both whetstones (NMI reg. nos E151:11 and 14) are roughly rectangular in outline; the largest measures L. 9.6cm, W. 3.35cm, T. 3.5cm.

In 1973 a series of four fulachta fiadh were discovered at Catstown during land-drainage operations. Two of these were subsequently partially excavated by Dr M. Ryan of the National Museum of Ireland. The majority of the finds were recovered from site 1 (E151:2, 8–11, 14 and 15). The largest of the stone discs (E151:13) was a surface find from near site 3 with no evidence of direct association between it and the site. Several modern finds were also recovered from site 1 (Ryan, this volume).

14. KILTRASSY, CO. KILKENNY
AXEHEAD, STONE
Broadly rectangular in outline with an oval cross-section; made of a schist which is found locally. L. 12.05cm, W. 4.5cm, max.T. 1.85cm. Recovered from within the remnants of a destroyed fulacht fiadh exposed by ploughing.

15. MABBOTSTOWN, CO. KILKENNY
SIDE-SCRAPER, FLINT
NMI reg. no. 1970:172
Irregular in outline, of uneven thickness though roughly triangular in cross-section. At least three chips of flint have been removed from its dorsal face. Retouch along the entire edge of one side with traces of cortex on the side directly opposite this. L. 3.8cm, W. 3.4cm, max.T. 9mm. This was a surface find approx. 6m from the site of a fulacht fiadh located in marshy land which has since been reclaimed.

16. OLDCASTLE LOWER, CO. KILKENNY
POT SHERD
NMI reg. no. 1987:39
Sherd of medieval cooking ware, roughly triangular in outline. The outer surface is reddish-buff with patches of dark grey, the inner surface is red. The fabric of the pottery contains traces of mica and quartz. A black carbonised substance adheres to the outer surface. L. 4.6cm, W. 3.1cm, max.T. 0.65cm. It was uncovered during ploughing from 20cm below the surface of the burnt stones of the site.

17. WEBBSBOROUGH, CO. KILKENNY
TWO CLAY BALLS, CHERT FLAKE
NMI reg. nos P1954:21–23
The balls are off-white in colour and are made of fired clay. One of the balls (P1954:21) has two black spots on its surface, a result of charcoal filling slight depressions on the face of the object. Diams. 2.30cm and 2.32cm.

The chert flake (P1954:23) bears no evidence of having ever been used as an implement.

The finds were recovered during excavation of the site; the clay balls were found on the floor of the trough (Prendergast 1955).

18. DOOROS, CO. MAYO (Pl. 4)
GOLD DRESS-FASTENER
NMI reg. no. 1934:5600
Undecorated with hollow, evenly-expanded terminals and a solid bow. The

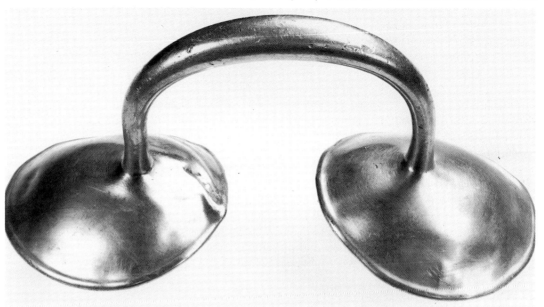

Plate 4—Gold dress-fastener from Dooros, Co. Mayo. (National Museum of Ireland).

surface of one of the terminals is slightly dented and the edges of both terminals are raised a little to form a rim. The bow is D-shaped in cross-section at the centre where it has a max. T. of 1.6cm; it narrows to 0.68cm at the junction of the terminals where it is circular in cross-section. Max.W. (from the extremity of one terminal to the other) 13.70cm. Diam. of terminals 5.83cm. Weight 176.73g.

19. TIROE, CO. TIPPERARY
END-SCRAPER, FLINT
NMI reg. no. 1969:840
Trapezoidal flake; no evidence for retouch on this scraper but it may have existed on the distal end where there is now a smooth polished strip running along its edge. A band of cortex runs along the entire length of one side of the scraper. L. 2.2cm, W. 1.5cm, max.T. 3mm. It was recovered from the material of a fulacht fiadh exposed by cattle disturbance.

20. CLONKERDON, CO. WATERFORD
THREE AXEHEADS
Quinlan (1885–6, 392) tells of three axeheads which he found 'within a few feet of the burned stones' of a fulacht fiadh he had opened at Clonkerdon. He describes the axeheads as being of Neolithic date, although NMI files record the axeheads as being made of bronze.

21. CROOKE, CO. WATERFORD
WHETSTONE FRAGMENT
NMI reg. no. 1976:69
Rectangular fragment; the faces are slightly concave and both faces and edges are very smooth from use. One end of the whetstone is marginally bulbous and the other end is broken. L. 8.4cm, W. at bulbous end 3.4cm, W. at break 3cm, max.T. 9mm. Recovered from the mound of a fulacht fiadh.

22. RATHCULIHEEN, CO. WATERFORD
FIVE SHERDS OF POTTERY
NMI reg. nos 1971:1056–1058, 1060–1061
Sherd 1 (1971:1056): rectangular sherd of North Devon Smoothware, orange. L. 5.75cm, W. 4cm, max.T. 1.7cm.

Sherd 2 (1971:1057): rectangular sherd of North Devon Smoothware, orange external surface and a green glazed inner surface. L. 5.6cm, W. 2.87cm, max.T. 6.5mm.

Sherd 3 (1971:1058): irregular-shaped sherd of Combed slipware; buff-coloured internal surface; outer surface yellow with a pattern of four parallel lines of brown conjoined semicircles. L. 4.1cm, W. 3.8cm, max.T. 7.25mm.

Sherd 4 (1971:1060): trapezoidal sherd of Tin Glazed Earthenware; only traces of glaze are now evident. L. 3.4cm, W. 2.7cm, max.T. 9mm.

Sherd 5 (1971:1061): trapezoidal sherd of Westerwald Stoneware; outer surface decorated with incised lines and patterns of grey and blue glaze, inner surface plain. L. 4cm, W. 2.4cm, max.T. 3.4mm.

ACKNOWLEDGEMENTS
I wish to thank the following: the National Museum of Ireland for access to records of previously unpublished material; Mr Victor Buckley, OPW; Mr Diarmuid Ó Drisceoil for access to the material from Fahee South, Co. Clare; Dr Michael Ryan and Ms Mary Cahill, National Museum of Ireland; Ms Rose Cleary and Professor Peter Woodman, University College, Cork. Photographs courtesy of the National Museum of Ireland.

REFERENCES

FAHY, E.M. 1960 A hut and cooking places at Drombeg, Co. Cork. *J. Cork Hist. Archaeol. Soc.* **65**, 1–17.

HODGES, H.W.M. 1955 The excavations of a group of cooking-places at Ballycroghan, Co. Down. *Ulster J. Archaeol.* **18**, 17–28.

Ó DRISCEOIL, D.A. 1980 Fulachta fiadh: a study. Unpublished M.A. thesis, University College, Cork.

O'KELLY, M.J. 1954 Excavations and experiments in ancient Irish cooking-places. *J. R. Soc. Antiq. Ir.* **84**, 105–55.

Ó RÍORDÁIN, S.P. 1938 Stone implement from Currafhcrowley West near Ballineen Co. Cork. *J.Cork Hist. Archaeol. Soc.* **43**, 56–7.

PRENDERGAST, E. 1955 Pre-historic cooking places in Webbsborough District. *Old Kilkenny Review* **8**, 1–10.

QUINLAN, J. 1885–6 The cooking-places of the Stone Age in Ireland *J. R. Soc. Antiq. Ir.* **17**, 390–2.

SMITH, M.A. 1959 Some Somerset hoards and their place in the Bronze Age of southern Britain. *Proc. Prehist. Soc.* **25**, 144–87.

The dating of fulachta fiadh

A.L. Brindley and J.N. Lanting

In 1980, a comprehensive programme aimed at establishing an absolute chronology for Irish prehistory was set up by J.N. Lanting (Groningen) and A.L. Brindley (Dublin), in cooperation with W.G. Mook (Radiocarbon Laboratory, Groningen). As part of this programme it was decided to date a series of fulachta fiadh to establish specifically their main period of use; for full details, discussion and references of data used here see Brindley *et al.* forthcoming). Fulachta fiadh are particularly suitable for dating by this process because of the characteristic and usually well-preserved wooden trough which provides integral samples from directly comparable contexts. The trough is always in an identifiable and normally primary position, and usually the wood species can be identified and the number of growth rings (i.e. its own age) estimated. The samples from fulachta fiadh troughs therefore provide optimum dating material. The premature identification of all occurrences of burnt stone as fulachta fiadh is incorrect as burnt stone debitage occurs as a result of various activities which have been practised at many times from the Mesolithic up to this century. For this programme, therefore, only sites which included a trough were sampled.

Figue 25 shows the 27 radiocarbon dates available for Irish fulachta fiadh by October 1988 and published dates from similar contexts in England and Scotland, but not from Wales. The Irish dates include re-dating of both Killeens I samples (K–I on Fig. 25), the Killeens II sample (K–II on Fig. 25) and both Drombeg samples (D on Fig. 25). In all cases, the duplicate samples produced more accurate results which agree well with other fulachta fiadh datings. The early result (? on Fig. 25) is from Cloghaclocka, Co. Limerick. The sample was taken from wood considered by the excavator to be possibly part of a fulacht fiadh trough. It is not clear why the date falls so far outside the expected range. However, the $\delta^{13}C$ content of the sample (too low for wood) suggests that the dated matter was in fact charcoal and not wood. Both date and $\delta^{13}C$ suggest that, inadvertently the wrong sample was used, and until a duplicate sample has been dated the result should be treated with caution. The two dates classified as 'possible' refer to unexcavated sites on Valentia Island where the samples were collected from spreads of burnt stone and charcoal which were interpreted as being fulachta fiadh. The radiocarbon dates indicate that this is likely.

Several dates have been excluded from Fig. 25 as not pertaining to fulachta fiadh, namely

(i) A sample of wood from Catstown, Co. Kilkenny, site 2, from later disturbance at the centre of the mound. This date is *terminus ante quem* for the fulacht fiadh).

(ii) Two samples from Ballycahane Lower, Co. Limerick, the first consisting of wood fragments in a peat layer thought to be part of a trough on the basis of a spread of heat-shattered sandstone and isolated limestone blocks. A scatter of pig bones was found nearby. The second sample was of peat below the shattered stone. Both dates indicate activity during the Early Mesolithic, unrelated to the spread of stones.

(iii) Charcoal from a spread of burnt stone uncovered during reclamation of a low-lying wet area at Fofannybane, Co. Down. No trough was noted at the site, which was not excavated. Either the site is not a fulacht fiadh or the sample was contaminated by younger material.

Previous discussions of fulachta fiadh have relied heavily on the Dublin and Chicago dates from Drombeg and Killeens I and II. Because of the importance of these dates, duplicate samples were analysed. The Groningen dates indicate that the Dublin samples were insufficiently pre-treated, resulting in dates which were too recent and thus appeared to

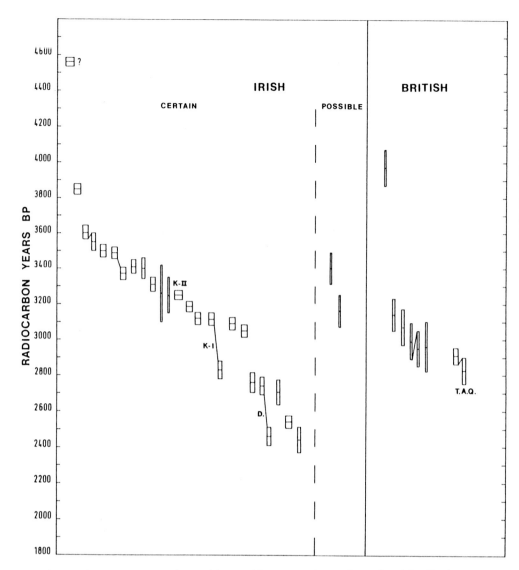

Fig. 25—The 27 radiocarbon dates available for Irish fulachta fiadh by October 1988 and corresponding English and Scottish dates.

substantiate a connection with cooking practices described in Early Historic texts. The Groningen dates, however, concur with other fulachta fiadh results. The Chicago dates for Killeens I and II were also duplicated, as analyses carried out by the solid carbon method during the early fifties are frequently inaccurate and have large standard deviations.

CONCLUSIONS

1. The figure shows that, with no exceptions, fulachta fiadh date to the Bronze Age and to a well-defined span within that period.

2. The term fulacht fiadh should be used only with reference to sites with troughs and mounds of burnt stone.

3. Fulachta fiadh, as defined above, have no connection with descriptions in Early Historic and later texts to practices involving cooking with stones. The practices described in these texts have not been identified so far archaeologically.

4. There is, therefore, no evidence or even compelling argument to indicate that fulachta fiadh are primarily cooking sites, although their widespread distribution and apparently fairly regular use might support such a function.

REFERENCE

BRINDLEY, A.L, LANTING, J.N. and MOOK, W.G. (forthcoming) The radiocarbon dating of Irish fulachta fiadh and their context. *J. Irish Archaeol.*

PART 2

SCOTTISH CONTRIBUTIONS

EDITED BY JOHN BARBER AND CHRIS RUSSELL-WHITE

WITH ILLUSTRATIONS BY KEITH SPELLER

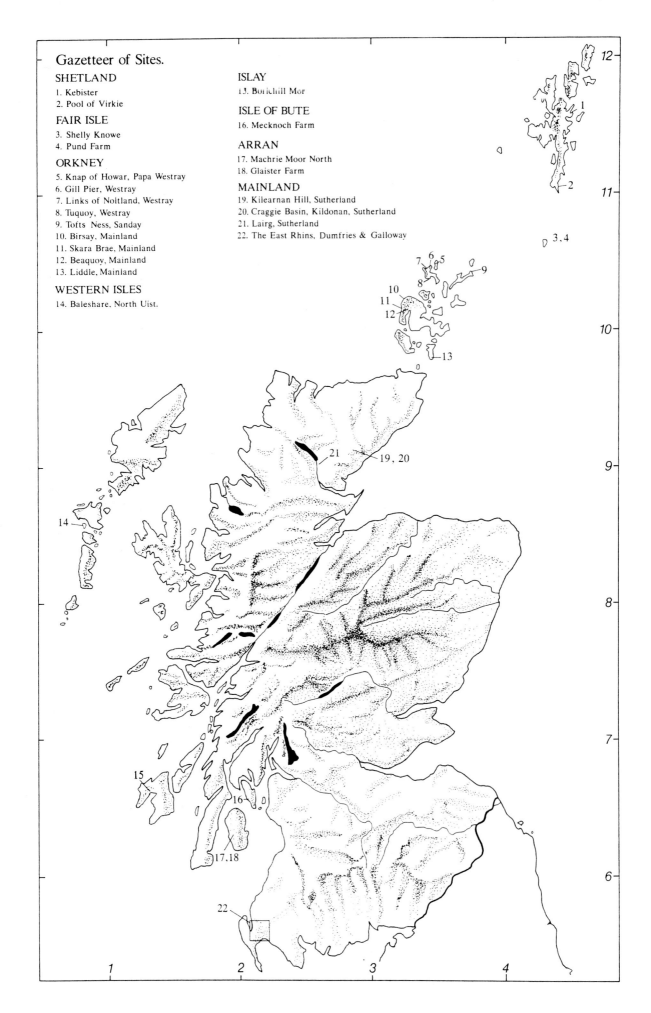

Gazetteer of Sites.

SHETLAND
1. Kebister
2. Pool of Virkie

FAIR ISLE
3. Shelly Knowe
4. Pund Farm

ORKNEY
5. Knap of Howar, Papa Westray
6. Gill Pier, Westray
7. Links of Noltland, Westray
8. Tuquoy, Westray
9. Tofts Ness, Sanday
10. Birsay, Mainland
11. Skara Brae, Mainland
12. Beaquoy, Mainland
13. Liddle, Mainland

WESTERN ISLES
14. Baleshare, North Uist.

ISLAY
15. Borichill Mor

ISLE OF BUTE
16. Mecknoch Farm

ARRAN
17. Machrie Moor North
18. Glaister Farm

MAINLAND
19. Kilearnan Hill, Sutherland
20. Craggie Basin, Kildonan, Sutherland
21. Lairg, Sutherland
22. The East Rhins, Dumfries & Galloway

Fig. 26—Gazetteer of sites in Scotland.

58

Preface

The occasion of the IBMSG conference in Dublin in 1988 provided both stimulus and forum for a review of burnt mounds in Scotland. The three penultimate papers in this section contain the substance of the contribution of the Historical Buildings and Monuments branch of the Scottish Development Department to that conference, to which we have added further papers in an attempt to present a balanced view of work on burnt mounds in Scotland.

The work of the Royal Commission on the Ancient and Historic Monuments of Scotland in the south-west of the country has not only revealed numerous burnt mounds but also, and more importantly, has led to the realisation that earlier surveys have simply failed to identify these sites in other areas. The implications of that realisation are discussed by Strat Halliday in the opening paper of this section. The National Monuments Record of Scotland, which is included within the RCAHMS, has provided the gazetteer of the known Scottish sites (Appendix 2).

John Hunter's continuing work on the small and appositely named Fair Isle is an important attempt to place the Scottish burnt mounds in their archaeological landscape. While we must await the results of excavation to establish which of the palimpsest of surveyed features are contemporaneous with the burnt mounds this is surely one of the main directions which burnt mound studies must take, particularly when, as he shows below, the burnt mound is often the sole surviving element of the original array of sites. Steven Dockrill's excavations of similarly complex landscapes at Tofts Ness parallels Historic Buildings and Monuments work on Arran, Kildonan, Kebister and elsewhere. Brief accounts of the excavations of burnt mounds revealed in the HBM projects appear below, but analyses of their relationships with the other elements in the archaeological landscape await publication of the projects. Dockrill's use of geophysical survey techniques to identify burnt mound deposits is particularly important for Scotland where the sites commonly appear as amorphous mounds, quite unlike the classic kidney-shaped fulacht fiadh of the literature.

Burnt mounds are, individually, among the most boring sites with which a field archaeologist must deal. Apart from a new date and a new spot on the distribution map, individual sites have little to contribute to our understanding of the past. However, as statistical entities, the patterns of their chronological and spatial distributions hold the promise of insights into the use of marginal and upland areas, while their relationships with other sites may begin to reveal something of the social patterning of emerging village life in the Scottish Later Bronze Age and its collapse with the transition to dispersed Early Iron Age settlement over upland Scotland. As indicators of more significant sites and events burnt mounds have the advantage of 'survivability', being recognisable even when ploughed flat. It seems to us, then, that the future of burnt mound studies lies, on the one hand, in the patient accumulation of further dating and distributional evidence and, on the other, in pursuing the study of their relationships with the other elements of the archaeological landscape. In this regard the IBMSG conference was a timely opportunity to take stock of the existing evidence and define future objectives.

Chris Russell-White
John Barber
AOC/HBM
Fleming House
28-31 Kinnaird Park
Newcraighall
Edinburgh EH15 3RD
April 1989

4. PATTERNS AND DISTRIBUTION

Patterns of fieldwork and the distribution of burnt mounds in Scotland

S. P. Halliday

Some fifteen years ago, an assessment of Scottish burnt mounds was published by John Hedges following his excavations at Liddle and Beaquoy (1975). (All references are located at the end of this section.) At the time, it appeared that there were two distinct distributions of burnt mounds in the British Isles, one in the north and the other in the west. Most of the Scottish examples fell in the northern distribution, which comprised the concentrations on Orkney and Shetland and a thin scatter across Caithness and Ross and Cromarty. The scatter known from Galloway, however, was grouped in the western distribution, along with those of Ireland, Wales and England. Rashly, perhaps, Hedges ventured the opinion that this reflected a real pattern of occurrence (1975, 61), and he went on to compare the distribution in the Northern Isles with that of the better agricultural land, concluding that there was a direct relationship between the two (1975, 64–5, 74).

There are now in excess of 800 burnt mounds known in Scotland, many of them recorded since Hedges conducted his survey. The purpose of this paper, however, is not only to examine the impact of the last fifteen years' work but also to explore the patterns of work that lie behind the distribution. Unlike scientific experiments, where fresh sets of data may be collected to confirm or deny earlier conclusions, distributions of archaeological material tend to represent the sum of cumulative knowledge gathered over a period of two hundred years or more. It is essential, therefore, to assess the sources of information from which a distribution is drawn in order to identify any bias that may have had an effect upon it. Some sources of bias are the result of the processes of survival and destruction (Stevenson 1975), but others reflect patterns of collection (e.g. Young 1986) and it is these that particularly concern me here.

The most comprehensive source of information for sites in Scotland is undoubtedly provided by the National Monuments Record cards, which extend the record card system built up by the former Archaeology Division of the OS (see gazetteer, Appendix 2). Indeed, for large areas of Scotland, little has been added to the cards since they were taken over by the NMR. It is often forgotten that this card system was established by the OS as a mapping tool, not as a record of the archaeology, and their contents were severely constrained by broad policies for the mapping of antiquities. The principal functions of the field sections were to establish that sites depicted on earlier editions of the maps or mentioned in the archaeological literature fulfilled the criteria by which they were eligible for depiction, and were shown in the correct place with the correct classification. There was limited scope for the sort of survey familiar to most archaeologists, where the main objective is to locate unrecorded monuments. With these constraints it is remarkable that so many new sites were recorded by the field sections, but it is inevitable that most of their work was directed into the areas where sites were already known. The implications for distributions drawn from the cards are considerable, particularly where comparisons are being made with data drawn from other sources. On Shetland, for instance, the apparent relationship observed by Hedges is not with the better agricultural land itself but with the other monuments, such as the burial cairns, the various types of settlements, or even the medieval castles and churches, which all tend to be found on the better soils. As yet there is no more wide-ranging survey available that can distinguish real gaps in the distribution from those that simply reflect the extent of the thick mantle of uncut peat.

More general problems arise with the wider distribution of burnt mounds in Scotland. Prior to the revision of the basic scale maps of Orkney and Shetland in the late 1960s and early 1970s, the OS field sections had little experience of burnt mounds and very few were identified on the mainland. In the late 1970s and early 1980s, however, they put the experience gained in the Northern Isles to good use, and a series of burnt mounds was recorded in Sutherland, Caithness, Ross and Cromarty, Inverness and Argyll. Most archaeologists realise, although few care to admit to it, that there is a tendency to record within limits set by experience and expectation. Interestingly, the present investigators of the Royal Commission on the Ancient and Historical Monuments of Scotland have been through a similar process to the archaeological surveyors of the OS, since the Commission's experience of burnt mounds in the field effectively ended with the completion of the Inventory of the Northern Isles (RCAHMS 1946). The northern field section of the OS had alerted us to the burnt mounds in the north, but we gained little experience in locating or recognising them until the survey of the East Rhins in Wigtownshire (RCAHMS 1987). The survey was conducted over a period of about eighteen months between March 1985 and October 1986, but the existence of the burnt mounds was not established until March 1986. Over the next few months we identified a total of 75, about 60 of them in the last 50 square kilometres to be surveyed. The uneven distribution, with its cluster in the lower reaches of the Luce valley, is unlikely to reflect anything other than the pattern of survey. Having gained the experience, however, we have located 28 examples in Perthshire (RCAHMS forthcoming), whilst a week's survey in Easter Ross identified at least four. One of the remarkable features of these burnt mounds is the uniformity of their shape and form. Of the 110 recorded by the Commission in Wigtownshire, Perthshire and Easter Ross, no less than 75 are characterised by a crescentic or penannular mound around a shallow hollow.

The available data for the distribution of burnt mounds are clearly unreliable, reflecting the patterns of work and experience of the various agencies involved, and it is no longer possible to separate confidently the burnt mounds in the north from those in Galloway. The burnt mounds that have now been located in Arran and Argyll, together with the possible example near Muirkirk, Ayrshire, are beginning to fill the gap, whilst those in Perthshire and possible examples in Kincardine (RCAHMS 1984a, 42, no. 283), Midlothian (RCAHMS 1988, 32–3, nos 172, 178–9), Berwick and Roxburgh hint at a much wider distribution across the whole of Scotland. It is this possibility of a wider distribution that fieldwork must explore over the next few years.

ACKNOWLEDGEMENTS
I should like to thank my colleagues in the Commission for commenting on an earlier draft of this paper, particularly J. L. Davidson and N. K. Blood for their help in the sections dealing with the pattern of Ordnance Survey fieldwork.

5. RECENT RESEARCH

Recent research into burnt mounds on Fair Isle, Shetland, and Sanday, Orkney

J. R. Hunter and S. J. Dockrill

According to antiquarian records, field monuments composed of burnt stone have long been recognised as ancient landscape features in the Northern Isles. Only recently, however, have questions regarding their social and economic significance been posed, largely stemming from the results of a detailed sites and monuments survey which have shown a distribution considerably more widespread than hitherto supposed. Lamb's systematic cover of over 20 likely sites on Sanday (RCAHMS 1980, nos 32–52) and 16 from neighbouring Stronsay (RCAHMS 1984b, nos 99–114) are both surprisingly high considering the extent of modern agriculture and the relative sparsity of marginal land.

BURNT MOUNDS IN THE LANDSCAPE

Elsewhere in the north other detailed work, notably by Parry on West Burra, has attempted to identify the burnt mound as a specific component of relict landscapes (Hedges 1984, 47). Similar investigations on Fair Isle, Shetland, and at Tofts Ness, Sanday, Orkney (Fig. 26), have also been carried out by the authors but directed towards more broadly-based issues of early settlement, combining both survey and excavation. In the case of Fair Isle this paper pre-empts excavation work scheduled for 1989 but nevertheless serves to illustrate a localised group of mounds which, given the natural boundaries imposed by an island landscape, might be argued to represent a definable infrastructure. At Tofts Ness, on the other hand, sample excavation work in an area of remarkable prehistoric activity has already demonstrated the importance of environmental and geophysical parameters in studies of this kind (Dockrill 1988).

Work on Fair Isle was undertaken seasonally from 1984 until 1987 and involved a total landscape analysis from prehistoric to post-medieval times. The underlying designs for this have been discussed elsewhere (Hunter 1984, 1) although one factor in particular, namely the level of monument preservation brought about by relative inaccessibility and absence of modern development, is worthy of further emphasis here. In common with Fetlar, Foula and Papa Stour, Fair Isle is physically divided by a major landscape feature of arguable antiquity, a 'feelie' dyke constructed of earth and turf which separates pasture from hill land. In the case of Fair Isle this bisects the island from east to west thus separating (or indeed creating) two distinctive zones of land use, namely pasture and modern habitation to the south of the dyke and moorland to the north. Documentary evidence suggests that settlement and cultivation in historic times have been restricted to the southern zone almost exclusively, and that the area of pasture delineated in modern times (Fig. 27) represents the maximum expansion of post-medieval agriculture. Given, therefore, the density of occupation in this zone, which reached a recorded peak of around 360 souls in the mid nineteenth century according to census returns and which affected land division and continual cultivation, it would be remarkable if anything other than minor indications of earlier occupation had survived. Indeed, the contrast in the monuments record from either side of the modern fence line that defines this pasture shows the importance of marginal land even within a densely populated area.

What is perhaps surprising, therefore, is that the distribution of burnt

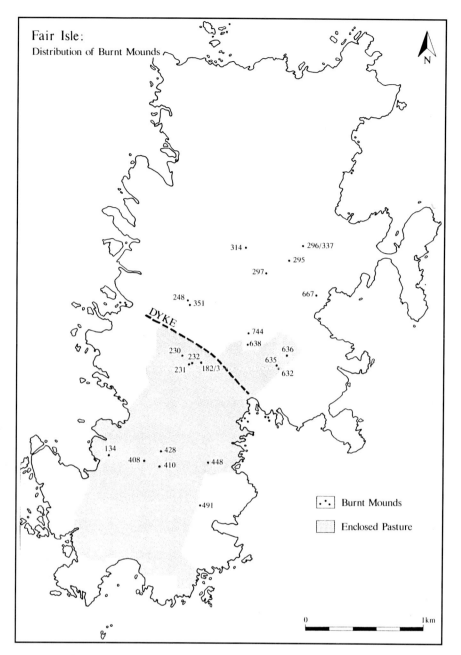

Fig. 27—Distribution of recorded burnt mounds in Fair Isle in relation to area of post-medieval enclosed land.

mounds (Fig. 27) is by no means restricted to areas outside the southern zone of settlement. Of the 24 likely sites identified, 11 were located where their survival might be anticipated whereas the other 13, located in the pasture zone, have survived in spite of intensive post-medieval occupation and land use. This is not to say that erosion had been obviated, as was evident from ploughing, quarrying and the Funniquoy mill system, but the indications suggested that the recorded distribution of burnt mounds is a reasonable reflection of their original distribution. Physical stature is presumably a major factor in this survival, but the nature of the composition is equally relevant. Mounds of stone, whether cairns or burnt mounds, are difficult and time-consuming to shift and, unlike linear earthen features, pose little in the way of hazard to formal agriculture. Even on Fair Isle, where useful stone for building purposes is at a premium, burnt mounds are effectively valueless and are more likely to be continuously supplemented as clearance cairns than to be robbed for building. To some extent this makes identification difficult, but no more so than distinguishing mounds of burnt character from those evolving from burial or settlement, for example by observation of characteristic geophysical properties (below).

The Fair Isle mounds differ widely in recorded stature and form, although a proportion appear to conform to a crescent shape, presumably

63

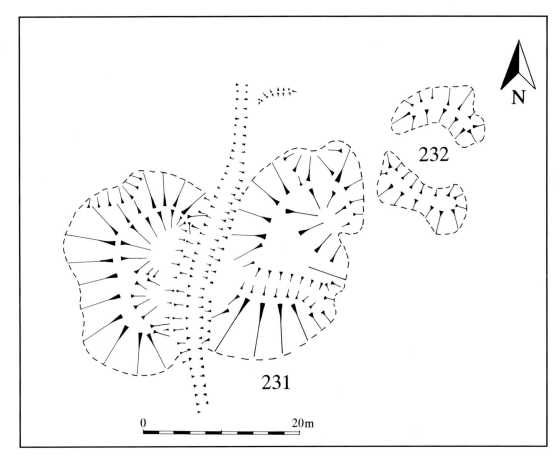

Fig. 28—Fair Isle sites 231 and 232.

232

231

0   20m

reflecting either an original discard pattern or robbing or a combination of both activities. The most substantial example (site 231; RCAHMS 1946, no. 1196) covered an area of approximately 40m x 30m, standing to a height of about 1.5m (probably the largest of its type in Shetland), and is bisected by a modern cable/pipe trench (Pl. 5). Another example, site 744 (RCAHMS 1946, no. 1195), damaged during road construction in the later nineteenth century, contained possible cremations which appear to relate to secondary activity. Others have suffered plough damage (notably sites 182 and 183), another from the intrusion of a watercourse (site 134), and a further (site 428; RCAHMS 1946, no. 1202), although noted on the current Ordnance Survey map, has been completely obliterated.

The remaining monuments were ostensibly unaffected by major erosion and varied in ground area between *c.* 8m x 5m (site 633) and *c.* 19m x 13m (site 232) with a surviving height typically of between 1m and 1.5m. Although some were fairly isolated (e.g. site 491), others were clearly identifiable in groups, and in some cases could be interpreted as being integral to groups of other monuments. Sites 295, 296 and 337, for example, could be argued to belong to a relict landscape containing field boundaries, cairns and associated structural remains (Hunter 1985, fig 5). They could, in effect, be seen in context rather than as individual unrelated features. Sites 248 and 351 occupied a similar position in relation to a series of turf-based and stone-based forms derived from inferred earlier settlement (Hunter 1985, fig. 3), and a similarly early environment was postulated for site 297. At both these locations, however, the precise nature and extent of the associated remains requires clarification. Near the farm of Pund, however, at the location of the three largest mounds on the island (sites 230, 231 and 232, Fig. 28), no such associations were evident, probably as a result of drainage and cultivation. The same argument presumably applies to another group (sites 408, 410 and 428) where the mounds also appear to stand in isolation within the pasture zone. The final group (sites 632, 635 and 636) also lies within this area of modern pasture, but at the extreme north-east in an area of 'reclaimed' marginal land where cultivation has been less intensive. Here traces of earlier remains are still evident in the vicinity, presumably attesting to the relatively short duration of post-medieval agricultural use.

The mounds themselves, therefore, are seen as indicators of early settlement locations, and on the Fair Isle evidence are argued to be particularly strong archaeological survivors.Their distribution is seen to survive major agricultural changes and, in those places where the landscape is marginal, associated archaeological monuments with which they stand as integral components are still evident.

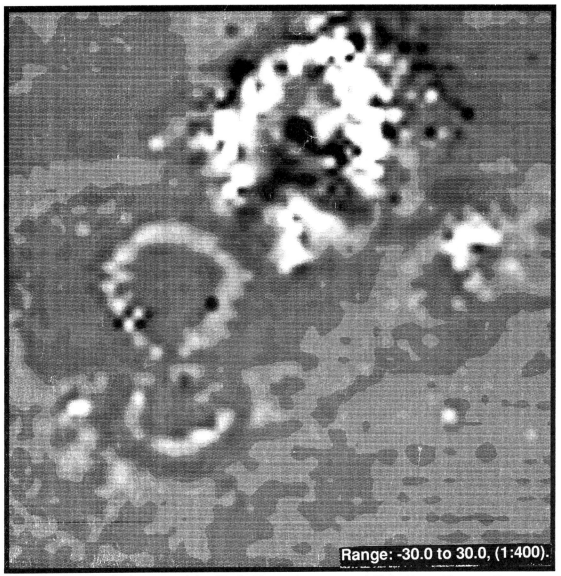

Fig. 29—Geophysical survey of the Shelly Knowe burnt mound, Tofts Ness. The curvilinear features to the south-west are interpreted as structural remains.

BURNT MOUNDS AND GEOPHYSICAL SURVEY

Research designs can be set to test this modelling, but one important prerequisite lies in the identification of burnt mounds in the first instance, given the turf-covered nature of most examples recorded. Roasted stones within the mounds show an enhanced magnetic susceptibility (in as much as this has been tested on the geology of the Northern Isles) which can be observed as a characteristic magnetic signature. Pioneering work in this respect was conducted at the Liddle and Pickaquoy burnt mounds, Orkney (A. Aspinal, pers. comm.), and further tests have since been conducted on the Fair Isle mounds using upgraded equipment to provide greater discrimination between mounds of different function types.

Ultimately it will be feasible to provide definitive numbers of extant or former burnt mound sites on the basis that even ploughed-out scatter should offer a characteristic magnetic response. On Fair Isle, for example, there are a further seven putative burnt mound sites whose character requires definition preferably by non-excavational means.

Similar work, supplemented by excavation, has been carried out on the peninsula of Tofts Ness, Sanday, a prehistoric landscape covering an area of some 150 hectares preserved largely by burial in blown sand and described at length by Wood, a local antiquarian, in the mid nineteenth century (NSA 1845, 136). His investigations suggested the presence of funerary monuments, some of which contained evidence of inhumations as well as cremation. Recent field survey has drawn attention to the varied range of monument types present (Stevenson 1980), and an archaeological assessment was subsequently implemented ahead of a scheduling programme. This combined conventional and geophysical survey with sub-surface sampling and a programme of excavation. One major burnt mound complex was identified within the archaeological landscape, known locally as Shelly Knowe (Fig. 29) and consisting of a number of earthworks dominated by a single large mound formed in the shape of a crescent. Together with the presence of burnt stone exposed in the north face, this characteristic form suggested that the site was a burnt mound, although the presence of large quantities of shell midden offered some ambiguity about the overall nature of the site. However, a fluxgate gradiometer survey undertaken by J. Gater showed a response typical of burnt mound sites and additionally indicated the presence of two structural features in a low adjoining mound to the south. Some 250m to the west similar signals had been received from the walls of a round house (since excavated) and were seen to be caused by midden either incorporated within the wall core or abutting the walling lines. Using this analogy, a similar interpretation was applied to the anomalies forming these two circular structures.

Examination of the surrounding landscape adjacent to the burnt mound complex showed a further area of magnetic enhancement although many of the surface features had been lost by ploughing and clearance. Sub-surface sampling and excavation have since revealed that this magnetic anomaly corresponds to a buried anthropogenic soil (in places over 0.5m deep) sandwiched between layers of windblown sand. Similar anthropogenic soils have been identified elsewhere within the excavation programme, notably sealed by a later cultivated sand-based soil which in turn was sealed by Late Bronze Age/Early Iron Age midden deposits derived from the round house complex. These soils indicated areas of intensive arable cultivation in the vicinity of settlement sites and argue for a high degree of 'land management', itself indicative of permanent rather than seasonal exploitation of the palaeolandscape.

Evidence from the main excavation programme has shown that the settlement mound containing the round house contains occupation from the Neolithic through to the Early Iron Age, and it seems probable that the remains of the Shelly Knowe burnt mound complex are equally widely dated. Two TL dates from stratified burnt stones at the exterior surface of the main mound give values of 360 ± 300 BC (SUTL70) and 90 ± 310 BC (SUTL71), indicating a late use for this type of monument notwithstanding the sampling difficulties involved. Provisional dating of the round house itself suggests that the two sites may have partly functioned together in the first millennium BC, the house being interpreted as a domestic site engaged in arable cultivation as well as animal husbandry and the exploitation of marine resources. Surprisingly, therefore, burnt stones were not observed either within the dwelling or its associated middens and thus the particular cooking method traditionally interpreted from burnt mounds seems not to have been employed at the dwelling itself, although a stratigraphically earlier structure on the same site yielded a stone tank and floor plan (Pl. 6) almost identical to the features recovered by Hedges

66

Plate 5—Fair Isle site 231, one of the largest burnt mounds in Shetland, seen from the south-west.

Plate 6—Excavated tank feature at Toft's Ness.

at the Liddle burnt mound (Hedges 1975, fig. 2, reproduced here as Fig 40). However, no burnt stones were encountered in association and this draws into question the significance of major burnt mounds of the Shelly Knowe type which might be seen as having a more specialised function within the palaeolandscape. As at Fair Isle, the strategy shows the importance of considering the burnt mound within the widest possible context and by applying complementary techniques.

ACKNOWLEDGEMENTS

The investigations on Fair Isle have been supported by the National Trust for Scotland, the Shetland Amenity Trust, the Russell Trust and the Society of Antiquaries of Scotland. Work at Tofts Ness has been carried out on behalf of the Scottish Development Department (Historic Buildings and Monuments).

6. EXCAVATION

Excavation and sampling of burnt mounds in Scotland

C. J. Russell-White

INTRODUCTION

Between 1980 and 1988 the Central Excavation Unit (now AOC) of HBM was involved in the excavation and sampling of a number of burnt mounds. Between 1980 and 1981 nine mounds were excavated and surveyed before afforestation on Machrie Moor, Arran. Also in 1981, damage was noted on a burnt mound at Borichill Mor on Islay which was sampled. In 1983 at Killearnan Hill, Sutherland, four mounds were excavated before afforestation. The following year (1984) a single mound, threatened by coastal erosion, was excavated at Gill Pier, Westray, Orkney. As part of a large project, in 1987, several mounds were investigated at Kebister, Mainland, Shetland. In the same year, in the East Rhins of Galloway, seven mounds threatened by forestry, road bypass, or drainage ditches were excavated, sampled or both. In 1988 the Buteshire Natural History Society excavated Mecknoch Farm on the Isle of Bute; and during evaluation work in the Craggie Basin, Kildonan, Sutherland, one mound was sampled.

For the purpose of this chapter the sites have been divided into two parts: those whose main place of publication is this work, and those which will appear elsewhere. The first part contains the mounds from the East Rhins of Galloway (nos 1–7), the Arran mounds (8–16) and the Gill Pier mound from Westray (17). The second part includes Killearnan Hill (20–2) and Craggie Basin (29), both in Kildonan, Sutherland, Kebister, Shetland (23–28), and notes on Bute (18) and Islay (19).

6a.

The East Rhins of Galloway

C. J. Russell-White

INTRODUCTION
The East Rhins of Galloway form an upland area bordered on the east by the Moors of Galloway, by Loch Ryan and Stranraer to the west and Luce Bay to the south. Most of the land is grass moorland (typical of Galloway) lying above 150m. There are no very high hills here and much is plateau land cut by one notable valley, that of the Water of Luce, which runs south into Luce Bay.

The local bedrock comprises greywackes of the Lower Palaeozoic together with shales, and some very limited igneous and metamorphic

The Burnt Mounds of the
East Rhins of Dumfries & Galloway.

Existing Burnt Mounds. △ ▲

1. Dervaird
2. Auld Taggart 2   3. Auld Taggart 4
4. Cruise 1   5. Stair Lodge
6. Gabsnout Burn 1   7. Claddy House Burn

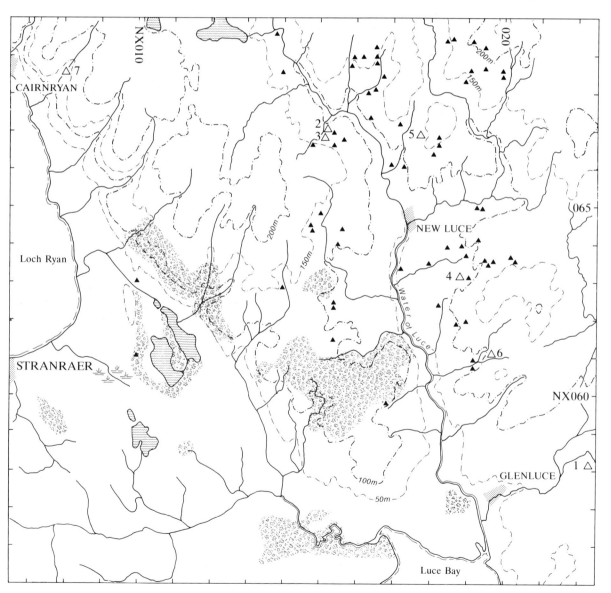

Fig. 30—The burnt mounds of the East Rhins of Dumfries and Galloway.

70

inclusions of porphyrite dikes and granites of later date. The soils vary greatly throughout, but the investigated sites all lay on soils of the Ettrick Association. These were mostly Brown Forest Soils and related types derived from the greywackes and shales and formed on glacial tills and boulder clays.

In the summer of 1987 damage to a number of the mounds was noted by the RCAHMS. In response, seven mounds were investigated by the CEU, with a view to establishing a chronological and morphological framework for burnt mounds in south-west Scotland. The work was carried out in two stages. Dervaird, mound 1, outside the area of the RCAHMS survey, was investigated in one week by a team supervised by J. Barber. Several weeks later another team excavated the other six, within the survey area, over a period of three weeks (Fig. 30).

Dervaird, Glenluce, was threatened by road improvement. Five of the remainder lay within a few kilometres of New Luce. Four were damaged by field drainage; the fifth, at Gabsnout Burn (mound 6), had been ploughed for forestry. The final mound, at Claddy House Burn, mound 7, overlooking Loch Ryan, was cut by the drainage ditch of a forestry road.

The mounds were all situated at the edge of wetland or burns, but often on or near comparatively well-drained slopes. Although none of the sites could be associated directly with any other structure, all lay within a few hundred metres of either open settlement, agricultural remains or cairns. This is the densest area of probable funerary cairns in Dumfries and Galloway (Yates 1984).

Three levels of excavation and recording were undertaken. Three sites (Auld Taggart 4, mound 3, Cruise 1, mound 4, and Dervaird, mound 1) were substantially or partially excavated. Three (Claddy House Burn, mound 7, Auld Taggart 2, mound 2, and Stair Lodge, mound 5) either had existing areas of damage sectioned or were box-sectioned. The final site (Gabsnout Burn 1, mound 6) was sampled for radiocarbon and possible thermoluminescence dating, as were the other six.

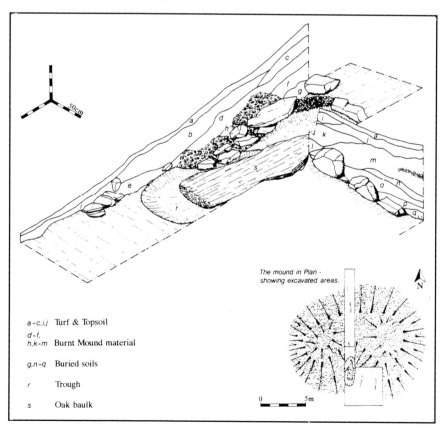

Fig. 31—Dervaird Burnt Mound:
Isometric reconstruction.

a-c,i,j   Turf & Topsoil

d-f,
h,k-m   Burnt Mound material

g,n-q   Buried soils

r   Trough

s   Oak baulk

The mound in Plan -
showing excavated areas.

0   5m

71

EXCAVATION
Mound 1, Dervaird NGR NX 224 582
This mound lay immediately S of the A75 and 3 miles E of the township of Glenluce. It was excavated in the light of its envisaged destruction by the realignment and widening of the A75 road and has since been completely destroyed. It was kidney-shaped in plan, measuring some 16m by 8m (Fig. 31), and was sited in a wet hollow immediately adjacent to a small

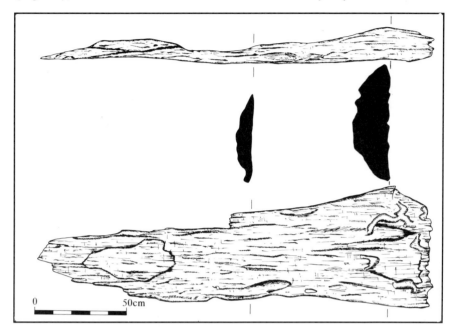

Fig. 32—Rotted oak baulk: Dervaird.

stream. Some 10m away were the remains of a second burnt mound, now cut by a meander of the stream.

Excavation revealed a cooking pit cut into the boulder clay between the enclosing arms of the mound. The pit had been partly lined with stone slabs at two different levels. These may have been intended to revet and preserve the clay sides of the tank as they did not present a continuous face and could not, alone, have retained water. The base of the pit had been lined with a large oak timber which was relatively well preserved. It was triangular in plan, only 0.75m wide across its base and approximately 2.25m long. Its thickness varied from just over 0.17m at its wider end to less than 1cm at its apex and it was plano-convex in cross-section, flat face uppermost (Fig. 32). Like the side slabs, this seems to have been used to prevent the erosion of the clay floor of the pit rather than to provide a full lining.

The kidney-shaped mound consisted of heat-shattered stones set in a dark matrix, rich in charcoal. The stones were mainly sandstones and the charcoal was, for the greater part, oak. Charcoal and the 20 outer rings of the oak plank were submitted for radiocarbon dating, producing dates of 1210 ± 50 bc (GU-2331) and 1280 ± 50 bc (GU-2330).

Auld Taggart
A group of four mounds lay near the remains of a turf sheiling along the SE side of the Lingdowey Burn, c 500m SSE of its confluence with the Water of Luce. Two, 40m apart, were investigated.

Mound 2, Auld Taggart 2, NGR NX 1516 6700 (Fig. 33). This mound lay beside the old track to the ruined farmstead at Auld Taggart. It could barely be seen as a mound, showing mainly as a scatter of broken stones on the surface and in the bottom of a drainage ditch. This prevented the extent of the mound being determined. No structure could be discerned, and to avoid the problem of flooding encountered in the other mounds it was only sectioned. A section was cut at about 45 degrees to the ditch,

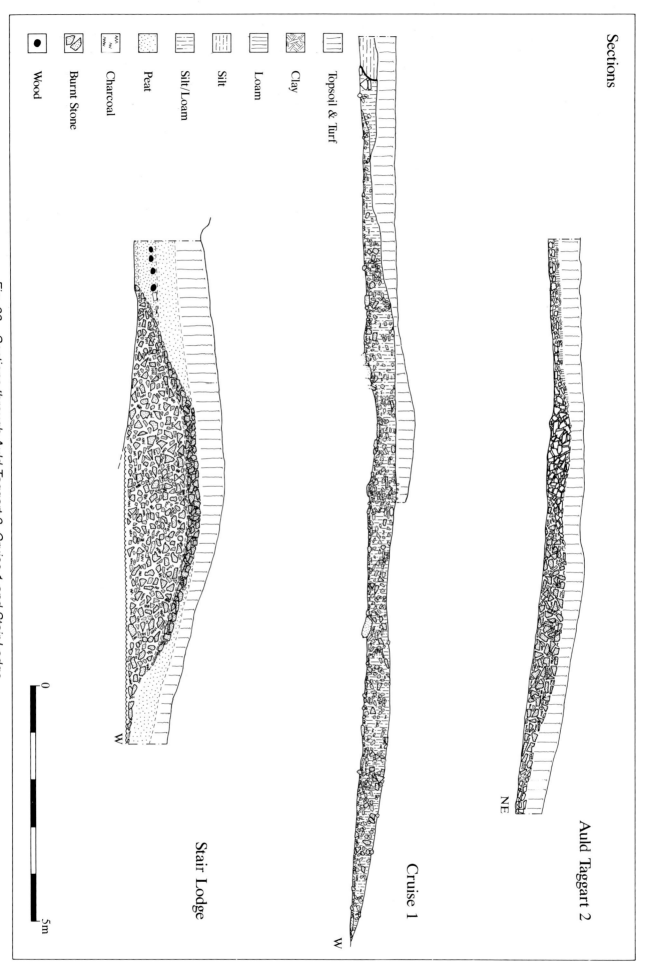

Sections

Topsoil & Turf

Clay

Loam

Silt

Silt/Loam

Peat

Charcoal

Burnt Stone

● Wood

Auld Taggart 2

NE

Cruise 1

W

Stair Lodge

W

0

5m

Fig. 33—Sections through Auld Taggart 2, Cruise 1 and Stair Lodge.

73

running roughly N–S. About 2m by 1.5m of the mound was in evidence on the surface but a length of over 7m was visible in section.

The mound material consisted of pink heat-cracked stones (mostly greywackes) in a charcoal-rich soil matrix. The surface of the mound where the roots were densest formed a hardened crust. Between mound and subsoil was a buried soil. This very clayey humic loam with quantities of roots and very small stones was best preserved at the S. Here, it overlay a compressed layer of broken stones; a similar area packed with stones was seen in the more waterlogged N end. The mound was radiocarbon-dated to 1060 ± 50 AD (GU-2416) with charcoal of *Betula* sp. and *Alnus glutinosa*.

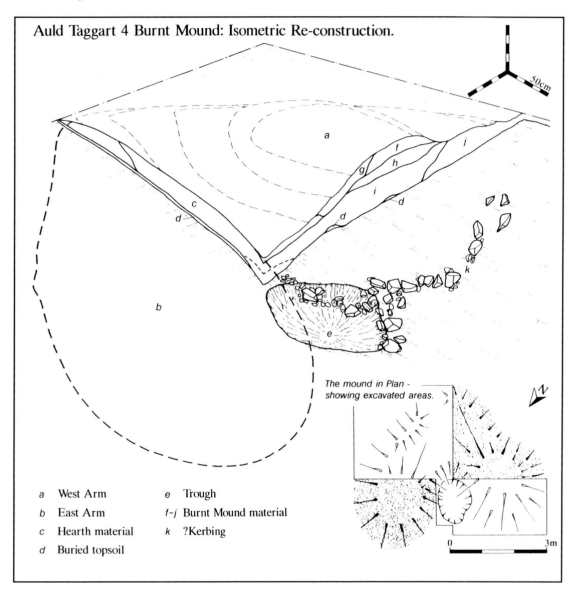

Auld Taggart 4 Burnt Mound: Isometric Re-construction.

The mound in Plan - showing excavated areas.

a	West Arm	e	Trough
b	East Arm	f-j	Burnt Mound material
c	Hearth material	k	?Kerbing
d	Buried topsoil		

Fig. 34—Auld Taggart 4: isometric reconstruction.

Mound 3, Auld Taggart 4 , NGR NX 1513 6696. Auld Taggart 4 lay some 40m NE of Auld Taggart 2. It was almost complete although clipped on the NW side by a drainage ditch. Crescentic in plan, it had a fairly boggy hollow located between the two wings, less than 1m high, on the NW. The mound measured a maximum of 6m wide and 4.5m from trough to back. Since its shape and extent could be seen in plan, it was excavated by quadrant. The mound was divided on NW–SE and NE–SW axes and the E and W quadrants were excavated (Fig. 34). On completion of the quadrants the trough area was investigated.

The mound consisted of loosely-packed heat-cracked stones, the lower parts of which sat in a matrix of charcoal-rich soil. This was held together by a skin of more compacted, rooted stones in a loamy matrix. On the higher SW side, patches of charcoal were noted further up the section amongst the looser stones.

A platform lay between the two wings. The make-up of this, which sloped gently down towards the trough, was fine small stones set in a charcoal-rich matrix. It seems likely that this was the hearth site.

Both parts of the mound stood upon a possible buried topsoil which, under the combined effect of the weight of stone and of waterlogging, appeared to merge into the subsoil. An arc of more compacted stones in a loamier soil lay under the edge of the E quadrant, appearing to blend into the possible buried topsoil. The looser stones had slumped over this apparent kerb.

Because of flooding it was not possible to excavate the trough area cleanly, but it was noted that material from all sides of the mound had slumped into the hollow, obscuring the trough edges. The trough (1.40m x 1m) had also silted up with a waterlogged peaty fill which contained twigs and from which rushes grew in abundance. It was cut into the subsoil (to a depth of 0.32m) and functioned well as a water tank. Its incomplete lining consisted of stones on the NW and SW sides. The bottom, which could not be fully revealed, seemed to be covered with very small, sharp, angular stones, presumbly derived from heat-shattered stones. Radiocarbon dating samples were taken from charcoal from the body of the mound (1150 ± 50 AD (GU-2414)), the surface of the 'hearth' area (1000 ± 50 AD (GU 2413)) and from beneath the mound (1060 ± 50 AD (GU-2417)).

Mound 4, Cruise 1, NGR NX 1881 6314 (Fig .33)
This mound was part of a dispersed group on the boggy plateau at the source of the Cruise Burn. It lay immediately S of an old road (now the Southern Uplands Way) 250m SSW of the ruins of Dernemullie Farm. Between 2.5m and 3m of the mound was visible in the roadside drainage ditch. It survived to a height of about 0.3m.

A section was cut parallel to the ditch, aligned ESE–WNW. There was the suggestion of a hollow towards the W end of the mound and the excavation was dog-legged at the W end to uncover the most likely siting for the trough. Sondages were also sunk between the ditch and road and on the N side of the road.

As well as being cut by the modern drain, the mound had been cut by another, now silted, ditch to the E. The topsoil was a silty, rather clayey, loam which covered most of the excavated area. On the W of the mound this overlay a greasy charcoal-rich loam, which in turn lay immediately on the burnt stones. There was no evidence for *in situ* burning. Within the mound material, separate tip-lines could, in places, be discerned and compacted stones were noted at the base of the mound, trampled into the subsoil. The stones, all greywackes, were heat-cracked and burnt and were in a matrix of well-rooted humic loam in some places and in others charcoal-rich loam from which charcoal radiocarbon dated the mound to 1590 ± 50 bc (GU-2411).

Mound 5, Stair Lodge, NGR NX 1771 6686 (Fig. 33)
This mound was one of a very scattered group centred on Barlure and Stair Lodge 1–1.5km N of New Luce. It lay in the rushy area on the edge of a bracken-filled gully *c.* 350m NE of Stair Lodge. As with Cruise 1, drain damage had revealed a semicircular section through mound material. The mound survived to a height of *c.* 0.50m.

The section was straightened and cut parallel to the ditch, aligned ESE–WNW. Because of the proximity of the ditch, and the subsequent flooding, full profile depth of the mound could only be seen for about half of the section's length.

Two thick layers of peat covered the mound. An upper light red peat lay over the top of the mound and some way down the sides. Below this was a darker, greasier peat. At the interface of these two layers, on the E of the mound, lay several parallel small birch logs. There was no sign of cithor trough or hearth The burnt material formed a clear dome in the section. Within the mound the only clear variation was trom the upper/outer crust of root-compacted stones and charcoal to the looser inner fill. Below the mound, burnt material had become compressed into the grey/yellow clay subsoil. In places between mound and subsoil were faint traces of a putative buried topsoil showing as waterlogged peaty loam. Although part of the trench was flooded, it was quite evident that the subsoil, a very wet greasy clay, dropped sharply to the W. Charcoal retrieved from the main body of the mound dated it to 1730 ± 50 bc (GU-2412).

Mound 6, Gabsnout Burn, 1 NGR NX 1968 6103

This was one of a group of three mounds at the foot of the N side of Camrie Fell. It was located between two burns, the Gabsnout and its tributary, on land ploughed for forestry, about 50m to the W of a large knoll and 30m N of improved land. Although standing to about 1m, its full extent and shape were somewhat masked to the E and W by severe plough damage. Its dimensions are cited, by RCAHMS (1987), as 12m by 7.7m. This seems to apply to the full extent of the material rather than the main body of the mound which does not extend beyond the furrows and only measures some 4m N–S. The mound was radiocarbon-dated to 1000 ± 50 bc (GU-2415). No trough was noted. The mound was, however, rich in charcoal and dating material has been retrieved.

Mound 7, Claddy House Burn, NGR NX 0800 6849

This was an isolated mound in a small valley cut into the steep slopes overlooking Loch Ryan, c. 400m NE of the ruins of High Croach farmstead. Much of it had been destroyed by the realignment of the forestry road and the construction of a drainage ditch. It was still visible as a low mound through the shallow turf, measuring some 4m NE–SW by 2.8m. Its maximum height was c. 0.60m.

In the section, a length of over 6m of mound material was visible beneath a thick turf-line devoid of topsoil. The mound material was of heat-cracked stones set in a matrix of charcoal-stained soil. The stones were bound together in lumps of iron pan and disturbed by roots. At the SW end of the section the material levelled out to a 0.10m-thick layer and became finer. No buried soil was apparent between these deposits and the glacial subsoil. The subsoil was a yellow-grey sand with large rounded boulders and bedrock outcrops. No charcoal suitable for radiocarbon assay was retrieved from this mound even after flotation of samples taken for this purpose.

ACKNOWLEDGEMENTS

For access to the land and permission to excavate we must thank the landowners: Stair Estates (Auld Taggart 2 and 4, Stair Lodge and Cruise 1), Mr and Mrs Wallace (Claddy House Burn), Mr Kay, representative of David Goss and Associates (Gabsnout Burn 1), and Mr K. Brooks (Dervaird); and tenants Mr and Mrs Mitchell (Auld Taggart 2 and 4), Mr and Mrs Donan (Stair Lodge) and Mr and Mrs Goad (Cruise 1). We are also grateful for the sterling assistance offered by the excavators in both teams and to the Whithorn Trust whose workers we inherited and whose accommodation we used for the second team. Finally, our thanks go to S. J. Halliday of the RCAHMS for informing us of the deteriorating condition of the sites, and to Jane Murray, postgraduate of Edinburgh University, whose research into and knowledge of the area, and whose help as a member of both teams, were very valuable.

Arran: Machrie North and Glaister

Excavation by J. Barber
Report by D. Lehane

INTRODUCTION

Survey work, undertaken in the Machrie North area before and after forestry ploughing, revealed ten burnt mounds. The majority of these mounds were identified when the plough exposed characteristic deposits of fire-shattered stones in blackened soil. They were usually revealed as low mounds, roughly circular, which often appeared to sit on small natural rises in the slope. The exceptions, 24/02 (mound 8) and 24/53 (mound 9), had been recognised as burnt mounds from surface indications, the former displaying the classic kidney shape. All of these sites were located below the 80m contour on gently sloping ground in wet, sedge-covered areas. The mounds lay close to small streams; the two exceptions, 24/02 (mound 8) and 24/53 (mound 9), lay in badly drained boggy areas.

THE MACHRIE NORTH SITES
Mound 8, site 24/02, NGR 8997 3438

Introduction. This site had been identified as a burnt mound by the OS Archaeological Division and was situated on a small, level and very boggy area below the 70m contour. The site first appeared as a crescentic bank, slightly flattened on top, opening to the E. The horns of the crescent were roughly symmetrical with a slight depression between them. The objectives of the excavation were to establish the form and construction of the mound, to retrieve dating material and to examine the surrounding area for signs of contemporaneous settlement.

Excavation. Initially an area 10m by 13m was opened with a 0.50m baulk running E/W across the site. After the removal of the peat the mound was found to consist of a mass of burnt stones set in a black matrix *c.* 9.65m N–S by *c.* 7.40m E–W. The mound appeared to have been built up around a small rise, shown by excavation to be a natural clay hillock in an otherwise flat area. A number of 3m squares were also opened in the environs of the mound to examine the possibility that settlements, seasonal or permanent, were associated with it: none were found.

The mound. A 2m strip across the mound was excavated and the mound, in section, was found to consist of compacted fire-shattered stones in a matrix of dark grey gritty soil. The bulk of the mound was fairly homogeneous, but a number of discrete layers or lenses could be distinguished, mainly on the basis of their charcoal content. In the W end of the section a deposit of large unburnt stones was noted within a matrix of heavily root-disturbed sandy material.

The trough. A trough was located in the depression between the horns of the mound. It was rectangular, shallow and flat-bottomed, measuring 1.70m E–W by 0.60m N–S, cut into the subsoil. The trough was filled to 0.50m of its depth with a deposit of grey gritty sand with charcoal flecks, over which was a 0.03m-thick deposit of charcoal, sealed by 0.10m of burnt mound material, which was also piled up against the W edge of the trough. To the west of the trough a small, roughly crescentric ridge of redeposited pink-brown gritty sand was noted.

Interpretation. Although a number of different layers were identified on the basis of their relative concentrations of charcoal, the mound displayed no chronologically significant stratification. A trough had been cut into the

77

subsoil and the excavated material formed the ridge of gritty sand described above. The mound itself was then built up as the stones used in the subsequent cooking were removed from the trough and piled on top and to either side of the clay hillock. Subsequent dumps of burnt stone were deposited over this and resulted in the distinctive crescentic shape of the mound. The deposit of burnt stone which sealed the trough and which was piled against its W edge appeared to represent spillage from the mound when the trough was no longer in use. Two samples of charcoal were dated from this mound at 1875 ± 65 bc (GU-1566) and 1850 ± 65 bc (GU-1569).

Mound 9, site 24/53

Introduction. This site was a well-defined kidney-shaped mound measuring 12m by 9m. Similar in shape and location to site 24/02, it was built up around a small natural hillock in a very boggy area, no great distance from 24/02. A brief examination only was undertaken to confirm that the sites were similar and to retrieve dating material.

Excavation. A 1m square was excavated in the crown of the mound to determine its composition. This revealed the characteristic fire-shattered stones, which were in a matrix of black gritty charcoal-rich sand. This deposit had a maximum depth of *c.* 0.50m, and no separate dumps of material could be distinguished. An area 2m square opened in the depression at the NE side of the mound revealed the corner of a shallow oval trough. It was cut into a deposit similar to the fabric of the mound, and although its full extent was not exposed it could be estimated at approximately 2m by 1.5m. The trough was filled to a depth of *c.* 0.20m with a deposit of grey clay, over which was 0.10m of grey-brown clay. Above this was 0.15m of black silty sand, sealed by 0.10m of dark loam.

The trough exposed on the northern edge of the site appears to represent a secondary use of the site because it was cut into burnt mound material. The trough was clay-lined. The mound was radiocarbon-dated to 1910 ± 65 bc (GU-1567).

Mound 10, site 24/54

Introduction. A Forestry Commission plough-furrow had bisected this site and exposed large quantities of fire-shattered stones in a blackened soil matrix. The site measured *c.* 9.9m E–W by 11.3m N–S, and had no apparent depressions or indentations in its circuit.

Excavation. Limited excavation revealed that the mound was composed of fire-shattered stones in a black, gritty, charcoal-rich matrix, with no discernible layers or lenses. On the NW side of the mound a corner of a sub-rectangular trough was located, and although not fully excavated it was at least 1m square and 0.50m deep. The trough was filled to a depth of 0.01m by a deposit of grey clay, over which was a deposit, 0.01m thick, of burnt stones in a grey-black matrix. This was in turn covered by a further deposit of grey clay, *c.* 0.01m thick, over which lay 0.20m of burnt stone in a black gritty sand matrix sealed by a 0.10m-thick deposit of burnt mound material.

Interpretation. The trough was clay-lined; the second deposit of clay within it was interpreted as a relining of the pit, a feature also noted at the excavations at Rhos Carne Coch, Dyfed, where the largest pit associated with mound A had been partially relined (H. James, pers. comm.). The mound was dated to 1455 ± 115 bc (GU-1568).

Mound 11, site 24/100 (Fig. 35)

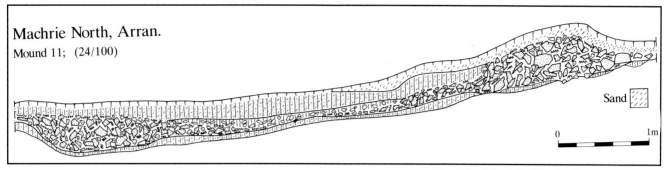

Fig. 35—Machrie North, Arran, section.

This site was cut by a Forestry Commission plough-furrow which revealed, in its section, the composition of the mound and the presence and extent of a trough. The mound itself consisted of a deposit of fire-shattered stones in a black matrix, which had a maximum depth of 0.50m. No separate dumps of material were noted, the deposit having been dispersed by the ploughing. At the bottom of the slope of the mound, c. 4m from its crown, a flat-bottomed trough was noted. About 1.2m long and 0.1m to 0.15m deep, it was covered by a deposit of mound material.

Mounds 12 and 13, sites 24/104 and 24/105

These two sites lay almost in the middle of the Machrie North area and were respectively 100m NE and 50m E of site 24/02. They consisted of spreads of burnt stone lying in a matrix of black, charcoal-rich grit, no more than 0.2m thick. No other features were found in association with these spreads but their composition suggests that they were burnt mounds.

THE GLAISTER FARM BURNT MOUNDS

Mounds 14, 15 and 16, sites 24/101, 24/102 and 24/103

These mounds formed a distinctive group along a single stream. Site 24/103 was visible since it had been eroded by the stream which may have been diverted to feed the site. A square-cut trough, 0.65m deep and at least 2m across, was visible in section. The mound was of the usual composition and survived to a height of 0.70m. Site 24/101 has been cut by a Forestry Commission plough-furrow which revealed burnt mound deposits c. 0.30m to c. 0.40m high. The final site, 24/102, was not investigated.

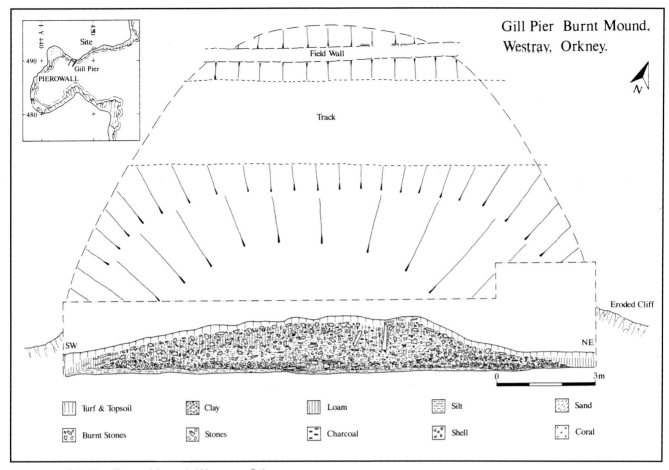

Fig. 36—Gill Pier Burnt Mound, Westray, Orkney.

Gill Pier burnt mound, Westray, Orkney
Mound 17, HY 4502 4922 (Fig. 36)

D. Lehane

Excavation. This site, situated on the shoreline 400m NE of Gill Pier, Westray, Orkney, was being eroded by the sea. It was described on the OS cards (1970) as 13m long E–W, 5m wide and 0.6m high. By June 1983 its maximum width had been reduced to 2.5m (RCAHMS 1983, 27).

The sea had cut through the site on an E–W axis, forming a low cliff and revealing an irregular section through the mound. This was straightened, cleaned and recorded. A narrow trench, 0.25m wide, was cut at right angles to the section to determine the inland extent of the mound. The monument was found to extend for 8.40m behind the section. It was visible as a mound for approximately 3.30m of that extent, standing to a maximum height of 1.70m. In section the mound was found to be composed almost entirely of densely-packed burnt sandstone and shale with little intervening material. Five separate phases of activity could be identified, each represented by a separate dump of material.

Interpretation. Phase 1 represents the earliest use of the site and the section revealed no traces of associated structures. Phase 2, a second dump of burnt stone, also contained a small and enigmatic deposit of unburnt stones. The exact nature of this feature was not discernible in section. It may have been the remains of a hearth, but the stones show no traces of heat-cracking and the clay matrix was not scorched. It is therefore more likely that this is the remains of a revetment preventing encroachment of the mound material on an area of activity such as a hearth or pit. Phases 3 and 4 were both small dumps of burnt stone and may represent successive episodes of use separated by a short time-span. Abundant seashell remains were noted in the section's phase 3 deposits. The largest dump of burnt stones was deposited in the final phase of activity on the site. Two large angular stones located at the E end of the section may also be traces of a revetment. It is probable that they are the remains of a stone-lined trough associated with the final phase of activity on the site.

6b.

Bute and Islay

The burnt mounds on Islay and Bute seem to be exceptional in that they lie outside the main areas of currently-known distribution. There is, however, nothing in their form or content to distinguish them from the mounds of Arran or the Scottish mainland.

MECKNOCH FARM, ISLE OF BUTE
Mound 18, NS 045 588

Excavated by Miss D. N. Marshall, Bute Natural History Society
Note by C. J. Russell-White

Mecknoch Farm lies on the W coast of the island about 7.5km SW of Rothesay. It is the only burnt mound to be noted on the island, although burnt mounds occur on the neighbouring island of Arran and the adjacent mainland in Kintyre.

The mound is situated on a lightly wooded slope above a burn whose course may have been re-routed. The vegetation cover is grass and bracken. Roughly oval, 11m by 8m by 1m high maximum, the long axis of the mound runs downslope (N–S) to stop short of the burn on a flat area, possibly the old stream bed. The mound consisted of fire-cracked stones in a matrix of very fine black loam from which no charcoal has been retrieved.

Two areas of flat stone flags were noted close to the mound. The first, at the bottom of the slope (on the S), was possibly the remnant of a trough. The other area was on the W side up the slope and may have been the remains of a paved surface. No stratigraphic relationship between these and the mound itself could be determined.

BORICHILL MOR 1, ISLE OF ISLAY
Mound 19, NR 3074 6524

Sampled by J. Barber

This site is one of a group of four in this part of the island. It is cut by the road from Coullabus to Bridgend just N of Borichill Mor. Occupying the top of a local eminence, bounded by the road on the W and by a streamlet on the N, the mound is horseshoe-shaped in plan with the open end facing N. It is cut on the W and S sides, revealing the typical heat-shattered stones of a burnt mound lying in a charcoal-packed soil. One radiocarbon date was retrieved from this mound, 1745 ± 60 bc (GU-1465).

Kilearnan Hill

Excavated by A. Haggerty

Kilearnan Hill is situated S of the River Helmsdale *c.* 10km inland from the town of Helmsdale in Sutherland. The underlying geology is sandstone and metamorphosed sandstones overlain by glacial till between 1m and 3m. The sites, which were on N-facing slopes, are just three of a large number of sites of various types and dates, surveyed and excavated in advance of forestry.

Mound 20, site 15 (NGR 9534 1747)

NMRS name: Oulmsdale Burn

Recorded by the OS in 1976 as 14m E–W by 12m N–S by 1.5m high, with a depression in the E opening onto a dried-up stream bed, this site was recognisably kidney-shaped. The mound lay on a slope of *c.* 1:10 on free-draining, stony, sandy loams. The mound was dominated by grass rather than the surrounding mixture of heather and grass. A small-scale excavation was undertaken as one element of the 1982 programme of sampling and survey. Bad weather delayed its full excavation until 1983. The following phasing was observed.

Firstly, a pit of uncertain size had been cut into the subsoil and the heat-shattered stones were piled to SW and SE of it. Next, the pit was cut by another revetted pit (3m by 1.5m by 0.5m deep) and stones piled to S, NE and NW. Thirdly, this second pit was recut (1.5m square and 0.65m deep) and revetted with boulders at E and W, and stones were piled on the W with some to the N and S. At all times the E was left free. The dates from the mound were all from the first millennium bc (870 ± 85 bc, GU-1921; 710 ± 95 bc, GU-1912; 800 ± 80 bc, GU-1913; 865 ± 60 bc, GU-1914) with the exception of one date from the Middle Ages (1440 ± 60 ad, GU-1915) which came from a hearth set on the top of the mound.

Mound 21, site 17 A and B

Ploughing exposed the stone of these two mounds. The NW mound, B, was *c.* 5m in diameter and stood some 0.5m above the surrounding surface. The SE mound, A, was an oval, 3.5m by 2.5m, rising to *c.* 0.3m high. A stream flowing immediately to the E apparently caused intermittent flooding, forming silt layers among and over the deposits of shattered stones. No trough was discovered in the small area investigated but it seemed likely that it lay between the two mounds which, in practice, constitute two arms of the same monument. The soil matrix of the mound material contained no charcoal.

Mound 22, site 18

This monument had not been recorded previously and was noticed during work on site 17. The mound was crescentic and lay some 35m N of site 17 on the opposite side of the same stream where it ran through a 3m-deep channel. A plough-furrow had exposed burnt stone on the extreme E side but otherwise the mound was untouched and obscured by heather. A revetment of large boulders protruded from the W side above the stream. It is possible that the course of the stream had been deliberately altered at this point. The presence of this site may have represented the transference of activity from site 17 to a position less likely to be flooded.

Craggie Basin, Kildonan, Sutherland

Excavated by C. E. Lowe

Mound 29, Kildonan 28 (NGR NC 9157 1840)

NMRS name: Allt A'Choire Mhoir

This kidney-shaped burnt mound (12m by 10m by 0.85–1m high) was sampled during the 1988 pre-afforestation evaluation. It was situated about 2km WNW of Kilearnan Hill on the NE flank of Cnoc Craggie Beag. The monument appeared as a grassy mound in the reedy surround of a dried-up stream bed. The supposed trough area was to the E and on the SW side there was a platform (6.5m by 5.5m) which may have been the hearth area. The mound has been dated to 920 ± 50 bc (GU-2483).

Kebister: burnt mounds and burnt mound material

Excavated by O. Owen
Report by C. E. Lowe

INTRODUCTION

The site of Kebister lies on Dales Voe, Mainland, Shetland. It was excavated in advance of construction of an oil rig supply base in 1985, 1986 and 1987. Two burnt mound sites were recorded during the survey at Kebister in 1987. One, to the SE of the excavation area, had previously gone unnoted; the other, to the NE, was shown to be more complex than previously recorded.

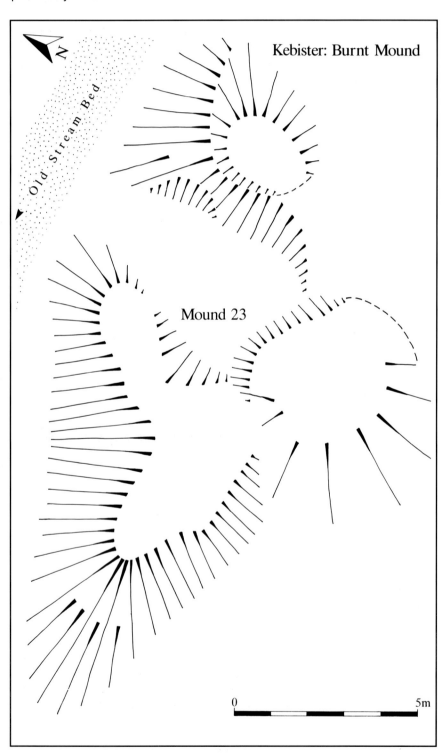

Fig. 37—Kebister: burnt mound.

BURNT MOUND: SURVEY BLOCK H
Mound 23, HU 4574 4543 (Fig. 37)

The site is located 80m SE of the excavation area at approximately 19m above OD. It is sited above and on the S side of a dried-up watercourse or gulley which runs down from the hillside above, to the E. Crescentic in form, the monument measures roughly 18m E–W and 11m N–S and appears to comprise three distinct elements. The larger W mound is grass-covered and sub-triangular with concave faces to the N and E (10m E–W, 6.50m N–S and 1–1.50m high). The smaller mound to the E (*c.* 5m in diameter and 0.50–0.75m high) is covered with *Sphagnum* and grass and has a concave face to the W. An open *Sphagnum*-covered area (3m E–W by 4.50m N–S), the possible trough site, extends between these two parts of the monument. To the S of these features there is a low amorphous sedge- and sphagnum-covered mound, 6m in diameter.

Small test-pits were dug into the tops of the mounds which comprised dense concentrations of medium angular and sub-angular burnt and fire-shattered stones in a dark grey silty clay matrix. A large sherd of coarse

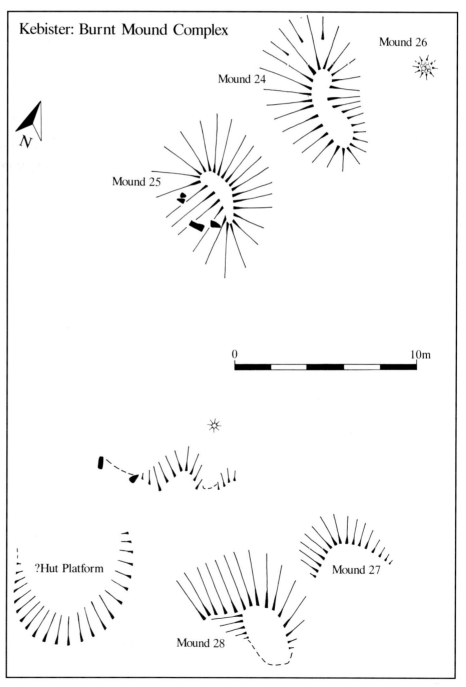

Fig. 38—Kebister burnt mound complex.

pottery, comprising the base and part of the body of a pot, was also recovered from one of the test-pits.

BURNT MOUNDS COMPLEX: SURVEY BLOCK G
Mounds 24 to 28, HU 4593 4567 (Fig .38)

Two large and four small burnt mounds are located together in a cluster, approximately 290m NE of the excavation area, 15m above OD, and to the N of a possible hut platform. The two larger mounds had previously been recorded by Peter Moar as `Viking Graves' (in Winham 1978). They were, however, correctly identified by Winham (1978, 20; 1980) in 1978. Nevertheless, the adjacent monuments have previously gone unrecorded.

Burnt mound G14 (mound 24) is of an elongated oval form, aligned roughly NW–SE (8.50m by 5.50m and 0.80m high) with a concave face on its NE side.

Burnt mound G15 (mound 25) lies close by, to the SW. It is of sub-circular form (*c.* 6.50–8.50m in diameter by 0.80m high) with a concave face to the W. There are also traces of a possible wall line on the same side, about half-way up the mound. This is defined by three or four large protrusive stones, with sides up to 0.50m long, which form an arc.

Samples of the buried soil were recovered from a small trial trench which extended across the lower part of the NE side of the mound and into the area between mounds G15 and G14.

A small mound of burnt stones (G13, mound 26, 1.70m in diameter and 0.25m high) was located to the NE of G14. Two similar but slightly larger mounds (G8 and G9, mounds 27 and 28), located a few metres to the S, appear to have been formed against the side of a natural break of slope. These mounds may be associated with feature G10, which is situated on the flat ground below. Feature G10, possibly the site of a building, is represented by a series of low amorphous mounds of burnt stones. The feature appears to be delimited on the W by two or three large earthfast stones.

Small test-pits were dug into the mounds, in each case revealing a dense concentration of burnt and fire-shattered stones of sub-angular and sub-rounded form in a brown to black loamy soil matrix. Traces of a manganese precipitate were also noted on some of the stones.

Synthesis

C. J. Russell-White

SIZE, SHAPE AND CONTENT

The Scottish sites vary greatly in size. The largest known is the site of Vaasetter, on Fair Isle, which is nearly 40m across. At the other end of the scale are sites like some of those at Kebister which apparently measure less than 2m across. The bulk of the sites lie between 5m and 15m across and are less than 1m high.

This variability in size is matched by a variability in shape. The classic burnt mound is said to be crescentic or kidney-shaped, but of the 40 sites recently examined in SW Scotland only 15, roughly one third, could be said to possess the classic shape. Halliday notes (*supra*) that 75 out of 110 sites recorded by the RCAHMS in Scotland are kidney-shaped, whilst Hunter notes that a 'proportion' of the Fair Isle sites are crescentic in form. The others range, throughout Scotland, from amorphous mounds or groups of mounds to multi-peaked annular settings with central or peripheral hollows. There is some degree of correlation between size and shape, with the larger sites tending to be more irregular or amorphous.

Some seven sites were examined by the Scottish CEU in the East Rhins area of Wigtown District in 1987. Two of these were crescentic, both of them revealing, on excavation, cooking troughs. The base of one of the troughs had been lined with a crude oaken plank. Troughs were not located on the other sites. On Arran seven of ten sites were examined, four of which proved to have troughs. A trough was found at only one of the two sites excavated at Kilearnan Hill. None of these sites revealed hearths and indeed, of all the sites examined, only three sites, Gill Pier, Auld Taggart 4 and Kilearnan 15, revealed possible hearths, with that at the third site clearly secondary.

There is a relationship between the morphology of the sites and the ease with which troughs can be located. The classic kidney-shaped site normally has a trough between the open arms. The more amorphous sites can overlie or sit eccentric to their troughs so that, unless excavation is extensive, the troughs will not be revealed. Furthermore, in the case of settlement-associated material the troughs may lie some distance from the deposits of burnt stone.

Scottish burnt mounds consist of burnt stone set in a dark soil matrix which also contains charcoal and ash. This material is so distinctive that it is termed 'burnt mound material' even when found in other contexts. Hard, unweathered and relatively heat-resistant stones were selected by the burnt mound users, the most common being hard sandstones. In the East Rhins sites the locally available greywackes were used, while on Arran metamorphic types were employed. The burnt mound material found on settlement sites in the Outer Hebrides (below) clearly shows the deliberate selection of suitable material. The greater part of the islands' bedrock is Lewisian Gneiss, which is reduced to a coarse granular mass by heating and quenching. Virtually 100% of the burnt stone comes from the less than 5% of the bedrock which is not Lewisian Gneiss.

Wood seems to have been the preferred fuel but peat was extensively used in the Northern Isles, where any forest cover that existed had been eliminated early in prehistory. Peat ash survives as readily identifiable deposits within the northern sites, while no trace of the more soluble wood ash seems to have been recorded even though its presence is clearly indicated by the abundant charcoal from the southern sites.

Routine analyses of the soils that form the matrix of the burnt mounds in the East Rhins area revealed that the soils were uniformly acidic (Appendix 1). The relative phosphate levels were higher for the burnt mound deposits than for the local topsoils or subsoils except for the two medieval mounds. The quantities of organic matter present in the soils were also high, as revealed by the 'Loss On Ignition' (LOI tests) Appendix i). High phosphates are normally indicative of the presence of decayed bone, while the high LOI values indicate that the soils of the deposits have been enriched by the addition of organic material. These tests seem, at face value, to support the contention that the burnt mounds were used for cooking. However, the high phosphate values might have been explained by the presence of wood ash from burnt fuel were it not for the two later mounds. It may, therefore, have some reflection upon the use. The high LOI values could result from the presence of the decay products of unburnt fuel. In the presence of an alternative explanation, neither the high phosphate levels nor the high LOI values can be accepted as firm indications that the sites were used for cooking.

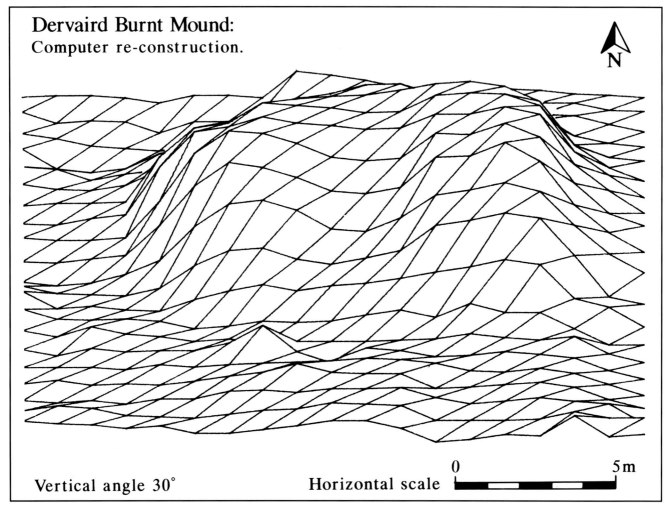

Fig. 39–Dervaird burnt mound, computer reconstruction.

FREQUENCY OF USE

That burnt mounds were used for cooking has been disputed, but there seems to be no disagreement that they represent the debris created as the result of heating water by the immersion of heated stones. Experiments by O'Kelly and others suggest that roughly 0.5 cubic metres of debris is generated by a single boiling. Using this figure, the volume of the Dervaird burnt mound (Fig. 39) would have been produced by some 42 boilings or, allowing for the imprecision of the calculations, 40 to 50 boilings. The frequency of use of the other sites for which the data are adequate have been assessed in proportion to this 'Dervaird standard'. The results suggest that frequency of use varied over two orders of magnitude, from 4 boiling events for the smaller mounds to nearly 200 for the larger mounds in Sutherland and at Kebister, with up to 400 times for the Beaquoy mound. Buckley (this volume) suggests that metamorphic or igneous rocks survived repeated quenching to a greater degree than sandstone and thus may generate less than 0.5 m³ per boiling. This is less significant in Scotland than in Ireland because most of the Scottish mounds are of sandstone. Furthermore, it does not alter the basic observation that these are small and very large burnt mounds, with relatively few of intermediate size.

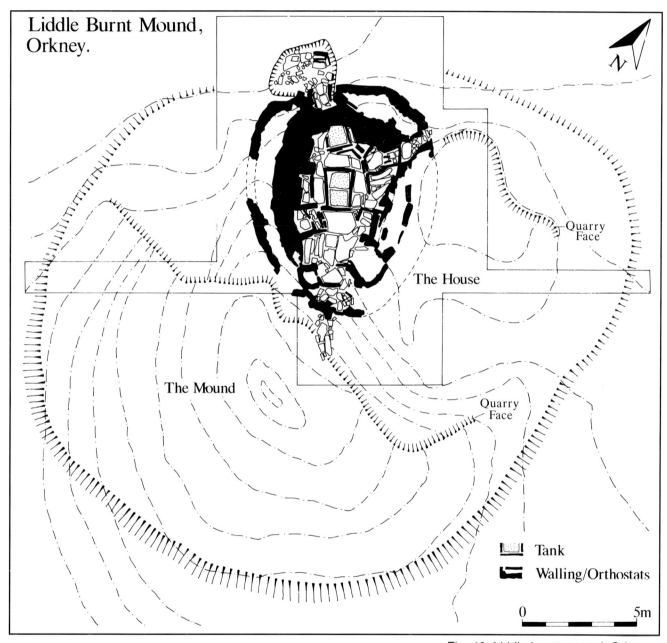

Fig. 40–Liddle burnt mound, Orkney.

LOCATION AND ASSOCIATED STRUCTURES

Burnt mounds are invariably located in the immediate vicinity of a source of water. This is all but inevitable given their primary purpose, which is the heating of water. Their distribution in respect of other sites is not so clearly definable. The area of the East Rhins, in the south-west of Scotland, has recently been surveyed (RCAHMS 1987) and an initial examination of the data does not reveal any clear distributional association with other sites. Analyses of this data set and of data from surveys at Lairg and Kildonan will continue to explore the hypothesis that burnt mounds 'service' monuments of some other type, from which they are set apart.

At Liddle and Beaquoy (Figs 40 and 41) Hedges (1975) recorded substantial stone structures, which he termed houses, associated with the

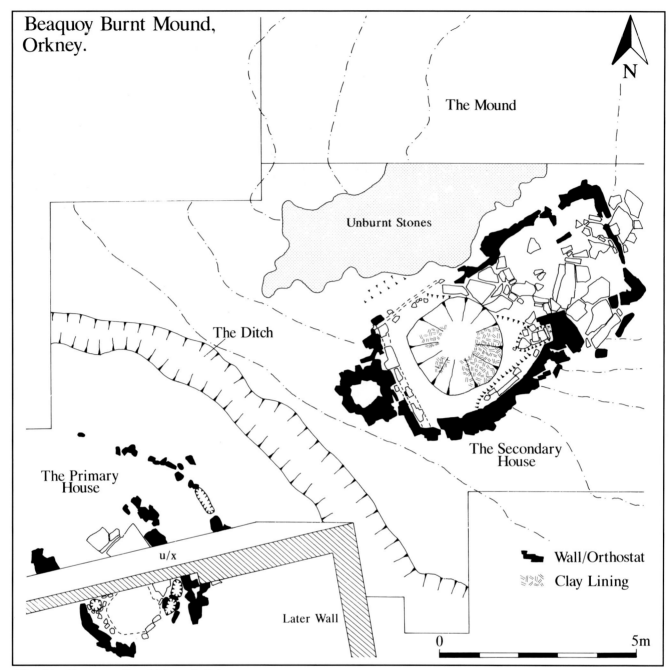

Fig. 41—Beaquoy Burnt Mound, Orkney.

mounds. He suggested that this may be more common. The only, very tentative, evidence that we have found for structures associated with the mounds is at Kebister on Shetland and at Auld Taggart in the East Rhins. At the former a group of small mounds less than 2m in diameter are close by the site of a possible building which is itself represented by a series of low amorphous mounds of burnt stones. This is apparently delineated on the west by two or three large earthfast stones. At Auld Taggart there is a group of four burnt mounds, which have been dated to about the tenth century AD, within 50m of a turf shieling and within 300m of a probable medieval farmstead. It should be noted that both of these possible associations concern groups not individual burnt mounds, and in the latter case include dates of mounds and assumed dates of other monuments.

CHRONOLOGY
There are both radiocarbon (Table 4 p.102) and thermoluminescence (TL) (Hedges 1975, appendix 2) dates for burnt mound sites in Scotland. The radiocarbon dates are most numerous for the southern area; nine are from

the East Rhins, four from Arran and one from Islay. There are also dates from the Strath of Kildonan, Sutherland, from two sites (Kilearnan 15 and Kildonan 28). The use of peat as fuel in the north has meant that most of the dating there is from TL.

The Northern Isles dates are generally Early Iron Age with one Late Bronze Age. Two radiocarbon dates from Liddle place it roughly in the tenth century BC (Hedges 1975). The Arran mounds are all Early Bronze Age. In the East Rhins a less uniform picture is apparent. Most of the burnt mounds from which samples were taken were on the east side of the Water of Luce. These were all Bronze Age. The two mounds that were excavated on the west of the river produced dates from the eleventh and twelfth centuries AD. The Kildonan site was also of the tenth century AD. Three of these samples come from different parts of one mound and the other from a mound 40m away. The available radiocarbon date distribution therefore gives the main body of dates between the twentieth and eighth centuries BC with an outlier of five dates from the Middle Ages. No burnt mounds as such fall into the 17-century gap between these. However, it is not devoid of dates associated with burnt stone deposits.

7. SETTLEMENT

Burnt mound material on settlement sites in Scotland

J. Barber

BURNT MOUND MATERIAL

Fulachta fiadh, whose use was apparently described by Seathrun Ceitinn (Dinneen 1908), are generally thought of as discrete, kidney-shaped mounds of burnt and fire-shattered stone set in a matrix of charcoal-rich, dark soil, the entire deposit produced by heating stones to boil water for cooking. This burnt mound material is distinctive, readily identifiable and quite characteristic. Thus Fahy (1960) and O'Kelly (1954), excavating classic fulachta fiadh, felt free to suggest that **all** burnt mound sites were simple hunting-stations. Hedges, finding structures on the two Orcadian sites he investigated (1975), suggested that all burnt mounds may contain or must have contained structures. Barfield and Hodder, interpreting their sites in Birmingham as saunas, seem to wish to reinterpret all other sites as saunas also (1987, 376).

Although these writers have disagreed quite strongly on the precise interpretation of burnt mounds, they seem to agree that all burnt mounds were produced by the same process and that they can all be interpreted in the same way. Clearly, the distinctive nature of burnt mound material has seduced us into believing that all deposits of this material are produced by the same mechanism and for the same functional reason.

IRON AGE SITES

However, burnt mound material is often observed on sites which are certainly not fulachta fiadh. In Scotland, deposits of burnt mound material are, for example, commonly found on brochs. A broch is, essentially, a fortified farmhouse (see Ritchie and Ritchie 1981, 101–8, for general description). They probably represent the prehistoric equivalent of the smaller Irish tower houses and, like the latter, they seem likely to have been the residences of locally powerful families. They are one element of the sequence of large drystone structures built in Scotland over a period of almost a millennium, from before 600 BC to AD 300, on present evidence. It seems likely that brochs date to the last 500 to 600 years of this period.

Stone-lined boxes are commonly found sunk into the floors of brochs (Pls 7a, 7b). These were sometimes clay-luted to make them watertight. They have in the past been interpreted as holding-tanks for shellfish (Clarke 1976). In his recent work on brochs, John Hedges refers to these tanks specifically as cooking tanks (1987, 18). Furthermore, he identifies, at the site of Bu, deposits of fire-shattered stone and ash, some of it from within the make-up of the secondary thickening of the main enclosing wall (*ibid.*, 11).

At the broch site of East Shore, Pool of Virkie, Shetland (Fig. 26), the foundation trench of the broch wall cuts through a midden rich in burnt material, including peat ash and burnt stone. This deposit contained, *inter alia*, part of a beehive-shaped quern. On the available evidence, this site probably dates to the period 300 BC to AD 200. Similarly, deposits revealed by coastal erosion on the margins of the large broch site at South Harbour on Fair Isle include one very clear deposit of burnt mound material (Barber *et al.* forthcoming). Pottery sherds and animal bones were also included in this deposit.

In earlier broch excavations the deposits *per se* were often ignored, attention being focussed on the artifacts they contained. However, the excavators' notes sometimes reveal that deposits of small angular stones set in a dark or ashy matrix were observed (J. Hedges, pers. comm.). Nor was burnt mound material restricted to broch sites. It was retrieved from several contexts at the multi-period settlement site of Kebister, on Mainland Shetland (Fig. 26), where it was found both as disturbed and *in situ* deposits.

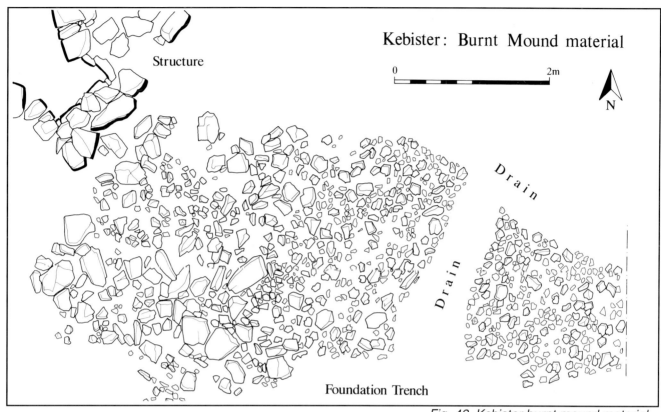

Fig. 42–Kebister burnt mound material.

One disturbed deposit at Kebister consisted of a stone spread containing a high proportion of burnt and fire-shattered stones. This partly overlay the remains of a circular stone structure, probably of Early Iron Age date. The deposit had been much disturbed, probably by medieval or post-medieval cultivation. Many prehistoric coarse pot sherds were recovered from the deposit, together with some glazed medieval sherds, steatite vessel sherds, other artifacts and slag.

One *in situ* deposit of burnt mound material consisted of a low mound of burnt stone, some 7m by 3.50m by 0.35m high (Fig. 42). The stones were contained within a lumpy brown silty clay in which discrete patches of charcoal and peat ash were also noted. Several sherds of coarse pot, a few crude stone tools, a piece of slag and a piece of worked steatite were retrieved from this deposit. Macroplant remains so far identified include carbonised cereals and charcoal of hazel and oak.

A second, smaller mound of burnt stones, of the same period, was found nearby and revealed an area measuring roughly 2m N–S, at least 1m E–W and 0.25m high. It consisted of burnt stones set in a dark brown clay containing patches of charcoal and peat ash. Carbonised oat seeds are among the macroplant remains from this deposit. Routine soil analysis revealed that the soils, with pH of 6.7, are of neutral status, and with LOI of 24.7% are rich in both phosphate and soil organic matter. (The writer is grateful to Ms O. Owen and Dr C. Lowe for access to this information on Kebister in advance of their own publication.)

LATER SITES

Substantial deposits, dating to the Norse/medieval period, have been noted at the site of Tuquoy, Westray (O. Owen, pers. comm.). Smaller deposits, rich in fish bone and dating to the seventh century AD, have been found beneath the parish church at Birsay, Orkney (Barber, in Morris forthcoming). It is probable that burnt mound material occurs on sites of other periods but that in general it has not been identified nor has its use as an interpretational tool been appreciated.

EARLIEST APPEARANCE

It would have been difficult to determine whether the absence of burnt stone from deposits of Neolithic date was real or apparent had it not been for the very high quality of the modern excavations of Neolithic middens in the north of Scotland. Dr D. Clarke confirms (pers. comm.) that burnt stone was not retrieved from the deposits he excavated at the sites of Skara Brae (1976) and Links of Noltland, and Dr A. Ritchie (pers. comm.) confirms its absence also from the Neolithic deposits at the Knap of Howar (1983). It is clear, then, that the technique of boiling water by plunging heated stones in a tank of water was introduced at the beginning of the Bronze Age. This conclusion is consistent with the evidence from Stephen Dockrill's work (*supra*) at Tofts Ness, Sanday, Orkney.

BURNT MOUND MATERIAL AS AN INTERPRETATIONAL AID

The presence of burnt mound material can be of assistance in interpreting the nature of the deposits in which it is found. In turn, these deposits and their contents cast some light on the function of the burnt mound material.

Deposits studied during a sampling excavation of the site of Baleshare provide a useful example. The small island of Baleshare lies off the west coast of North Uist in the Outer Hebrides (Fig. 26). It is an extensive midden site, covering an area at least 300m by 100m, with deposits up to 3.5m deep. Its deposits are, in the main, sandy loams, rich in archaeological materials. A variety of structures were erected at various times in the site's history and are set within the site's deposits.

During excavation, individual contexts, i.e. layers, pits, post-holes, etc., were grouped into blocks for ease of data handling and as an aid to understanding. A 'block' is defined as a group of contiguous contexts which have had a similar depositional or formational mechanism. The 29 blocks which comprise Baleshare contain some 246 individual contexts.

Table 1

Block no.	Type	No. of Contexts	No. with burnt stone	% of contexts with burnt stone	Average % burnt stone present	Index (col. 5 x col. 6)
7	Backfill	3	1	33.33	5	166.67
18	Cultivated	1	1	100	5	500.00
25	Cultivated	1	1	100	30	3000.00
22	Cultivated	1	1	100	20	2000.00
20	Cultivated	3	3	100	20	2000.00
26	Cultivated	4	4	100	40	4000.00
9	Ditch fill	1	1	100	10	1000.00
24	Dumped	15	6	40	10	400.00
17	Dumped	8	8	100	35	3500.00
5	Dumped	19	1	5.26	5	26.32
19	Midden site	4	4	100	10	1000.00
15	Midden site	14	10	71.43	15	1071.43
2	Midden site	28	21	75	15	1125.00
16	Midden Site	18	13	72.22	30	2166.67
11	Structure	41	6	14.63	10	146.34
23	Cultivated windblown	7	5	71.43	5	357.14
27	Cultivated	10	7	70	25	1750.00
3	Conflation	1	1	100	25	2500.00

Table 2 — Baleshare deposits with burnt stone	
Deposit type	*Mean score*
Structure	146.34
Ditch fill	500.00
Backfill	833.33
Cultivated windblown sand	1053.57
Dumped	1308.77
Midden site	1340.77
Cultivated midden/dump	2300.00
Conflation	2500.00

Burnt stone was found in 99 contexts, spread over 18 blocks. Thus some 62% of the blocks (40% of all contexts) contain burnt mound material (Fig. 43).

The non-structural stone from each context was weighed and the amount which had been burnt was calculated as a percentage of the weight. This ranges from 0% to a full 100%, with a relatively wide range of values exhibited in some of the blocks. An index of relative abundance of burnt stone, per block, was then calculated by multiplying the percentage of contexts containing burnt stone by the average percentage of burnt stone contained in the contexts for each of those blocks whose contexts contained burnt stone (see Table 1). A mean value was calculated for categories of blocks grouped by their perceived depositional mechanics. Thus in Table 2 all dumped deposits are grouped together, as are all cultivated deposits and so on.

There appears to be a relationship between the nature of the deposits and the relative abundance of the burnt mound material which they contain. In general structures, and features directly associated with them, contain less than other deposits. Windblown sand which has been cultivated and into which some midden material has been ploughed, as manure, scores higher than the structural features. Dumped deposits, i.e. clearly discrete dumps of material, and midden site deposits, i.e. deposits which accumulate in the immediate vicinity of habitations, consistently exhibit high relative abundance of burnt stone. Where such deposits are later cultivated the relative abundance score is even higher.

Cultivation acts on midden deposits as a form of anthropogenic conflation. To the already abundant supply of burnt stone, artifacts, etc.,

Fig. 43—Baleshare midden: block section.

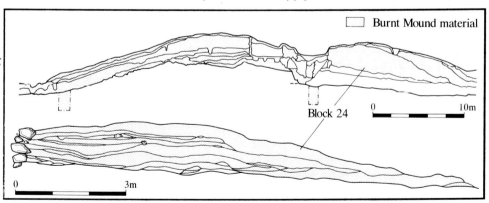

Burnt Mound material

Block 24

0   10m

0   3m

already present in midden deposits, repeated manuring adds more. Cultivation breaks down the more friable inclusions, like pot sherds, while the organic matter is gradually lost through natural soil processes, taken up by soil fauna and plants and broken down mechanically by the plough. Stone is not affected by these processes and eventually comes to represent a larger percentage of the reduced bulk of the deposit's inclusions.

Naturally-formed conflation horizons show the highest relative abundance of burnt stone. These horizons are created when the sandy matrix of a series of layers is removed by aeolian erosion. The layers' contents fall to the bottom of the erosion hollow, resting on top of the surviving midden. When this stabilises, it grows a vegetation cover and becomes invaded with worms, etc. Then bioturbation allows the deflated materials to sink into the surface of the deposit, enriching it with derived and asynchronous materials from the previously overlying deposits.

THE INTERPRETATION OF BURNT MOUND MATERIAL

Some indication of the function of the burnt mound deposits from settlement sites can be derived from the wealth of cultural materials with which they are associated. As we have noted above, deposits of burnt stone at Kebister, Fair Isle, Tuquoy and East Shore all yielded significant numbers of artifacts and 'ecofacts'. Table 3 shows the amounts of such materials retrieved from the stratigraphic blocks that contained burnt mound material at Baleshare. This demonstrates a strong correlation between the deposition of burnt stone and the deposition of domestic refuse. So strong is this correlation, at Baleshare and at the other sites discussed, that the burnt stone element of it can only be interpreted as domestic refuse too. Furthermore, its ubiquity shows that it was a common element in the domestic refuse of antiquity. It is therefore hard to escape the conclusion that it is mainly a by-product of cooking, perhaps the commonest of domestic processes.

Table 3 — Finds from Baleshare

Block	Bone	Pot	Snail	Seash.	Macro	Slag	Stone
7	1765	71	15.30	1432.1	24.1	-	132
18	909.2	87	17.03	1738	1.16	-	3014
25	1074	135	7.01	575	7.63	-	1660
22	3358	443	0.08	2925	0.59	2	4503
20	789.2	65	0.02	508	5.22	-	2465
26	1035.9	227	9.03	1371	18.18	-	3398
9	200	25	4.01	707	0.14	3	341
24	2137.3	217	41.8	20765	120.73	16	3464
17	744	109	0.26	710	15.29	8	3204
5	584.2	13	8.145	2305	82.03	7	327
19	584.1	48	8.42	1690	20.37	10	6072
15	3593.9	345	90.04	39334	217.23	92.3	10650
2	5426	495	153.4	44985	125.47	106	6653
16	6917	901	5.52	4714	103.67	79.9	25486
11	425.1	110	24.63	1083	521.57	-	3041
23	972	41	0.29	736	0.19	3	2844
27	818.8	55	3.09	662	41.29	-	2297
3	884.8	93	32.16	8868.7	0.68	1.7	1993.6

Plate 7a—Stone-lined tank and hearth in the Broch of Gurness.

Plate 7b—Stone-lined tank in the Broch of Gurness.

8. VARIATIONS ON A THEME

Scottish burnt mounds: variations on a theme

John Barber

In Scotland, burnt mound material has been recovered from four types of site, or rather from four classes of deposits. Deposits of class 1 are found in simple, isolated, kidney-shaped mounds, for which, we suggest, the name fulachta fiadh should be reserved. Class 2 deposits occur in close-set groups of mounds which are, individually, relatively simple, though not usually so clearly kidney-shaped as class 1 sites. We have described above sites in Arran, Fair Isle and Shetland where such groups occur. In such cases the location seems to have served as a *frequentus populi*, an area resorted to by some specific group of people.

Structures are found in direct archaeological association with burnt mound deposits of class 3. The sites of Liddle and Beaquoy are of this type, and we may now include one each of the Kebister and Auld Taggart sites. The excavated examples have produced small but significant amounts of settlement debris associated with the burnt mound deposits. Class 4 deposits occur on large settlement sites where burnt mound material is a common feature of the sites' deposits. These include, in Scotland, Later Bronze Age and Iron Age middens in the Outer Hebrides, Iron Age brochs, Iron Age settlements in Shetland, and Dark Age and Norse/medieval settlements in Orkney.

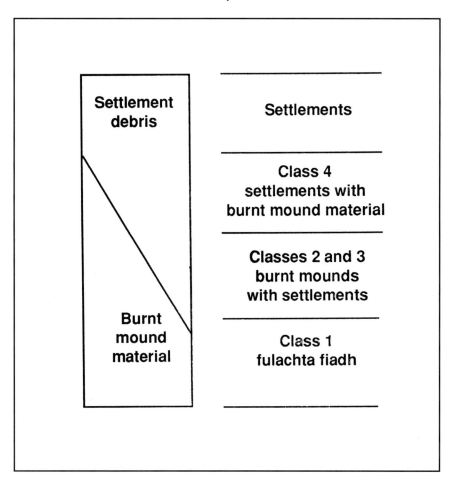

Fig. 44—Breakdown of burnt mound/settlement material.

This simple classification of burnt stone deposits distinguishes between the Scottish sites from which burnt stone has been recovered on the basis of their observed forms and associations. If, however, we concentrate not on the formal or associational differences between these four classes but on the ratio of burnt mound debris to domestic debris which each contains, perhaps we can see a unifying principle (Fig. 44). The four classes of deposits may then be seen as rather arbitrarily-selected points on a continuum which ranges from sites which are all burnt mound material and no settlement debris (class 1) to sites which are mainly settlement debris containing relatively small amounts of burnt mound material (class 4), with intermediate sites between these extremes (classes 2 and 3).

It is clear that we have much to learn about class 3 deposits, burnt mound material found in association with structures. TL dates from sites in the Northern Isles suggest that some of the class 3 sites may hold the key to the terminal Bronze and Earliest Iron Ages in the north of Scotland. Furthermore, it may well prove that class 2 sites are really sites of class 3. The existence of associated structures would explain the repeated use of a given location, and it is clear that at various times in the past, notably during the Neolithic and Early Bronze Ages, structures such as wooden houses were used which present little if any surface indication. The Arran group of class 2 deposits produced Early Bronze Age dates. But as they were revealed by forestry ploughing, the possibility that they were associated with, for example, free-standing wooden structures could not be explored.

In contrast, the area around the classic kidney-shaped site at Arran was sampled both by excavation and by chemical prospection to test for the presence of structures. None were found. Furthermore, it seems unlikely that the several tens of sites of this type now excavated (isupra) would not have revealed structures had such existed. The absence of evidence for structures with fulachta fiadh *sensu stricto* seems real and may support their interpretation as the sort of hunting-camps apparently implied by the early Irish literature (Ó Drisceoil 1988).

Should continuing work confirm the identity of class 2 sites as settlement-associated sites of class 3, the resulting classification may have implications which are cultural and chronological as well as formal and associational. In brief, class 1 sites, classic fulachta fiadh, could then be seen as hunting-station sites, indicative of the exploitation of 'wildscape' (*sensu* Fowler 1981, 9), introduced and used predominantly in the Bronze Age, to which period some 15 of the 18 dated Scottish sites are attributed. A resurgence is evidenced in the early medieval period in Scotland, attested to by three dated sites, two at Auld Taggart in south-west Scotland and one at Kildonan in the north-east (see Table 4). It must be assumed that upland Scotland had reverted from landscape to 'wildscape' in this latter period, an assumption which is not at odds with the growing body of palaeoenvironmental evidence.

Sites with class 2/3 deposits appear to be settlement sites on which the major surviving midden deposits are of burnt mound material. The Arran sites of this type have been radiocarbon-dated to the Early Bronze Age, while Liddle has been radiocarbon-dated to the very end of the Bronze Age.

The class 4 deposits occur on large settlement sites, the dates of which span the chronological gap between the Bronze Age fulachta fiadh and those of the medieval period. Their existence explains how two chronologically disparate groups of otherwise identical monuments can have occurred, the knowledge of the use of hot stones for boiling water being preserved on settlement sites during the intervening period.

THE FUNCTIONS OF FULACHTA FIADH AND OTHER DEPOSITS OF BURNT STONE

Barfield and Hodder suggest that there are four reasons for interpreting burnt mounds as saunas (1987, 371), or rather for not interpreting them as cooking sites associated with hunting-camps. These are (1) the absence of bone, (2) the absence of artifacts of cooking or settlement, (3) siting close to water which precludes permanent settlement, and (4) the very large quantities of stone which indicate use over a long period and preclude their accumulation during seasonal hunting.

It is important to note that in offering this alternative functional interpretation Barfield and Hodder have made the traditional assumption that all burnt mounds are of the same type, essentially that all are fulachta fiadh as defined above. Their four criticisms of the existing interpretation, that the sites are cooking places, are refutable in detail even if we only consider the fulachta fiadh, *sensu stricto*.

Class 1 sites, fulachta fiadh, do not occur in significant numbers on calcareous soils because roasting and quenching limestone or chalk produces slaked lime, in a solution of which cooking would not seem desirable, even if possible! It is significant that at the excavation of Fahee South, Co. Clare, a site in acidic soils but overlying a calcareous substrate, animal bones were recovered (Ó Drisceoil 1988, 675). Acidic soils, in which the vast majority of fulachta fiadh are sited, will have dissolved such bone as was left on site, but it is important to realise that no bone may ever have been left at the fulacht. The cooking pits are large, but could not have held a complete deer or pig carcass. Therefore only prepared joints can have been cooked at these sites, as is implied in Ceitinn's early seventeenth-century description of their use (Dinneen 1908). Thus the large numbers of bones discarded at the butchery stage would never have been deposited at the fulacht. Furthermore, consumption may have taken place away from the site. Indeed, this must necessarily have been the case, because the cooking pits were always sited in wet areas so that they would fill with water. Thus, bones discarded after consumption of the meat would, similarly, not have been deposited at the fulacht. There is therefore little reason to assume that large numbers of bones were ever deposited on fulachta fiadh and every indication that those which were so deposited have been dissolved by their harsh depositional environment. The high phosphate levels in fulachta fiadh deposits cannot, strictly, be used to confirm the latter contention, but they certainly do not weaken it.

With both the preparation and consumption of food taking place at some remove from the site, there is no need to anticipate, as Barfield and Hodder seem to suggest, that the artifact assemblages associated with these functions would be found at the site of the cooking. It is, perhaps, naive to assume that anything other than the primary function of a site must necessarily be mirrored in archaeological assemblages. It is clear, for example, that wood and peat were brought to the sites as fuel but there are no recorded finds of axes or peat-shovels from fulachta fiadh. The burnt stone and charcoal or peat ash mirror the primary function of these sites, which is the heating of water. The question to which Barfield and Hodder address themselves is the function of the heated water, and as this is secondary to the site formation process we need not be surprised to find little or no direct evidence of it.

It would be difficult to sustain the argument that proximity to water precluded permanent settlement at any time in the past. Rather, it is part of archaeology's received wisdom that settlements tend to cluster along watercourses and along shores and beaches. It is hard to see, therefore, why Barfield and Hodder suggest that the siting of burnt mounds in wet areas precluded permanent associated settlement. In any event, almost all class 1 sites visited by this writer, while set in wet areas, lie within a few metres of dry land suitable for settlement.

We have shown that the volumes of stone typically found on fulachta fiadh do not necessarily support the view that they were frequently used, or used over very long periods. The frequency of use of the sites in Scotland ranges from 40 to 400 'boilings', if we accept the experimental results of O'Kelly (1954). Victor Buckley has shown, also by experiment, that certain of the metamorphic and volcanic rock types can be quenched more often than sandstones, producing less detritus per boiling than the 0.5 m^3 produced in O'Kelly's experiments. However, the majority of the large Scottish sites are in the Northern Isles and north-east Scotland, where sandstones predominate and were used almost exclusively in the burnt mounds for which we have records. Even were we to allow that the frequency of use could be double or treble our current estimate, they still do not speak of lengthy duration of use.

An accumulation representative of 400 cookings, at the modest rate of ten cookings per year, would have completed the largest site's deposits in forty years, or roughly one generation. While it is readily conceivable that hunting parties might return to a convenient halt in successive years over this period, it is more probable, given the Scottish evidence, that the larger sites were associated with settlements and may have accumulated in far shorter periods. Furthermore, those fulachta for which multiple radiocarbon dates exist were used over periods of time which are not significant, with respect to the precision of the radiocarbon analyses (Table 4). This finding correlates well with the absence of turf regeneration horizons within excavated fulachta. Together, the closeness of multiple radiocarbon dates and the absence of periods of abandonment sufficiently long for turf regeneration suggest that the burnt mound deposits of classes 1 to 3 accumulated relatively rapidly.

Barfield and Hodder's refutation of the hypothesis that burnt mounds were used for cooking does not survive close scrutiny. However, it would be foolhardy indeed to suggest that these sites were used *solely* for cooking. Boiling water has many uses, and while cooking may be the most common of them it is certainly not the only one. There is no reason not to assume that some burnt mounds were used for bathing, washing, saunas and sweathouses and a range of semi-industrial functions of which we have as yet little indication.

Given the Scottish evidence for a diversity of types of site, the possibility exists that specific classes of site may have had specific functions. Were the class 1 fulachta, in general, contemporaneous with class 2/3 and 4 sites, the suggestion that they fulfilled some function other than cooking might be supportable. However, their chronological distributions are almost mutually exclusive. Their isolation and apparent distancing from settlement sites (but see Hunter and Dockrill, above) cannot, therefore, be adduced as evidence for their functional difference from the settlement site deposits.

Fulachta fiadh lie at the lowest point on a continuous scale, determined by depositional mechanics. Sites at the upper end and, indeed, at the middle of the scale show, by association, that burnt mound material is a common by-product of domestic activities associated with heating water. There seems no reason to suggest that sites at the lower end are produced by a different mechanism. That hot water has many uses and that steam extends the range of possible uses even further should not obscure the rather obvious fact that cooking is likely to have been by far the most common use and the major source of burnt mound material.

Table 4 — Scottish burnt mound radiocarbon calibration. Radiocarbon dates

No. Site (date no.)	Lab.no.	bc/ad	bp		1 Sigma		2 Sigma	
1 Dervaird (1)	GU-2331	1210 bc	3160	50	1512	1411 BC	1520	1320 BC
1 Dervaird (2)	GU-2330	1280 bc	3230	50	1591	1444 BC	1630	1420 BC
2 Auld Taggart 2	GU-2416	1060 ad	890	50	1039	1217 AD	1020	1250 AD
3 Auld Taggart 4 (2)	GU-2414	1150 ad	800	50	1208	1267 AD	1160	1280 AD
3 Auld Taggart 4 (3)	GU-2417	1060 ad	890	50	1039	1217 AD	1020	1250 AD
3 Auld Taggart 4 (1)	GU-2413	1000 ad	950	50	1018	1160 AD	990	1210 AD
3 Auld Taggart 4	AVERAGE	1070 ad	880	29	1058	1209 AD	1039	1225 AD
4 Cruise 1	GU-2411	1590 bc	3540	50	1948	1782 BC	2030	1750 BC
5 Stair Lodge	GU-2412	1730 bc	3680	50	2140	1985 BC	2200	1930 BC
6 Gabsnout Burn 1	GU-2415	1000 bc	2950	100	1376	1010 BC	1430	900 BC
8 Machrie 24/02 (2)	GU-1569	1850 bc	3800	65	2450	2141 BC	2460	2039 BC
8 Machrie 24/02 (1)	GU-1566	1875 bc	3825	65	2456	2147 BC	2470	2045 BC
9 Machrie 24/53	GU-1576	1910 bc	3860	65	2463	2207 BC	2560	2140 BC
10 Machrie 24/54	GU-1568	1455 bc	3405	65	1868	1640 BC	1890	1530 BC
19 Borichill Mor	GU-1465	1745 bc	3695	60	2194	1989 BC	2290	1930 BC
20 Kilearnan 15 (1)	GU-1915	1440 ad	510	60	1398	1440 AD	1299	1469 AD
20 Kilearnan 15 (2)	GU-1912	710 bc	2660	95	908	794 BC	1010	540 BC
20 Kilearnan 15 (3)	GU-1913	800 bc	2750	80	998	823 BC	1100	800 BC
20 Kilearnan 15 (4)	GU-1914	865 bc	2815	60	1041	907 BC	1158	830 BC
20 Kilearnan 15 (5)	GU-1921	870 bc	2820	85	1097	898 BC	1260	810 BC
29 Kildonan 28	GU-2483	920 ad	1030	50	974	1025 AD	890	1151 AD
Liddle (1)	SRR-701	876 bc	2826	75	1094	905 BC	1257	830 BC
Liddle (2)	SRR-525	558 bc	2508	45	792	537 BC	802	413 BC

Species id. by R.P.J. McCullagh (except)*

1 Dervaird (1)	*Quercus sp. and Betula
1 Dervaird (2)	* Quercus
2 Auld Taggart 2	Betula sp., Alnus glutinosa
3 Auld Taggart 4 (2)	Corylus avellana, Betula sp., Alnus glutinosa, Salix sp., Populus
3 Auld Taggart 4 (3)	Betula sp., Alnus glutinosa, Salix sp., Corylus avellana, Prunus
3 Auld Taggart 4	Betula sp. with Corylus avellana, Salix sp., Alnus glutinosa.
3 Auld Taggart 4 (1)	
4 Cruise 1	Quercus sp., Betula sp., Alnus glutinosa, Salix sp.
5 Stair Lodge	Quercus sp., Betula sp., Alnus glutinosa, Salix sp., Corylus avellana
6 Gabsnout Burn 1	Corylus avellana, Quercus sp.
8 Machrie 24/02	"wood charcoal"
8 Machrie 24/02 (1)	"wood charcoal"
9 Machrie 24/53	"wood charcoal"
10 Machrie 24/54	"wood charcoal"
19 Borichill Mor	"wood charcoal"
20 Kilearnan 15 (1)	"wood charcoal"
20 Kilearnan 15 (2)	"wood charcoal"
20 Kilearnan 15 (3)	"wood charcoal"
20 Kilearnan 15 (4)	"wood charcoal"
20 Kilearnan 15 (5)	"wood charcoal"
29 Kildonan 28	"wood charcoal"
Liddle (1)	*Organic detritus, mainly heather roots
Liddle (2)	*Peat

*Dr B.A. Crone

SCOTTISH REFERENCES

BARBER, J. 1981 *Discovery Excav. Scot. 1981*, 29. Edinburgh. CBA Scotland.

BARBER, J. (forthcoming) *Coastal erosion sites on Shetland.*

BARFIELD, L. and HODDER, M. 1987 Burnt mounds as saunas and the prehistory of bathing. *Antiquity* **61**, 370–9.

BETHELL, P. and MÁTÉ, I. D. 1989 The use of soil phosphate analysis in archaeology: a critique. In J. Henderson (ed.), *Scientific techniques.* Oxford Archaeological Monograph Series.

BOWN, C. J. and HESLOP, R. E. F. 1979 *The soils of the country around Stranraer and Wigtown.* Memoirs of the Soil Survey of Great Britain, Scotland. Macaulay Institute for Soil Research, Aberdeen.

BOWN, C. J., SHIPLEY, B. M. and BIBBY, J. S. 1982 *Soil and land capability, south-west Scotland.* Soil Survey of Scotland. M.I.S.R., Aberdeen.

CANTRILL, T. C. 1913 Stone boiling in the British Isles *Brit. Assoc. for the Advancement of Science,* 647–9.

CLARKE, D. V. 1976 *The Neolithic village at Skara Brae, Orkney: 1972–1973 excavations.* Edinburgh. HMSO.

COOK, S. F. and HEIZER, R. F. 1965 *Studies on the chemical analysis of archaeological sites.* Berkeley. University of California Press.

DAVIES, B. E. 1974 Loss-on-ignition as an estimate of soil organic matter. *Soil Sci. Soc. of America* **38**, 1050–1.

DINNEEN,, P.S. 1908 *Foras, Feasa ar Eirinn, II.* Irish Texts Soc. 326.

DOCKRILL, S. J. 1988 *Excavations at Tofts Ness, Sanday – Interim 1987.* Department of Archaeological Sciences, University of Bradford.

EIDT, R. C. 1973 A rapid chemical test for archaeological site surveying. *American Antiquity* **38**, 206–10.

FAHY, E. M. 1960 A hut and cooking places at Drombeg, Co. Cork. *J. Cork Hist. Archaeol. Soc.* **65**, 1–17.

FOWLER, P. 1981 Wildscape to landscape: enclosure in prehistoric Britain. In R. Mercer (ed.), *Farming practice in British prehistory*, 9–54. Edinburgh University Press.

HAGGERTY, A. (forthcoming) *Excavations at Kilearnan Hill, Kildonan, Sutherland.*

HAMILTON, J. R. C. 1956 *Excavation at Jarlshof, Shetland.* Edinburgh. HMSO.

HEDGES, J. 1975 Excavation of two Orcadian burnt mounds at Liddle and Beaquoy. *Proc. Soc. Antiq. Scot.* **106**, 39–98.

HEDGES, J. 1984 Gordon Parry's West Burra Survey. *Glasgow Archaeol. J.* **11**, 41–59.

HEDGES, J. 1987 *Bu, Gurness and the brochs of Orkney.* British Archaeological Reports 163, 164 and 165.

HUNTER, J. R. 1984 *Fair Isle survey, interim 1984.* Bradford University School of Archaeological Sciences, Occasional Paper No. 5.

HUNTER, J. R. 1985 *Fair Isle survey, interim 1985.* Bradford University School of Archaeological Sciences, Occasional Paper No. 6.

KEELEY, H.C.M. 1983 *The use of soil phosphorus analysis in archaeological prospection.* Ancient Monuments Laboratory Report 3851.

MORRIS, C. (ed.) (forthcoming) *Birsay: small sites.* Soc. Antiq. Scot. Monograph.

NSA 1845 *New statistical account of Scotland, vol. XV, Sutherland, Caithness, Orkney, Shetland—general index.* Edinburgh and London.

Ó DRISCEOIL, D. A. 1988 Burnt mounds: cooking or bathing? *Antiquity* **62,** 671–8.

O'KELLY, M. J. 1954 Excavations and experiments in ancient Irish cooking sites. *J. R. Soc. Antiq. Ir.* **84**, 105–55.

OWEN, O. and LOWE, C. E. (forthcoming) *Excavations of an early agricultural settlement at Kebister, Shetland.*

RCAHMS 1946 *Twelfth report with an inventory of the ancient monuments of Orkney and Shetland.* Edinburgh.

RCAHMS 1980 *Sanday and N. Ronaldsay.* Archaeological Sites and Monuments Series 11. Edinburgh.

RCAHMS 1983 *Papa Westray and Westray.* Archaeological Sites and Monuments Series 19. Edinburgh.

RCAHMS 1984a *North Kincardine.* Archaeological Sites and Monuments Series 21. Edinburgh.

RCAHMS 1984b *Eday and Stronsay.* Archaeological Sites and Monuments Series 23. Edinburgh.

RCAHMS 1987 *East Rhins.* Archaeological Sites and Monuments Series 26. Edinburgh.

RCAHMS 1988 *Midlothian (prehistoric to early historic).* Archaeological Sites and Monuments Series 28. Edinburgh.

RCAHMS (forthcoming) *North-east Perthshire: an archaeological survey.* Edinburgh.

RITCHIE, R. A. 1983 Excavations of a Neolithic farmstead at Knap of Howar, Papa Westray, Orkney. *Proc. Soc. Antiq. Scot.* **113**, 40–121.

RITCHIE, J. N. G. and RITCHIE, R. A. 1981 *Scotland: archaeology and early history.* London. Thames and Hudson.

SANCHEZ, P. A. and SALINAS, J. G. 1981 Low-input technology for managing oxisols and ultisols in tropical America. *Advances in Agronomy* **34**, 279–406.

STEVENSON, J. B. 1975 Survival and discovery. In J. G. Evans, S. Limbrey and H. Cleere (eds), *The effects of man on the landscape: the Highland Zone*, 104–7. Council for British Archaeology Research Report 11.

STEVENSON, J. B. 1980 Tofts Ness: Fieldwork July 1980. In RCAHMS 1980, 33.

WINHAM, R. P. 1978 *Discovery Excav. Scot. 1978*, 19–20.

WINHAM, R. P. 1980 Site morphology, location and distribution: a survey of the settlement archaeology of Shetland, investigating man—environment nteraction through time. Unpublished M. Phil. thesis, Southampton University.

YATES, M. J. 1984 *Bronze Age round cairns in Dumfries and Galloway (an inventory and discussion).* British Archaeological Reports 132.

YOUNG, R. 1986 Destruction, preservation and recovery: Weardale, a case study. In T. G. Manby and P. Turnbull (eds), *Archaeology in the Pennines*, 213–27. British Archaeological Reports 158.

PART 3

ENGLISH CONTRIBUTIONS

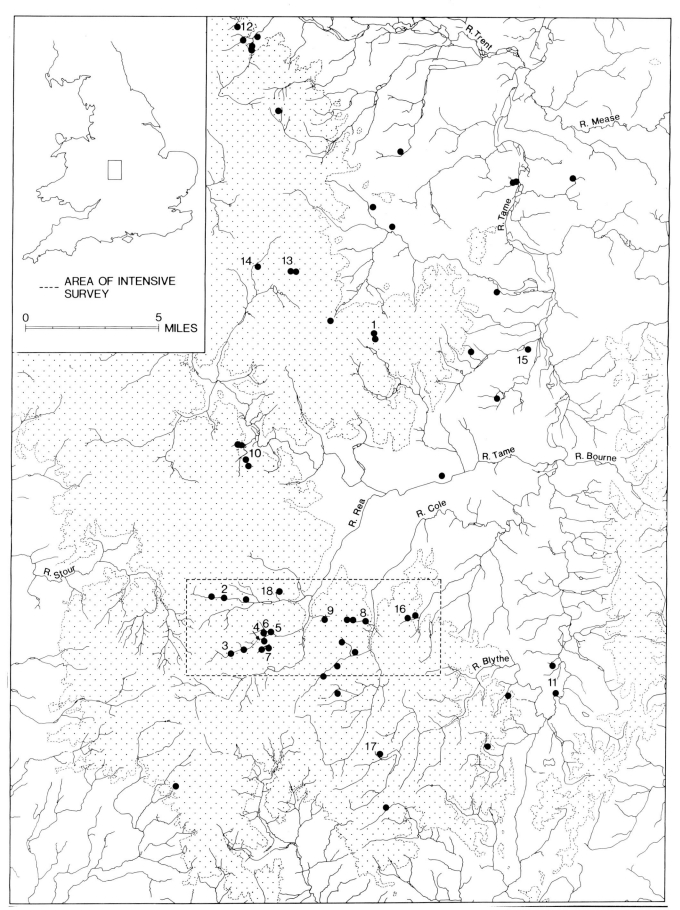

Fig. 45—Location of burnt mounds in the English West Midlands. Sites mentioned in text:

1. Sutton Park   **2.** Ridge Acre   **3.** Merritts Brook   **4.** Cob Lane   **5.** Yachting Pool   **6.** Police Station
7. Woodlands Park   **8.** Moseley Bog   **9.** Highbury Park   **10.** Sandwell Valley group   **11.** Barston
12. Rugeley area   **13.** Aldridge area   **14.** Pelsall   **15.** Middleton   **16.** Fox Hollies Park
17. Earlswood   **18.** Metchley   (Sharmer Farm is off the eastern edge of the map.)

9. WEST MIDLANDS

Burnt mounds in the English West Midlands

M. A. Hodder

INTRODUCTION: THE HISTORY OF BURNT MOUND RESEARCH IN THE REGION

Burnt mounds were first recognised in the region (for location see Fig. 45) in the early part of this century by T.C. Cantrill of the Geological Survey, who had also recorded burnt mounds in south Wales. Cantrill noted sites at Rugeley, Aldridge, Middleton and Pelsall, each of which consisted of a mound with a small hollow in it, lying adjacent to a stream. These sites were reported to the British Association for the Advancement of Science's meeting at Birmingham in 1913 (Cantrill 1913), and on the same occasion turf was removed from the Pelsall site, showing that the mound was composed of heat-shattered pebbles and charcoal (New 1915). In Sutton Park, north of Birmingham, a group of six mounds was discovered and partially excavated in 1926 (Bullows 1930). The mounds were arranged in an arc. Three were circular, one was oval, and the two largest were pear-shaped, with hollows in their highest and widest parts. Trenching showed that all were composed of heat-shattered quartzite pebbles, but no charcoal was present; there were pits under the two pear-shaped mounds corresponding to the hollows on top. In the 1950s and 1960s Michael Nixon located several sites in the south Birmingham area, each consisting of an exposure of heat-shattered pebbles and charcoal in an eroded stream bank (Nixon 1980). A radiocarbon date of 1010 ± 140 bc (Birm-697) was obtained for one of these sites, near the yachting pool in Bournville Park.

RECENT EXCAVATIONS

In 1980, trial excavations were undertaken by the Department of Ancient History and Archaeology, University of Birmingham, on one of the sites located by Nixon, in Cob Lane Park. A trench adjacent to the stream bank in which the mound was exposed revealed its surface and edges. A resistivity survey was then undertaken to locate the extent of the mound, and further excavations in 1981 exposed most of the mound (Fig. 46; Pl. 8; Barfield and Hodder 1980; 1981a; 1981b; 1981c). The mound was shown to have accumulated on a natural alluvial knoll in a former stream meander. The surface of the alluvium under the mound contained many stake-holes, though no pattern could be discerned. Adjacent to the former stream bank on the southern side of the mound was a rectangular area of heat-shattered pebbles and charcoal, removal of which revealed a square clay and timber-lined pit opening onto the stream bank, with a reddened oval hollow behind it. The pit is interpreted as a cistern and the hollow as a hearth. The deposits filling the former stream bed on the north side of the mound consisted of alternate layers of heat-shattered pebbles and alluvium, representing periodic erosion of the mound into the stream bed and the subsequent deposition of water-borne material over it. These deposits covered a group of large timbers laid parallel to the stream bank (Pl. 9), possibly belonging to a structure contemporary with the mound. The mound itself was excavated in arbitrary horizontal spits, there being no visible stratigraphy. The deposit of heat-shattered pebbles and charcoal was more clayey towards its base, but this was probably the result of a natural soil process. The whole of the excavated deposit was sieved, but nothing other than heat-shattered pebbles and charcoal was found. In particular there was no animal bone, despite the fact that the soil pH was neutral. A radiocarbon date of 1190 ± 90 bc (Birm-1087) was

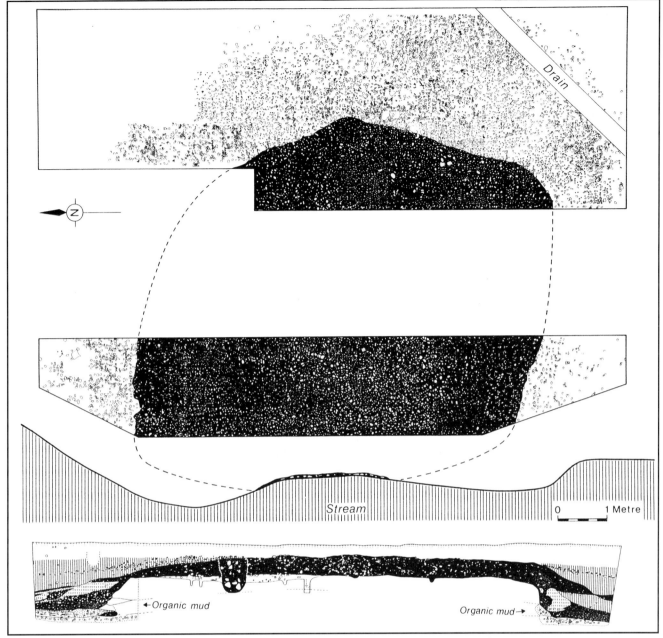

Fig. 46—Plan and section of burnt mound at Cob Lane.

obtained for charcoal at the base of the mound. The charcoal was predominantly alder, a wood which is best burnt as charcoal and which raises the question of whether it was made into charcoal before its use as fuel in the burnt mound (charcoal identification by Rowena Gale). The beetle species present in the waterlogged former stream bed suggested that there were grazing animals in the vicinity (identifications by Peter Osborne). The alluvium under the mound may have been deposited as a result of increased clearance and cultivation in the area before the establishment of the mound.

In 1983, a site in the Sandwell Valley, north-west of Birmingham, was partially excavated (Hewitt and Hodder 1988, 19–20). It was visible as an exposure of heat-shattered pebbles in a stream bank. Excavation revealed a mound *c.* 17m across and *c.* 50cm high, located, like the Cob Lane site, in a former stream meander. There were stake-holes and an oval pit under the mound. The charcoal was principally of ash and alder, and produced a radiocarbon date of 1020 ± 160 bc (Birm-1268). Sieving of the excavated material produced a single body sherd of nondescript coarse pottery. At least two much-eroded burnt mounds, with possible pits below them, were excavated at Metchley in south Birmingham in 1988–9 (A. Jones, pers. comm.).

RECENT FIELD SURVEY

The excavation of the Cob Lane site, described above, was followed by a systematic search of stream banks for burnt mounds, a survey method appropriate to a built-up area. An area measuring about 7 by 2 miles in south Birmingham was initially selected for intensive survey, but the survey has extended beyond this area because it is easier to follow individual drainage systems. Recording forms have been devised both for sites located, describing the nature and length of the exposure, and for each stretch of stream walked, describing the visibility of the stream banks at the time of survey. Three types of sites have been distinguished.

    (i)   A burnt mount *in situ* cut through by the stream, exposing heat-shattered pebbles and charcoal in section.

    (ii)   Heat-shattered pebbles eroded from a mound redeposited along the stream bank. In one case (Woodlands Park) the redeposited pebbles extended for 60m (Barfield and Hodder 1982).

    (iii)   Heat-shattered pebbles eroded from a mound and redeposited in the streambed.

Radiocarbon dates have been obtained for charcoal from stream sections as well as from excavated sites (Fig. 47); they cluster around 1100–1000 bc with one outlier.

    The distribution of sites located in past work and in the recent intensive survey is shown in Fig. 45. Within the area of intensive survey there are

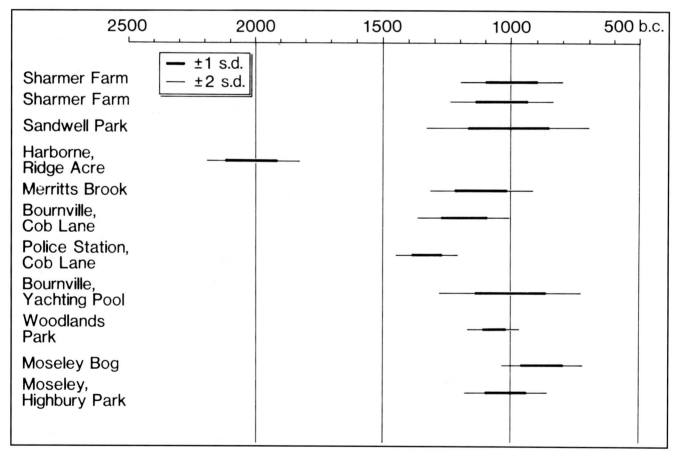

Fig. 47—Radiocarbon date chart. (Site locations are shown in Fig. 45).

23 sites in 22 miles of stream walked. The distribution is not even, but there is some clustering. Where two exposures are close together, they may represent two parts of the same site.

    The drawbacks of the stream survey method are that stream banks are exposed only in parks and open spaces in the built-up area and are otherwise culverted, and that sites are only seen where they lie on the present stream course. This latter factor is particularly demonstrated at

Plate 8—Burnt mound at Cob Lane under excavation, showing mound surface andstream bank.

Plate 9 —Cob Lane: large timbers in former stream channel.

the Police Station site, which lay between the Bournville Park and Cob Lane sites mentioned above but off the stream course. It was only revealed when a trench was cut through it to lay a new sewer pipe (Barfield and Hodder 1982).

Burnt mounds can also be found by conventional field-walking, for example at Barston, south-east of Birmingham, where two sites were visible as a low mound of heat-shattered pebbles and charcoal in a ploughed field (Burnett 1986; 1987). In the Sandwell Valley, a large open space north-west of Birmingham, all stream banks were searched. Four burnt mounds have been located: two were visible as exposures in stream banks (one of these was excavated, as described above), one was visible in the ploughsoil during field-walking, and one was found during the excavation of another site (Hewitt and Hodder 1988, 19–20).

RESISTIVITY SURVEYS

A resistivity survey at the Cob Lane site in 1981, mentioned above, demonstrated how the extent of a burnt mound could be determined by this method. A mound of heat-shattered pebbles is free-draining and offers a high resistance to an electric current; a contour plot of resistivity values reflects the contours of the mound itself. In addition, resistivity survey is a cheap, rapid and non-destructive method of studying the sites and their surroundings. Resistivity surveys have recently been carried out by Alex Jones in south Birmingham and by Chris Welch in south Staffordshire.

Jones surveyed sites at Fox Hollies Park and Earlswood, both originally located by Nixon (Jones 1988). The basic survey was carried out using a four-square array with readings at 0.5m intervals, the results being presented as dot-density plots. In addition, the 'Archres' pseudo-section device, developed by the Geology Department, Birmingham University, was used to establish the depth and profile of deposits. Readings of 'apparent resistivity' were obtained by passing a computer-regulated current to two electrodes in turn along a line of 25 electrodes inserted into the topsoil. A line of readings of resistance at a constant depth is thereby built up by advancing the point of measurement along the profile line. Readings at different depths can be obtained by varying the spacing between electrodes. At Fox Hollies Park the site located by Nixon consisted of a low horseshoe-shaped mound, open to the north, with heat-shattered pebbles in the adjacent stream bank. The resistivity survey showed the mound as an area of high resistance, and the area enclosed by it as of low resistance. The enclosed area is interpreted by Jones as a pit or trough, and the mound as heat-shattered pebbles upcast from it. The trough or pit must therefore be filled with material other than heat-shattered pebbles. Adjacent to the horseshoe mound, and on slightly higher ground, there were two sharply defined areas of high resistance. Augering showed that these were both composed of heat-shattered pebbles. At the east end of the site there were two old stream channels, visible as areas of low resistance, and a complex pattern of areas of high resistance. The latter consisted of a linear feature with two concentrations of high resistance and two sub-circular features with higher resistance in their centres, interpreted by Jones as possibly pits filled with heat-shattered pebbles.

Welch carried out both contour and resistivity surveys of two sites near Rugeley (Hodder and Welch 1990). The Smarts Buildings site was one of the sites originally located by Cantrill. It consists of a mound with a hollow in the centre. The contour survey revealed former stream channels around the mound. In the resistivity survey, the mound produced resistance values 250% above the mean, and two other adjacent areas of high resistance were detected. Another site nearby consisted of a very low mound, visible as an area of heat-shattered pebbles on the surface of a ploughed field. The contour plot again showed that the mound was bordered by a former stream channel which was possibly dammed. The mound itself produced high resistance values, and there was a smaller area of high resistance nearby.

DISCUSSION

Excavations and survey have shown that the burnt mounds of the West Midlands consist of oval mounds composed of heat-shattered quartzite pebbles and charcoal, originally located in meanders of small streams. The surviving mounds sometimes have a hollow in them, and in excavation stake-holes and a pit have been found under the mound. Resistivity surveys have shown the relationship of the sites to former watercourses and have revealed one or more subsidiary areas of heat-shattered pebbles. Intensive survey by stream-walking has demonstrated a dense distribution of sites in the region, with some clustering.

The radiocarbon dates (Fig. 47) could indicate that all the sites were in use either at the same time or successively. This problem may be resolved by obtaining more dates from each site rather than one as at present. The period of the burnt mounds is otherwise represented in the

110

region only by chance finds of metalwork, whose distribution is influenced by the distribution of modern built-up areas, and therefore the relationship of the burnt mounds to contemporary settlements is not known. The evidence of the beetles and alluvium at Cob Lane indicates agricultural activity nearby, but settlements associated with the mound are likely to have been on higher and better-drained ground rather than adjacent to the mound itself.

REFERENCES

BARFIELD, L.H. and HODDER, M.A. 1980 The excavation of two burnt mounds in south Birmingham: An interim report. *West Midlands Archaeol.* **23**, 14–26.

BARFIELD, L.H. and HODDER, M.A. 1981a Birmingham's Bronze Age. *Current Archaeol.* **78**, 198–200.

BARFIELD, L.H. and HODDER, M.A. 1981b Birmingham, West Midlands County. Survey of burnt mounds. *West Midlands Archaeol.* **24**, 51.

BARFIELD, L.H. and HODDER, M.A. 1981c Bournville, West Midlands County. Excavations on burnt mound at Cob Lane, second season. *West Midlands Archaeol.* **24**, 56–9.

BARFIELD, L.H. and HODDER, M.A. 1982 Birmingham, West Midlands County. Burnt mound survey. *West Midlands Archaeol.* **25**, 60–1.

BULLOWS, W.L. 1930 Notes on prehistoric cooking site and camping ground in Sutton Park, Warwickshire, excavated 1926. *Trans. Birmingham Archaeol. Soc.* **52**, 291–300.

BURNETT, W. 1986 Barston. *West Midlands Archaeol.* **29**, 63–4.

BURNETT, W. 1987 Barston. *West Midlands Archaeol.* **30**, 58–9.

CANTRILL, T.C. 1913 Stone boiling in the British Isles. *Rep. Brit. Assoc. for the Advancement of Sci. Birmingham 1913.*

HEWITT, N.R. and HODDER, M.A. 1988 A landscape survey of Sandwell Valley, 1982–87. *Trans. South Staffordshire Archaeol. Hist. Soc.* **28**, 14–38.

HODDER, M.A. and WELCH, C. 1990 Burnt mounds in the south Staffordshire area. *Staffordshire Archaeol. Studies* **4**, 15–24.

JONES, A.E. 1988 A geophysical and contour survey of burnt mounds at Fox Hollies Park, Acocks Green, Birmingham and Earlswood, West Midlands. Unpub. M.A. dissertation, University of Birmingham.

NEW, H. 1915 Stone boiling mound at Pelsall near Walsall. *Trans. Birmingham Warwickshire Archaeol. Soc.* **40**, 14–15.

NIXON, M.J. 1980 Burnt mounds in the south Birmingham area. *West Midlands Archaeol.* **23**, 8–11.

10. CUMBRIAN SURVEY

Some south Cumbrian burnt mounds — an initial survey

M. J. Nixon

In 1982, in the course of a geological mapping project in the Furness Fells, the opportunity was taken to survey for possible burnt mounds. The area surveyed was 9km² of the rocky low fells south-west of Coniston Water in the parishes of Torver and Blawith. The geological formations outcropping in the area are essentially Coniston Grit (sandstones) in the north-west and Bannisdale Slates (mudstones) in the south-east.

Four sites identified as burnt mounds were found on the Coniston Grit outcrop. No likely site has been observed on the Bannisdale Slates in the survey area. However, a site has been found on the Bannisdale Slates outcrop area 14 miles to the east at Plantation Bridge, near Staveley, between Windermere and Kendal.

The five sites are identified as burnt mounds on the basis of their shape, stream-side situation, the 'burnt' appearance of stone retrieved from the mounds, and the presence of a carbonaceous matrix deposit. More precisely, the stone fragments are rough-sided and angular, and commonly display large re-entrant angles (particularly on the coarser rock). Sometimes fragment surfaces display reddening or a network of fine irregular cracks. Such shapes and characteristics are typical of stones, often referred to as 'potboilers', that constitute the mound material of many other British burnt mound sites, particularly where the rock involved is quartzite or sandstone (Cantrill and Jones 1911; Ellis and Shotton 1973; Nixon 1980). The writer considers that such characteristics are more typical of the effect of sudden cooling on hot stones rather than of direct heat, where smoother plain or curved fractures sometimes develop. A petrological section of a reddened gritstone sample from site 4 demonstrates occasional fractured quartz grains not found in or to be expected in local fresh gritstone, helping to confirm that the mound material had experienced thermal shock.

Four of the five sites, those in Furness, are situated near the entrance of small, relatively broad, flat-bottomed valleys, roughly 250m long, surrounded by rocky fell sides or escarpments. These valleys tend to dry out considerably in summer but are very waterlogged or boggy in winter.

The Staveley site is situated in rough pasture in a col between rocky pastured hillsides and at the source of a stream.

On the basis of the similarity of these sites to others in the British Isles (some excavated and dated) (O'Kelly 1954; Cubbon 1964; Hedges 1974–5), the sites described here are interpreted by the writer as open-air cooking places at which water was boiled using hot stones ('potboilers'), and at which crescentic middens of fragmented and unusable 'potboilers' accumulated around the boiling trough. The relatively remote situation of the sites and the enclosed topography nearby suggest the possible association of cooking occasions with the herding or trapping of animals.

On the evidence of other English burnt mound sites, a Middle Bronze Age date range seems most likely for these Cumbrian sites also. On this assumption, one speculates whether there is a connection between the sites and the Bronze Age 'perforated implement' industry (Petrological Group XV). This industry used Coniston Grit as a source material (Coope 1979) and distribution studies suggest that the factories may have been in the Furness Fells area.

Local ancient monuments in the survey area appear to be a few cairns and two 'bloomery' sites, neither near to the burnt mounds. Ancient field systems, 'settlements' and 'stone circles' (probably ring-cairns) are noted on various Ordnance Survey maps in the lower-altitude land further south.

The five sites mentioned above are described in further detail below.

1. WOODLAND FELL, BLAWITH (Map ref. 26258880)

Two slight mounds of firmer ground rising from boggy land on the eastern bank of a narrow stream flowing northwards. Blackened angular ('potboiler'-shaped) fragments of gritstone were retrieved on one mound, from beneath peat at nearly 30cm depth. Maximum dimensions of mounds are 6m and 4m.

To the north of this site in the direction of site 2 is a level grassy platform (30m or so across), situated between the stream and a rocky escarpment in Coniston Grits.

2. WOODLAND FELL, BLAWITH (Map ref. 26278889)

Well-shaped steep-sided crescentic mound over 1m high, on north of and facing shallow stream. Dimensions: 9.7m x 8.7m with interior measurements of approx. 2m x 3m. Altitude: about 195m OD. Slightly reddened angular ('potboiler'-shaped) fragments of grit and mudstone, in a fine carbonaceous matrix, were retrieved from beneath 8cm of black humus. There is evidence of a buried straight kerb across the opening of this mound, and also of a very narrow ramp sloping up the inside of the eastern arm of the mound. The mound is covered with ling and bilberry, distinguishing it from the surrounding soft ground covered by grasses, bell-heathers and rushes.

About 375m ENE of this site is a cairn named 'White Borran', and another cairn 100m further away. About 500m to the SSW is a local peak of 248m OD.

3. NEAR PLAIN RIGGS, TORVER LOW COMMON (Map ref. 28109302)

Well-shaped crescentic mound about 0.7m high, on west of and facing slow stream. Dimensions: approx. 7.5m x 4.7m, with inside measurements of approx. 1.7m x 1.7m. Altitude: about 112m OD. Blackened angular ('potboiler'-shaped) fragments of gritstone were retrieved from the inner side of the mound.

The grassy mound is situated in grassy and marshy fell land, facing a Coniston Grit escarpment beyond the stream.

4. NEAR HAZEL HALL, TORVER LOW COMMON (Map ref. 27199285)

Very low firm mound, vaguely crescentic, on south-west bank of and facing shallow stream issuing from a small boggy valley. Dimensions: approx. 5m x 3m, with inner hollow about 1m across; height about 0.3m. Altitude: about 130m OD. Slightly reddened angular ('potboiler'-shaped) fragments of grit, mudstone and volcanic rocks were exposed in the low stream bank at the side of the mound and scattered in the stream bed at this point. The mound has more ling than the surrounding ground, and is situated shortly before the stream rapidly descends a high Coniston Grit escarpment.

5. PLANTATION BRIDGE, NEAR STAVELEY (Map ref. 48159709)

Low crescentic mound, up to 0.75m high, near source of small stream and facing towards lowest ground of SW-dipping pasture field. Dimensions: 8m x 9m with 3.5m-long interior depression. Altitude: about 95m OD. Reddened angular fragments of mudstone, in a fine blackish matrix, were observed in an erosion hole in the side of the mound.

REFERENCES

CANTRILL, T.C. and JONES, O.T. 1911 Prehistoric cooking-places in south Wales. *Archaeol. Cambrensis* **11**, 253–65.

COOPE, G.R. 1979 *The influence of geology on the manufacture of Neolithic and Bronze Age stone implements in the British Isles.* C.B.A. Research Report 23, 98–101.

CUBBON, A.M. 1964 Clay head cooking place sites. *Proc. Isle Man Natur. Hist. Antiq. Soc.* 566-96.

ELLIS, N. and SHOTTON, F.W. 1973 Radiocarbon and thermoluminescence dating of a prehistoric hearth and pit, near the Fosse Way, in Harbury parish, Warwickshire. *Proc. Coventry Nat. Hist. Sci. Soc.* **4**, 204–8.

HEDGES, J. 1974–5 Excavation of two Orcadian burnt mounds at Liddle and Beaquoy. *Proc. Soc. Antiq. Scot.* **106**, 38–98.

NIXON, M.J. 1980 Burnt mounds in the south Birmingham area. *West Midlands Archaeol.* **23**, 9–11.

O'KELLY, M.J.1954 Excavations and experiments in ancient Irish cooking places. *J. R. Soc. Antiq. Ir.* **84**, 105–55.

PART 4

WELSH CONTRIBUTIONS

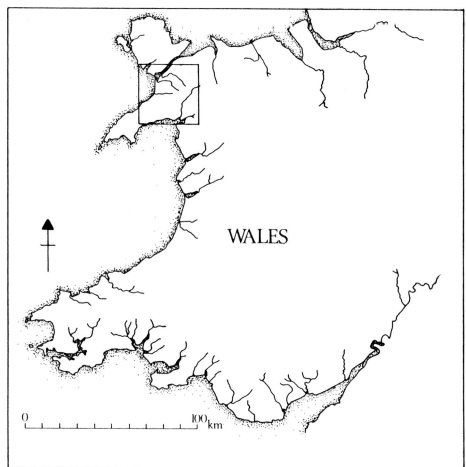

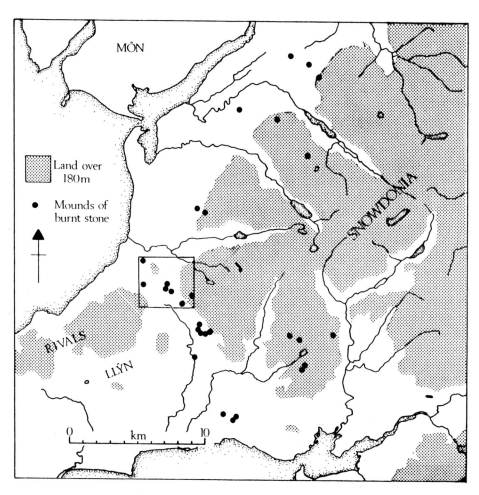

Fig. 48 —The Graeanog burnt mound: site location and the distribution of burnt mounds in central Caernarvonshire, Gwynedd (based on RCAHM 1960 , xxxiii, fig. 4).

11. RECENT WORK

Recent work in north-west Wales: the excavation of a burnt mound at Graeanog, Clynnog, Gwynedd, in 1983

Richard S. Kelly

A burnt or boiling mound at Graeanog farm in the parish of Clynnog, Gwynedd (OS NGR SH 46164945), was excavated between June and August 1983 by the Gwynedd Archaeological Trust, with funds provided by Cadw: Welsh Historic Monuments, in advance of gravel extraction. The site was the fifth in a series of excavations to be conducted in the Graeanog area by the Trust since 1977 (Kelly 1982; 1983), while work on a sixth site was recently completed in 1988. The burnt mound was the first Bronze Age site to be excavated although several burial cairns of the period occur in the area, whilst a remarkable stray find of late Bronze Age gold-plated 'ring money' was recently brought to light, having been originally discovered only a short distance from the mound (Green 1988).

THE SITE

The Graeanog burnt mound was first described and published by the Royal Commission (RCAHM 1960, 56b, no. 868). In addition, the Trust's pre-excavation contour survey showed that part of the mound's south-east side had been obliterated under the track-bed of the now-dismantled Caernarvon to Afonwen railway line.

The site lay on a gentle slope above a shallow valley bottom at the north end of the wide col joining the Rivals mountains and the Lleyn peninsula to Snowdonia (Fig. 48), and just beneath the steeper slopes of a kame mound which forms the Graeanog ridge (Fig. 49). It was located between dry ground to the north-west and an extensive marsh to the south in which the Desach and Dwyfach rivers rise; however, its relationship to a local water source was not apparent before the excavation and was presumed to have been obscured either by the construction of the railway or by the cutting of drainage ditches in more recent times.

The mound was fairly typical of its type (Fig. 50), being roughly crescent-shaped, up to 0.5m high and about 10m by 17m in maximum extent, and well within the range and proportions recorded for burnt mounds in the county of Caernarvon (RCAHM 1964, lxii–lxiv). It belonged to a dispersed scatter of single and groups of burnt mounds situated on the Lleyn – Snowdonia col between the 75m and 220m contours (Fig. 48, lower, based on RCAHM 1964, xxxiii, fig. 4). However, the original population of sites in this area might have been considerably higher, as fieldwork preliminary to the excavation led to the discovery of a further three conjoined or 'triple' mound sites, 250m to the south, in the middle of what is now a forestry plantation (Fig. 49, nos 4314–16). Their frequent occurrence in such locations, or on the edges of marshes where peat growth has obscured the original topography, has probably precluded the discovery of many more sites.

THE EXCAVATION

An excavation trench was laid out to include the whole of the visible extent of the mound and adjacent areas of flat ground to the north, west and south. Obviously, it would have been an advantage to open a larger proportion of the surroundings, but the area available was constrained by the old railway embankment on the east, a drystone field wall on the west,

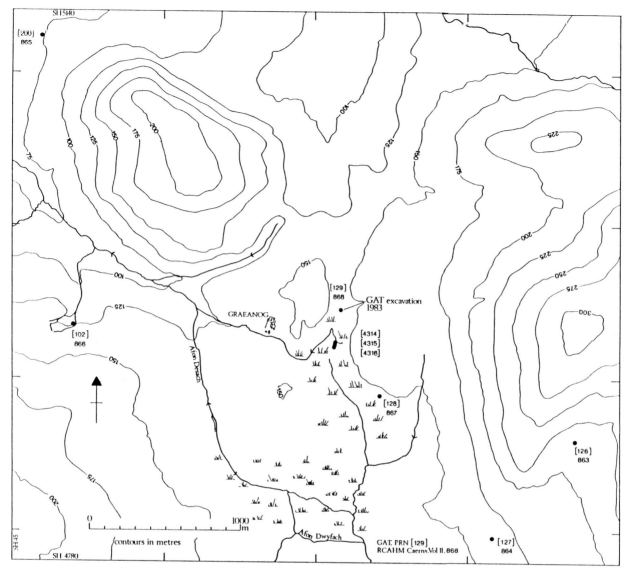

*Fig. 49—The Graeanog burnt mound: site location and the distribution of
burnt mounds in the area.*

and waterlogged ground to the south.

The site was initially stripped of a mixture of turf and topsoil on the
north-west and substantial deposits of peat on the south-east, differences
which soon became apparent as the 'dry' and the 'wet' sides of the mound
respectively (Pl. 11 and Fig. 51). A 1m-wide main section baulk was laid
out from north-east to south-west across the crest of the mound and this
was retained until the last stages of the excavation.

The excavation involved the complete removal of the mound and an
investigation of its constituent stratigraphy and the surfaces beneath and
outside. During this process, any features found within, beneath, or
outside the mound were individually examined as appropriate.

A sampling strategy for plant macro-remains was devised on the
observed stratigraphy but, apart from wood charcoal, this produced
disappointingly negative results. Geological samples were collected on a
similar basis, while fine particle recovery was investigated by water-
sieving, although this latter technique also failed to produce any evidence.
Samples of wood charcoal were taken from several contexts for ^{14}C dates
and also for the identification of the species present.

The soils on the site were examined in some detail and found to
comprise a brown podsolic soil up to 0.3m deep on the dry, north-west
side of the mound and a peat or peaty gley of similar depth on the
opposite, wet side, the variations representing different drainage
conditions over essentially the same parent material, a sandy clay loam of

Fig. 50—The pre-excavation contour survey of the Graeanog burnt mound.

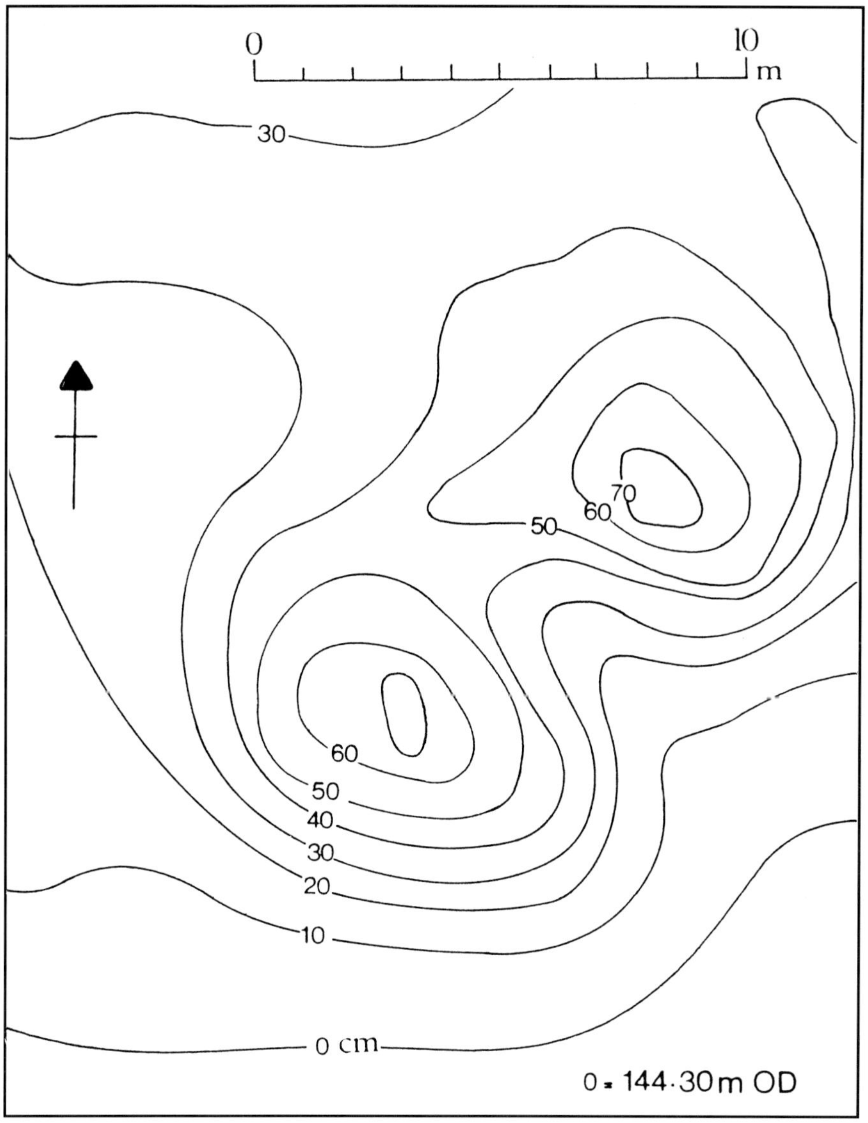

fluvio-glacial origin. Several stages of peat growth were observed in the peat profile, but the mound itself accumulated on a surface just above the parent material. This surface may have originally been overlain by a thin humic topsoil; however, this was not clearly distinguishable beneath the mound or elsewhere on site.

A soil pollen sample was taken from immediately beneath the mound, and although the pollen in this was poorly preserved, the range of species present indicated human activity with the pollen of wheat and weed species, but generally a more wooded environment than at present, typical of a streamside location.

Several 'layers' in the conventional archaeological sense were recognised, both within the mound and in the soil and peat profiles outside, but their individual significance in an overall site sequence is discussed more fully in the excavation report (Kelly forthcoming). Suffice it to mention here that the deposits in the mound comprised the typical agglomerations of disaggregated burnt stones, humus and charcoal commonly found on these sites. Plate 12 shows a typical portion of the main section and Fig. 52 the principal layers recognised in this.

There were three irregularly-shaped pits associated with the mound (Fig. 53), two beneath it, M 12 and M 14, and the third, M 11, cut through it at some later stage. M 14, depicted in Pl. 13, was clearly the central and largest pit, around which the mound had accumulated. Apart from the few sherds of possible Bronze Age pottery from the top of the latest pit, M 11, there were no finds from the site.

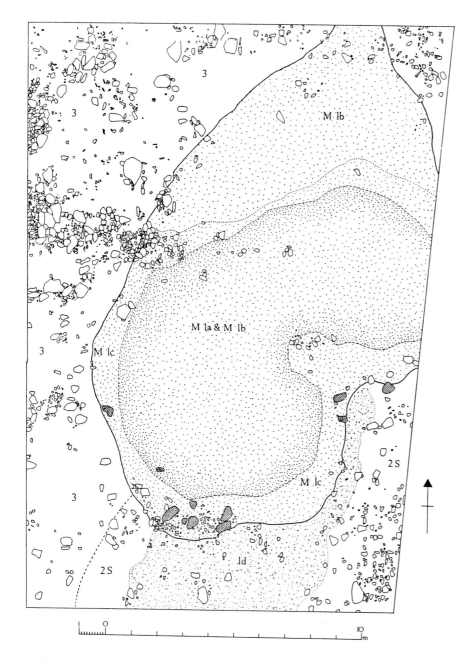

Fig. 51—The Graeanog burnt mound after de-turfing: M 1a, 1b and 1c, mound material; 1d, charcoal 'delta'; on top of 2S, stream deposits, and 3, 'natural' fluvio-glacial materials.

DATING

Two groups of closely matching ^{14}C dates were obtained, statistically consistent within themselves but about a millennium apart, based on their respective average values (Table 1). The earlier group, made up of CAR-713, 714 and 715, ranges between 2577 and 1880 cal. BC at two sigma, and is for wood charcoal from contexts which stratigraphically represent the initial period of activity on the site. The later group, comprising CAR-716, 717, 718, 719 and 720, ranges between 1253 and 790 cal. BC at two sigma, and is for wood charcoal from contexts belonging to the main period of activity, with four of these dates relating to the use of the central pit, M 14. As noted, however, the date of the pottery from the latest pit, M 11, is open to question beyond a tentative Bronze Age designation.

SITE USE AND HISTORY

On the basis of the excavation results, the purpose and the manner in which the Graeanog mound accumulated may be suggested, although the cultural context of this type of activity still remains largely enigmatic, both in Wales and elsewhere.

It is clear that a location with a plentiful water supply was essential. A small stream once ran past the site (Fig. 53) and two of the pits associated with the mound, M 12 and M 14, had been sited either on or

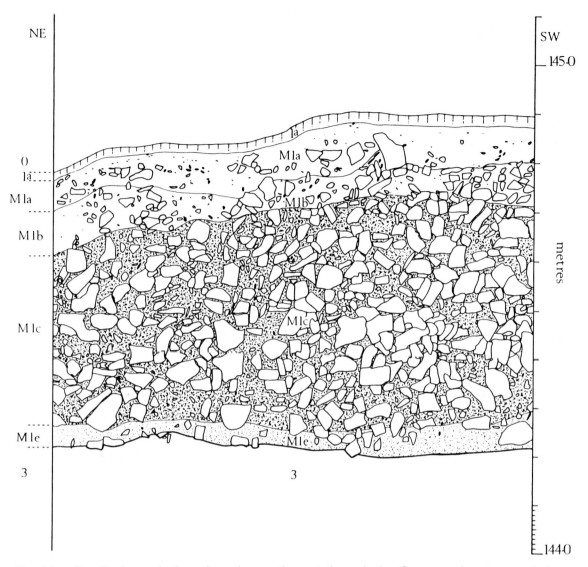

NE

SW

145·0

0

1a

M 1a

M 1b

M 1c

M 1e

3

3

144·0

metres

Fig. 52 —Detail of a typical portion of a section cut through the Graeanog burnt mound: 1a, modern turf cover; M 1a and 1b, weathered mound material; M 1c, mound material; and M 1e, interface between the latter and the 'natural', 3.

close to its bank where water was most easily drawn. However, both pits might have been inundated most of the time as the parent material into which they had been dug was largely impermeable.

The results of several successful field experiments (O'Kelly 1954, and more recently James 1986) suggest that, once filled, these pits would have been charged with heated stones in order to raise and sustain the temperature of the water sufficiently to cook food. Here, as in other reported cases, the stones had been collected locally and selected for their hardness (rhyolites — 47%; quartoze sandstones — 34%; microgranite type — 7%; dolerite — 6%; tuffs — 5%; others — 1%) and then heated close to the pits, possibly within the rough setting of large stones shown hatched on Figs 51 and 53, using firewood which had also been felled or gathered locally (average percentage weight of species in all contexts: hazel/alder — 29%; birch— 28%; ash — 24%; oak — 8%; indeterminate — 11%). The stones were apparently used until they cracked (Conway 1986; James 1986) and the resulting debris of disaggregated burnt stones, charcoal and ash cleared out and cast to the sides to form the mound. At Graeanog, some of the charcoal from the central pit, M 14, floated out in a distinctive black delta downstream (Pl. 10; Figs 51 and 53, layer 1d). None of the ash would have survived owing to the acid soil conditions. Whilst in use the central pit, M 14, might have had a temporary screen or canopy, probably of skin or some other light

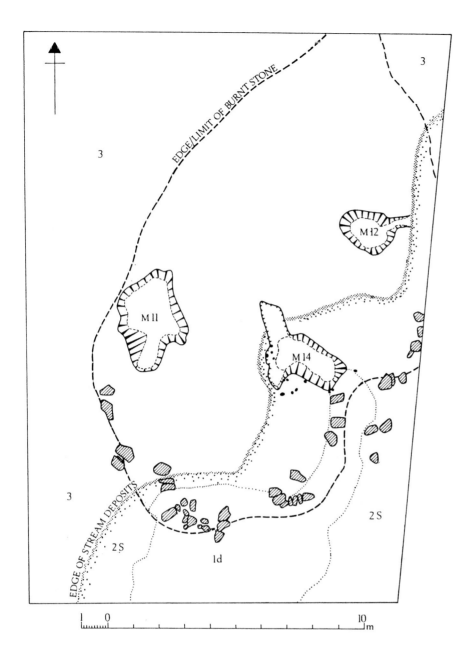

Fig. 53—Features revealed beneath the Graeanog burnt mound: 1d, 2S and 3 — as in Fig. 4; M 11, 12 and 14 — the pits associated with the mound.

organic material, secured to the surrounding stakes indicated in Fig. 53.

Whether or not the third pit, M 11, functioned in the same way is difficult to say as it had been dug through the mound at some distance from the stream; in any event, it resulted in the final accumulations of debris, after which the site was abandoned, possibly because water had ceased to flow in the stream over which peat deposits were forming.

The ¹⁴C dates confirm two of the periods of activity on the site: the first during the late third to early second millennium BC in pit M 12, and the second, main, period during the late second to early first millennium BC in the central pit, M 14. The final period in pit M 11 occurred during an unknown stage, but on stratigraphic grounds could not have been long after the second.

The precise deposits corresponding to each period of activity could not be easily identified since one of the principal layers in the mound, although appearing to be stratigraphically discrete and homogeneous, produced varying ¹⁴C dates. Many of the apparent differences found between deposits could therefore be the result of post-depositional changes rather than patterns of accumulation, a phenomenon also alluded to on other Welsh burnt mound sites, e.g. Carne, Pembs., where the stratigraphy did not wholly accord with the ¹⁴C dates (James 1986, 254).

Table 1— The Graeanog burnt mound: ¹⁴C dates

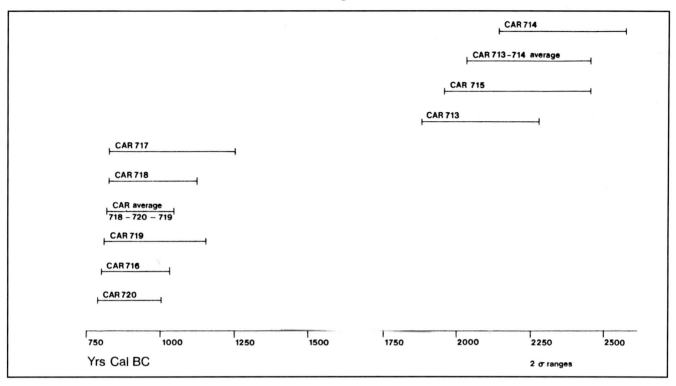

On the same site James postulated the rate at which a burnt mound might have accumulated and the frequency of use required to achieve this (*ibid.*, 262). Using her data, the Graeanog mound could represent the debris from at least a hundred operations, the majority of which occurred in the central pit, M 14, around which the mound was principally disposed. The absence of a definite surface under the mound is also paralleled on other Welsh sites (Felin Fulbrook, Cards. (Williams *et al.* 1987, 231), and, in the same county, Morfa Mawr (Williams 1985, 184)). It may be suggested that in the west of Britain, where there is higher than average rainfall, the surfaces on these sites were being continually exposed with little vegetation or soil cover ever developing, particularly along stream banks susceptible to flooding and degradation.

CONCLUSIONS

The weight of the evidence from both excavations and field trials overwhelmingly suggests that burnt mounds were primarily used as cooking places, at intervals from the early Bronze Age to historic times (O'Kelly 1954; Hedges 1975; James 1986). The evidence from Graeanog accords well with this although, if required, it could also be made to fit another, albeit highly unlikely, purpose which has recently been suggested, namely their use as saunas or sweathouses (Barfield and Hodder 1987). Obviously, no one function explains all the evidence (Bradley 1978, 83), and the full explanation must be sought not only by examining and comparing the results of individual excavations but also by thoroughly investigating the relationship of burnt mounds to other contemporary sites and events in the archaeological record, of which, so far, little is known in Wales.

The scope of the Gwynedd Archaeological Trust's involvement in the Graeanog area with the excavation of sites and related pollen studies, so far dating from the earliest period on the burnt mound to the medieval period (Kelly 1982), may in future provide the opportunity to adopt such an approach, but in the interim it is only pertinent to set the results against the known background.

The distribution and character of burnt mounds in the British Isles generally has been discussed by Hedges (1975) and the local pattern in north-west Wales was appraised by the Royal Commission (RCAHM 1964). The Graeanog burnt mound, one of the fifty or so in the area, had obviously been sited in a typical location on the edge of a bog and next to a stream; however, within the area excavated there was no evidence of any associated settlement or of any of the other features commonly found associated with these sites, such as the stone or wooden troughs, cisterns, hearths, areas of stone flagging, and so on. This seems to be the picture emerging on most of the Welsh sites recently investigated: Carne, Pembs. (James 1986), Felin Fulbrook, Cards. (Williams *et al.* 1987), and Morfa Mawr, Cards. (Williams 1985), although the absence of a fabricated trough is simple enough to explain in areas with impermeable glacially-derived soils. Likewise, apart from the few sherds of possible Bronze Age pottery from the latest pit at Graeanog, there were no finds and at least two, if not three, periods of activity indicated, something again noted in south Wales at Carne, Pembs. (James 1986, 260).

The cultures associated with the Welsh burnt mounds or, more specifically, the conditions which led to their recurrent use thus appear to have been materially austere in the extreme. However, the dearth of artifacts and other evidence is almost too apparent to be real, even for Wales, and must surely reflect the function of these sites rather than the impoverishment of the folk who used them. The key to this must lie on the contemporary settlements to which burnt mounds relate, where more evidence might have survived, but until such time as these have been identified and properly examined there will be no full answers, either here in Wales or elsewhere.

ACKNOWLEDGEMENTS

I am grateful to the Gwynedd Archaeological Trust and Cadw: Welsh Historic Monuments for the provision of the materials to prepare this contribution.

REFERENCES

BARFIELD, L. and HODDER, M. 1987 Burnt mounds as saunas, and the prehistory of bathing. *Antiquity* **61**, 370–9.

BRADLEY, R. 1978 *The prehistoric settlement of the British Isles*. London. Routledge and Kegan Paul.

CONWAY, J. 1986 'Pot-boilers' from the Ty Mawr hut-circles, Holyhead. *Archaeol. Cambrensis* **135**, 39–53.

GREEN, H.S. 1988 A find of Bronze Age 'ring-money' from Graianog, Llanllyfni, Gwynedd. *Bulletin of the Board of Celtic Studies* **35**, 87–91.

HEDGES, J. 1975 Excavation of two Orcadian burnt mounds at Liddle and Beaquoy. *Proc. Soc. Antiq. Scot.* **106**, 39–98.

JAMES, H.J. 1986 Excavations of burnt mounds at Carne, nr. Fishguard, 1979 and 1981. *Bulletin of the Board of Celtic Studies* **33**, 245–65.

KELLY, R.S. 1982 The excavation of a medieval farmstead at Cefn Graeanog, Clynnog, Gwynedd. *Bulletin of the Board of Celtic Studies* **29**, 859–908.

KELLY, R.S. 1983 Cairn at Cefn Graeanog, Clynnog. *Trans. Caerns. Hist. Soc.* **44**, 172–3.

KELLY, R.S. (forthcoming) The excavation of a burnt mound at Graeanog, Clynnog, Gwynedd in 1983. *Bulletin of the Board of Celtic Studies* .

O'KELLY, M.J. 1954 Excavations and experiments in ancient Irish cooking-places. *J. Roy. Soc. Antiq. Ir.* **84**, 105–55.

RCAHM 1960 Caernarvonshire II (Central). *Inventory*. HMSO.

RCAHM 1964 Caernarvonshire III (West). *Inventory.* HMSO.

WILLIAMS, G. 1985 A group of burnt mounds at Morfa Mawr, Aberaeron. *Ceredigion*, 181–8.

WILLIAMS, G.H., BENSON, D.G., HEYWORTH, A., HUNT, C. and TAYLOR, J.A. 1987 A burnt mound at Felin Fulbrook, Tregaron, Ceridigion. *Bulletin of the Board of Celtic Studies* **34**, 228–43.

Plate 10—The Graeanog burnt mound: the central pit, M14

Plate 11—Graeanog after de-turfing.

Plate 12—The Graeanog burnt mound. Detail of a typical portion of the main section, showing the principal constituents of disaggregated burnt stones, humus and charcoal.

Plate 13—Trowelling at Graeanog.

Plate 14—Carne mound B, from west. Stone dumps partially removed: pit 77 cut by pit 80 (photo: A. Waters).

Plate15— Carne mound B, pit 80 (photo: A. Waters).

Plate 16—Felin Fulbrook. Mound embedded in silt, overlain by peaty soil (photo: C. Stenger).

Plate 17—Stackpole Warren site A. Stone building and hearth complex, standing stone in background (photo: D. Benson).

Plate 18—Stackpole Warren site A. Detail of hearth complex from south; scale lying on stone platform (photo: G. Williams).

12. SOUTH-WEST WALES

Burnt mounds in south-west Wales

George Williams

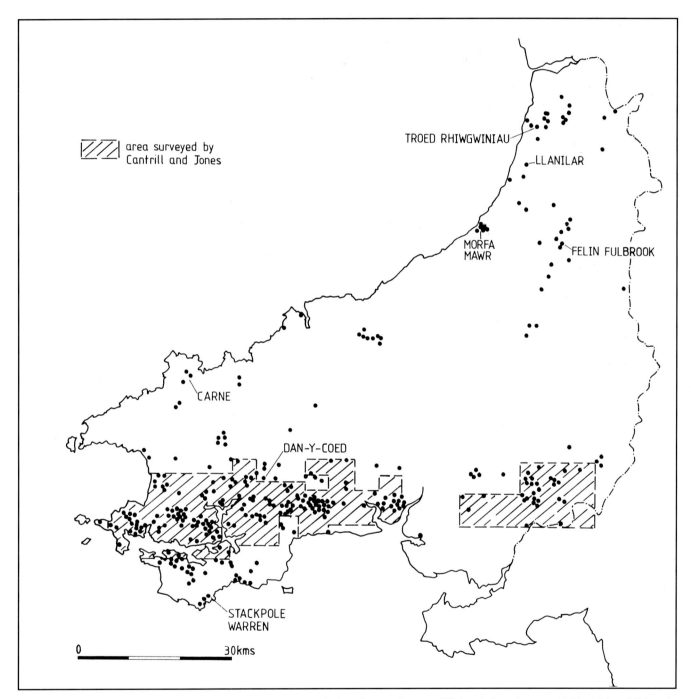

Fig. 54 —Burnt mound sites in south-west Wales (after James 1986, with additions).

INTRODUCTION

Since 1977, in south-west Wales, a programme of excavation of burnt mounds threatened with destruction has been carried out by the Dyfed Archaeological Trust. In addition, burnt mounds have been discovered incidentally by the Trust during the excavation of other, apparently more complex classes of site. The mounds date from the second millennium BC

129

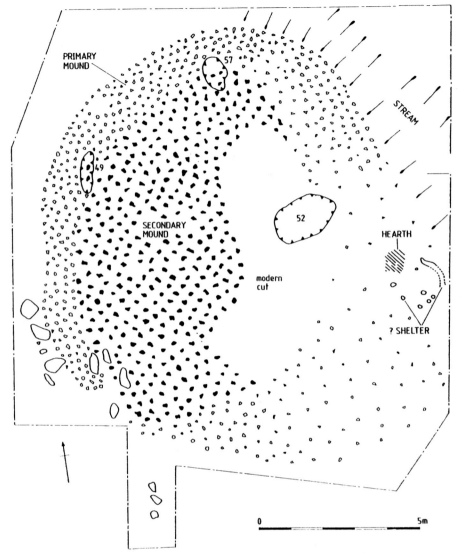

PRIMARY
MOUND

STREAM

57

49

SECONDARY
MOUND

52

HEARTH

modern
cut

? SHELTER

0   5m

Fig. 55 —Carne, Fishguard,
Pembrokeshire — mound B
(after James 1986).

(uncal.) to the first millennium AD. A pattern of variation in date and function is, perhaps, beginning to emerge. Experiments in heating water and cooking, which reproduced local conditions, also accompanied the most important excavation at Carne.

EARLY FIELDWORK AND DISTRIBUTION

The majority of the burnt mounds of south-west Wales (the modern county of Dyfed) were recorded in the late nineteenth and early twentieth centuries by the geological surveyors T.C. Cantrill and O.T. Jones (1906; 1911). They worked in southern Dyfed only, which is reflected in the distribution of mounds in the county (Fig. 54): although other examples have since been discovered, the county has clearly suffered from a lack of systematic, expert fieldwork.

Cantrill's mounds were typical fulachta fiadh. They were frequently associated with streams and springs and boggy ground. They were low and varied from 6ft to 50ft across. They were generally irregular, horseshoe-shaped examples being rare. Stones of hard rock were preferred and mounds were most common on Old Red Sandstone or granite. Artifacts were very rare: only in two instances were flints definitely associated. Structural features were also rare: Cantrill noted one mound associated with a possible trough and two others with possible pits. Possible hearths were associated with two of the mounds. Another worker, A.L. Leach, recorded a kerb on a mound at Marros, Carmarthenshire (Leach 1911).

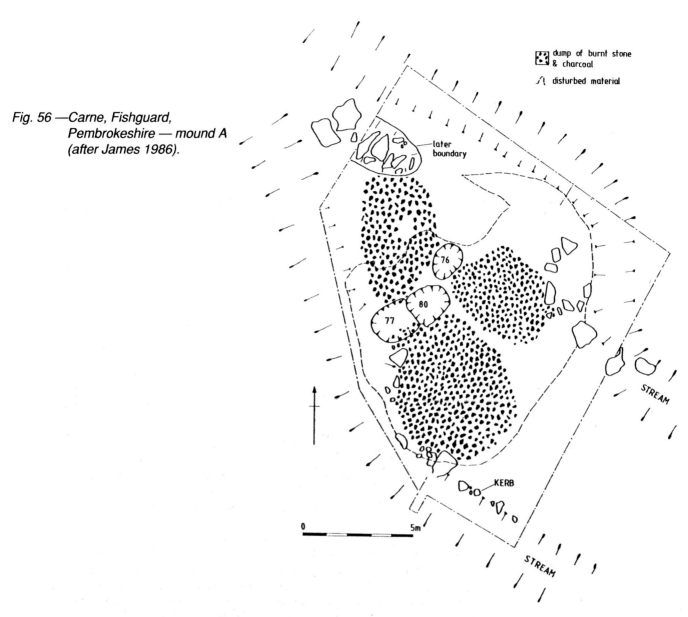

Fig. 56 —Carne, Fishguard,
       Pembrokeshire — mound A
       (after James 1986).

dump of burnt stone
& charcoal

disturbed material

later
boundary

STREAM

KERB

0   5m

STREAM

THE EXCAVATIONS
Dan-y-Coed, Llawhaden, Pembrokeshire (Williams 1983; 1988)

A burnt mound belonged to the immediately 'pre-rampart occupation' of a
late Iron Age defended enclosure. It was associated with a round-house,
later phases of which post-dated the rampart. The sequence provided
radiocarbon dates from the second century BC (uncal.) to the first century
AD (uncal.), the mound having a date of 130 ± 65 BC uncal. (CAR-705).

Carne, Fishguard, Pembrokeshire (James 1986)
This was the most important of the Trust's burnt mound excavations. The
site lay in a boggy area of boulder clay adjacent to a stream. Two mounds,
each approximately 10m across, were excavated, as well as a limited
surrounding area. A poorly-developed pre-mound soil had been eroded by
trampling in places.

The mounds consisted of locally-collected surface stones, harder rock
being preferred. They were associated with simple pits dug into the
underlying clay. At each mound there was a succession of such pits,
accompanied by a number of separate dumps of burnt stone, although the
mounds had been disturbed and the details of the sequences were not
always clear. At mound B (Fig. 55) there were two or three separate
dumps of stone: material from pits 76 and 77 may have contributed to an
early phase of the dumps; a later phase of dump seems to have derived
from a secondary pit, 80. The situation at mound A (Fig. 56) was less
certain: two pits, 49 and 57, were sealed by a primary mound while a third

131

pit, 52, was sealed by a secondary mound. Various permutations of relationship between these features at mound A can be suggested; however, it is clear that in the later phases the pits were completely sealed by burnt debris and could not have contributed to the mound.

A possible hearth and adjacent flimsy shelter were associated with mound B. No other traces of settlement were found in the (admittedly limited) areas excavated around the mound.

Periodic use of the sites may be suggested by the succession of features and by the fact that debris in some of the pits had been sealed by material slumped in from the side before the pit was re-cut: observation and experiment suggested that this probably resulted from a phase of disuse. The probable use of the pits for boiling can be emphasised: they clearly had had hot stone introduced into them and then cleared out; the sides were not scorched; they were water-retentive and, in wet weather, filled up naturally.

A number of experiments were carried out based on the results of the Carne excavations. One series suggested that, using local surface boulders, it was possible to boil water and produce debris of the type seen in the mounds. Other experiments proved that, with practice, it was possible to cook a leg of lamb in a pit full of water similar to those excavated, using similar hot stones. The experiments, although approximate, suggested that, given the conditions at Carne, relatively large quantities of debris could have been produced — on average 70kg/boiling. From this it could be estimated that mound B, for instance, could have resulted from between 20 and 60 uses of the pits.

There were no finds from the site. A radiocarbon date (Fig. 61) of 1840 ± 70 BC uncal. (CAR-292) came from the final fill of pit 52 in mound A. Radiocarbon dates from mound B were problematical. A date of 1820 ± 90 AD uncal. (CAR-497) was from disturbed and undoubtedly contaminated material. The others span a range from the twenty-first to the thirteenth centuries BC uncal. The early pits have dates of 2010 ± 65 BC uncal. (CAR-589) and 1760 ± 65 BC uncal. (CAR-591), but the stone dumps have produced dates of 1450 ± 70 BC uncal. (CAR-496) and 1255 ± 70 BC uncal. (CAR-498). While the later dates may relate to a late phase and vice versa it is perhaps difficult to envisage periodic usage over such a long time.

Felin Fulbrook, Tregaron, Cardiganshire (Williams *et al.* 1987)

This was a small burnt mound, approximately 3m across (Fig. 57), one of a number located on the edge of Tregaron bog. Much of the mound was excavated in advance of stream erosion. The mound was embedded in silt deposits and was obviously situated in an area which was flooded for part of the year. Only a limited area was excavated around the mound, without result, although no features were noted in the adjacent stream section. The mound overlay a number of irregular pits and hollows, although these could not have been used for direct cooking operations.

The mound produced a radiocarbon date of 1925 ± 70 BC uncal. (CAR-469) and a neighbouring mound produced a broken possible barbed and tanged arrowhead during drainage operations.

The silt deposit preserved a pollen sequence which could be related to the well-known sequence from Tregaron bog (Turner 1964) and gave some evidence of environmental change in the area of the mound. Before and after the use of the mound the pollen record showed a relatively dry environment, consistent with sub-Boreal conditions. The area was fairly heavily wooded, but there were indications of cereal cultivation. At a later stage the development of a peaty soil corresponded to an increase in the pollen of wet-loving species, presumably representing the onset of wetter, Sub-Atlantic conditions. There were also large-scale clearances for grassland in this phase, together with a decrease in cereal cultivation (and also a decrease in silt deposition which may also correlate with a decrease in arable cultivation upstream: Martin Bell, pers. comm.).

132

Fig. 57 —Felin Fulbrook, Tregaron,
Cardiganshire – features
below mound and section.

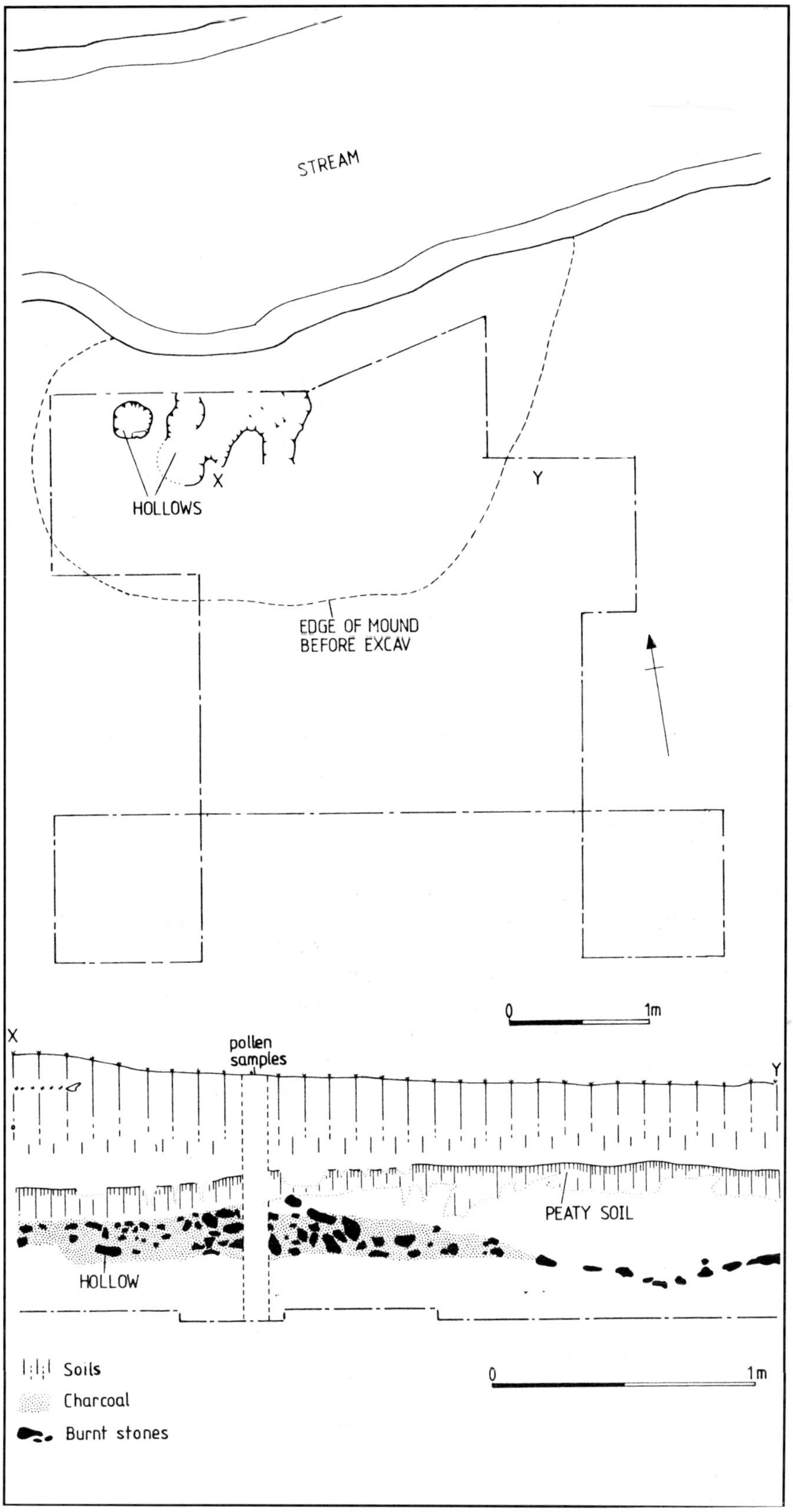

Llanilar, Ceredigion (Marshall and Taverner forthcoming)

A series of pits was excavated, dating from the Neolithic to the Early
Bronze Age, with evidence of 'structured deposition' culminating in
cremation deposits of the Early Bronze Age. Two somewhat different pits
contained burnt mound debris and one may have been associated with a
hearth, but no burnt mound survived on the heavily ploughed site and the

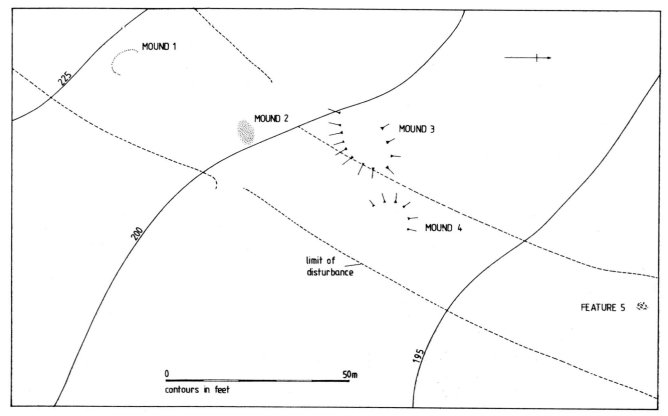

Fig. 58 —Morfa Mawr, Aberaeron, Cardiganshire.

dating of the pits was unknown.

Morfa Mawr, Aberaeron, Cardiganshire (Williams 1985b)

Salvage excavation was carried out, during road construction, on a group of burnt mounds lying in an area of extensive glacial deposition.

Three definite and two possible mounds were revealed (Fig. 58), but it was only possible to investigate two of them. Mound 2 was partially excavated. It was very small (7m x 4m across) but apparently contained two deposits of burnt stone. It gave a radiocarbon date of 770 ± 60 AD uncal. (CAR-458). A section only through a much larger mound, 3, was obtained. It clearly showed two deposits (perhaps suggesting discontinuous use as at Carne). The upper levels of the buried soil were not detected at either mound.

The machining of the whole length of the road in the area of the mounds was observed. Allowing for the limitations imposed by the watching brief, no other features were observed.

Stackpole Warren, Pembrokeshire (Benson 1977–9; *Current Archaeology* 82 (1982), 338; Williams 1985a)

This is a coastal dune site. Extensive excavations were carried out by the Trust in conjunction with University College Cardiff in advance of proposed cultivation.

The Warren was a focus of settlement from the Neolithic. It was engulfed in blown sand from the later Bronze Age. Permanent settlements associated with burnt mounds dated from this period and the Iron Age/Romano-British period.

Site G (Later Bronze Age).

A limited excavation was carried out on an enclosure, apparently overlain by a burnt mound. The site proved to be a settlement, surrounded by a substantial wall. The wall had collapsed after a short period of time. What was apparently a simple burnt mound on the surface was resolved into a complex series of occupation deposits overlying the ruined wall. These included charcoal and burnt stone but

134

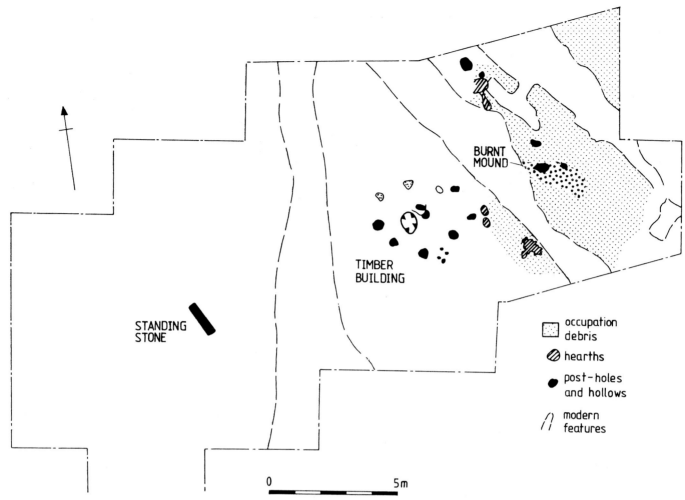

Fig. 59 —Stackpole Warren, Pembrokeshire — site A, burnt mound and timber building.

also fired clay, bone and shell and, surprisingly, coal. These were part of an apparently extended and fairly sophisticated settlement. The site produced quantities of pottery, including barrel- and bucket-shaped jars, with similarities to 'Middle Bronze Age' pottery from eastern Wales (Savory 1980, 32–3) and two radiocarbon dates of 820 ± 60 BC uncal. (CAR-845) and 760 ± 70 BC uncal. (CAR-843).

Sites A and B (later Iron Age/Romano-British). Phases of settlement were separated by incursions of blown sand. But although discontinuous, settlement was not temporary or sporadic: some phases boasted substantial buildings — at first of timber but later stone-built (it is not possible here to detail the full sequence of Iron Age/Romano-British occupation). The sequence lasted from the third century BC uncal. at site B into the second and third centuries AD at site A. Burnt mound debris and more discrete burnt mounds were found throughout the occupation sequence (radiocarbon dates of 285 ± 60 BC uncal. (CAR-103) and 105 ± 60 BC uncal. (CAR-102), from a relatively early phase of this occupation, were from bone from occupation deposits only indirectly associated with the burnt mounds).

A few general points can be made with regard to the mounds. They were of limestone with some sandstone. Partially-reduced pebble pot-boilers of both materials occurred on the sites and reflect locally available material. Limestone was often reduced to very small fragments, under 5cm across. In some instances the stones, while shattered, were not obviously burnt. Also, charcoal was not common in the better-defined mounds, although it occurred in association with more diffuse spreads of burnt stone and other occupation debris.

At site A, settlement overlay a complex surrounding the Bronze Age

135

standing stone. A small and not very well-defined burnt mound was associated with an early phase of settlement, but the main features of this type belonged to a late Iron Age/Early Roman phase. This phase (Fig. 59, also Plates 17 and 18) included a number of hearths; a spread of occupation debris including burnt stone, bone and charcoal; and a small,

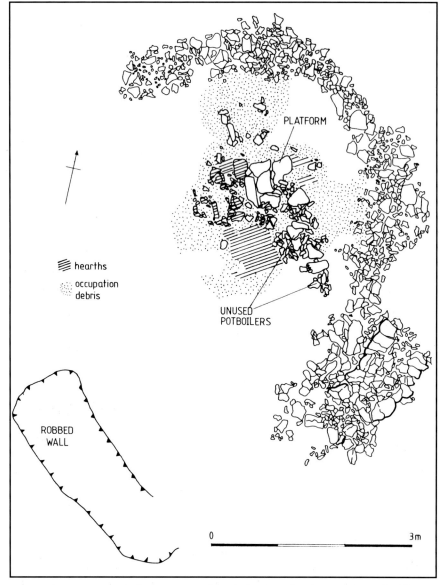

Fig. 60 —Stackpole Warren, Pembrokeshire — site A, stone building and hearth complex.

somewhat crescentic burnt mound 'pointing' at the largest hearth. These features were probably external to a timber building of uncertain plan.

The timber structure was rebuilt (Fig. 60) as a more substantial, sub-rectangular building with stone wall footings. A spread of burnt stone (not illustrated) lay just outside, actually dumped around the base of the standing stone (possibly, in part, as consolidation), although unfortunately it was not directly stratigraphically relatable to the stone building. Finds from the 'burnt mound' included food debris, Iron Age pottery and slag, although the last could have been due to contamination.

In the centre of the building a series of hearths surrounded a stone platform. There was a deposit of burnt stone on top of the platform (not illustrated) and a possible store of unused 'potboilers' by its side. There were indications that the structure had raised sides, but it could never have held water: neither was it burnt, so roasting does not seem an option. In this case, use as a sauna may be envisaged.

Site B was only partially excavated. The earliest Iron Age feature excavated was a burnt mound: again it was slightly crescentic and it also had a possible rough kerb. No cooking structure or hearth was recognised. Associated surfaces were strewn with bone and shell and a few post-holes may have been associated.

This phase was succeeded by a group of timber structures. A later phase included a fairly small and diffuse burnt mound with a central hearth, lying near a pit partly lined with clay. Shell and bone debris were scattered over the mound. Spindle-whorls and a possible quern were also associated.

Troedrhiwgwinau, Upper Vaenor, Cardiganshire (Castledine and Murphy forthcoming)

A limited excavation was carried out on a small burnt mound revealed in a pipe trench. A stream originally ran close to the site. The mound gave a radiocarbon date of 1320 ± 70 BC uncal. (Car-1046). Like Felin Fulbrook, the mound was embedded in alluvial deposits. Pollen analysis of deposits below the mound gave a similar picture to that at Felin Fulbrook — of a wooded environment with some clearance and probably some cereal cultivation. No features contemporary with the burnt mound deposits were noted in the pipe trench.

DISCUSSION

Although many of the Dyfed mounds are situated near streams or on boggy ground, this may possibly, to an extent, be an accident of survival: at Stackpole and Dan-y-Coed mounds were discovered during excavation in other locations, and many mounds may have been destroyed on better-quality, intensively-cultivated land.

Ideally, a larger area should have been opened up around many of the mounds — although we are beginning to understand what happened in the mounds themselves we have a much less clear idea of what went on around them. This emphasis on the obvious, above-ground monument, to the exclusion of its wider context, of course bedevils the study of many prehistoric sites, secular and ritual.

But although the evidence from south-west Wales is limited, it is tempting to suggest that two types of site may be represented, with different functions and date ranges. The mounds at Stackpole and Dan-y-Coed were associated with permanent settlements and dated from the Later Bronze Age and Late Iron Age/Early Roman period (Fig. 61). These sites may prove to be fairly typical of the undefended settlements of the period in the area (which are not well known). The mounds, if distinctive, are not the dominant features of the sites which include substantial buildings. Artifacts were also well represented.[1]

Other mounds — Felin Fulbrook, Morfa Mawr, Carne and Troedrhiwgwinau, all classic burnt mounds as described by Cantrill — may represent a different phenomenon. They may represent activity peripheral to the main settlement pattern, this being suggested by their occurrence on marginal land and by the lack of associated settlement evidence.[2] This difference is emphasised by the wide range of dates for these mounds, spanning the period from the late Neolithic to the early medieval period, the majority falling within the second millennium BC uncal. This activity may be temporary (in the case of very small mounds such as Felin Fulbrook) or recurrent, perhaps seasonal: recurrent use is strongly suggested by the evidence from Carne.

Other observations are relevant to these points. The experiments at Carne tend to confirm the evidence from other sites that relatively large mounds could result from comparatively few cooking episodes on presumably temporary settlements. Interestingly, many of the mounds associated with permanent settlement at Stackpole were very small. It is possible that burnt stone was periodically removed elsewhere. Accumulations of great quantities of burnt stone may, in some instances, have been less acceptable on a permanent settlement than on a temporary one.

Evidence as to use is only found on some of the south-west Welsh

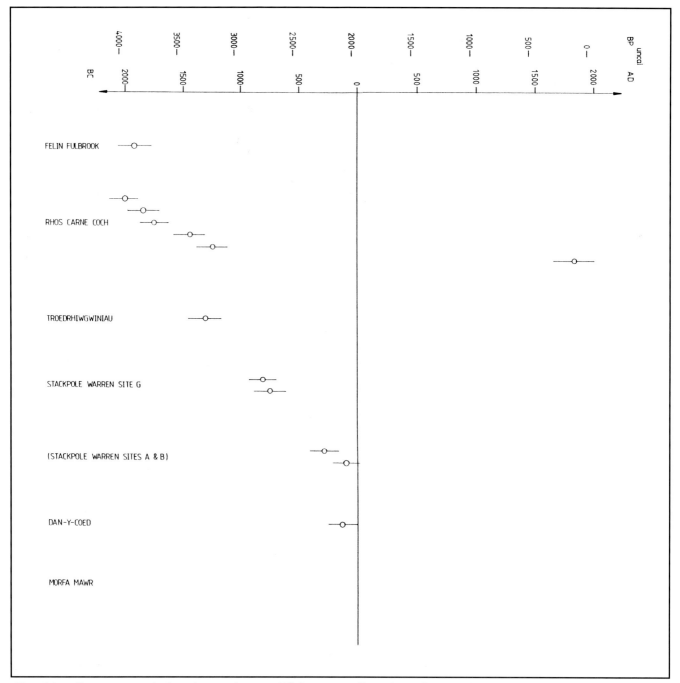

Fig. 61 —Burnt mound sites in south-west Wales — radiocarbon dates (all obtained from charcoal except Stackpole sites A and B which were obtained from animal bone).

sites. This, in general, suggests cooking. The evidence from Carne suggests that the pits had been used for boiling, and the same can be suggested for the clay-lined pit at Stackpole. Stackpole was unique in south-west Wales in having an alkaline environment, and shell and bone were recovered from in and around the majority of the mounds. It can be emphasised that uncalcined bone would not have survived the acid soil conditions on any of the other Dyfed sites. (It can also be mentioned that flotation for seed remains was carried out at Carne, Felin Fulbrook, Morfa Mawr and Troedrhiwgwinau, with negative results.)

The structure within the building near the standing stone at Stackpole is more of a problem. Interpretation as a sauna seems possible. This possibility is especially intriguing given the suggested ritual aspects of sauna bathing (Barfield and Hodder 1988, 374) and the proximity of the standing stone at Stackpole.

Attention can be drawn to a number of minor points. No troughs have

138

been recorded in Dyfed (apart from the doubtful example noted by Cantrill): the soils of Dyfed are generally not suitable for the preservation of wood. Turf and topsoil were missing below a number of mounds, an observation also made by Cantrill, but at Carne this was proven to be merely due to trample. A more puzzling feature, found at Carne (and perhaps Felin Fulbrook) as well as on some burnt mounds elsewhere, is the fact that pits were totally overlain by burnt debris and could not be seen as readily contributing to a final phase of the mounds.

ACKNOWLEDGEMENTS

This paper owes much to Heather James's publication of Carne. I am grateful to Mrs James and Mr K. Murphy for useful comments on the text. I am also grateful to the Trust for permission to use material on Dan-y-Coed, Llanilar (Clare Marshall and Nic Taverner), Stackpole Warren and Troedrhiwgwiniau (Ken Murphy) in advance of publication. The final drawings are by Peris Harries.

NOTES

1 Burnt mounds are also recorded from within the great hillfort on Carn Goch, Carmarthenshire (Cantrill and Jones 1906, 25; 1911, 261).
2 Although, admittedly, only limited areas have been excavated around the majority of these mounds, and associated structures may have been missed, a dearth of artifacts is very marked.

REFERENCES

BARFIELD, L. and HODDER, M. 1988 Burnt mounds as saunas, and the prehistory of bathing. *Antiquity* **61**, 370–9.

BENSON, D.G. 1977–9 *Archaeology in Wales* **17**, 27–8; **18**, 44; **19**, 24.

CANTRILL, T.C. and JONES, O.T. 1906 The discovery of prehistoric hearths in South Wales. *Archaeol. Cambrensis*, 6th ser., **6**, 17–34.

CANTRILL, T.C. and JONES, O.T. 1911 Prehistoric cooking-places in South Wales. *Archaeol. Cambrensis*, 6th ser., **11**, 253–86.

CASTLEDINE, A. and MURPHY, K. (forthcoming) A Bronze Age burnt mound at Troedrhiwgwiniau, near Abersytwyth, Dyfed.

JAMES, H.J. 1986 Excavations of burnt mounds at Carne, nr. Fishguard, 1979 and 1981. *Bull. Board Celtic Stud.* **33**, 245–65.

LEACH, A.L. 1911 Prehistoric cooking-places on the Pembrokeshire and Carmarthenshire coasts. *Archaeol. Cambrensis,* 6th ser., **11**, 433–6.

MARSHALL, C. and TAVERNER, N. (forthcoming) Further excavation of a Neolithic and Bronze Age complex at Llanilar, Cardiganshire.

SAVORY, H.N. 1980 *Guide catalogue of the Bronze Age collections.* National Museum of Wales, Cardiff.

TURNER, J. 1964 The anthropogenic factor in vegetational history 1. Tregaron and Whixall Mosses. *New Phytol.* **63**, 73–90.

WILLIAMS, G.H. 1983 *Archaeology in Wales* **23**, 26–30.

WILLIAMS, G.H. 1985a *Archaeology in Wales* **25**, 25.

WILLIAMS, G.H. 1985b A group of burnt mounds at Morfa Mawr, Aberaeron. *Ceredigion* **10**, no. 2, 181–8.

WILLIAMS, G.H. 1988 Recent work on rural settlement in later prehistoric and early historic Dyfed. *Antiq. J.* **68**, 30–54.

WILLIAMS, G.H., TAYLOR, J.A., HUNT, C., HEYWORTH, A. and BENSON, D.G. 1987 A burnt mound at Felin Fulbrook, Tregaron, Ceredigion. *Bull. Board Celtic Stud.* **34**, 228–43.

PART 5

INTERNATIONAL CONTRIBUTIONS

13. SWEDISH MOUNDS

Skärvstenshögar — the burnt mounds of Sweden

Thomas B. Larsson

INTRODUCTION

The present paper highlights a particular type of prehistoric feature that seems to be highly correlated with Bronze Age activities in northern and north-western Europe, namely the *burnt mounds, fulachta fiadh* or *Skärvstenshögar*, using the English, Irish and Swedish nomenclature.

The heating of stones, later to be used for cooking or roasting purposes, is a well-known anthropological phenomenon from many parts of the Old World (Lerche 1969) and the accumulation of fire-cracked stones at certain Indian sites in the New World was a thing that also puzzled Binford in the early phase of his career (1972,128):

> In fact, the hall outside Griffin's office was filled with fire-cracked rock; the newly opened lab was filled with fire-cracked rock. When Griffin saw all this rock the expression on his face (and lips) was one of total disbelief: 'What in God's name are you going to do with all that fire-cracked rock?' I answered knowingly, 'Why, count and weigh it, of course.' What I could possibly do with such data, I didn't know, but it was part of the archaeological record, and there must be something you could learn.

I believe that Binford's last words still hold true, particularly for Bronze Age archaeology in Ireland, Britain and Sweden. Even if the chronology of burnt mounds is rather well documented, a number of problems and questions still remain to be addressed and solved; there are indeed a lot of new things we can and ought to learn about this phenomenon.

One of the main reasons for writing this paper, to be published in an Irish archaeological publication, is the lack of knowledge about the Swedish burnt mounds among archaeologists in Britain and Ireland. I will therefore try to give an outline of what is known about *skärvstenshögar* in Sweden — a short review of the current state of affairs.

The word *skärvstenshög* can roughly be translated as 'a mound or heap consisting of fire-cracked stones' (Anderson 1984; Larsson 1986, 150ff). To avoid this long sentence, I will instead use the Swedish word *skärvstenshög*.

THE *SKÄRVSTENSHÖGAR* OF SWEDEN

The main distribution of *skärvstenshögar* in Scandinavia is clustered in the eastern parts of central Sweden (Fig. 62), in particular the provinces of Västmanland, Uppland, Södermanland and Östergötland. These provinces are marked by V, U, S and Ö on the map in Fig. 62. The total number of registered monuments of this type in these provinces is hard to specify without a closer examination of the Ancient Monuments Register (the Central Board of National Antiquities, Stockholm), but an estimate is 6000.

Adopting a geological perspective, it is interesting to see how the main distribution of *skärvstenshögar* coincides with the southern part of a belt of migmatised quartz–diorite (mainly gneiss and gneiss–granite) following the Swedish east coast (Fig. 63). The pure granites covering a large part of southern Sweden are perhaps more resistant to heating when used as cooking or roasting stones, a hypothesis that would explain why the numbert of *skärvstenshögar* is less in the southern parts of Sweden. The

142

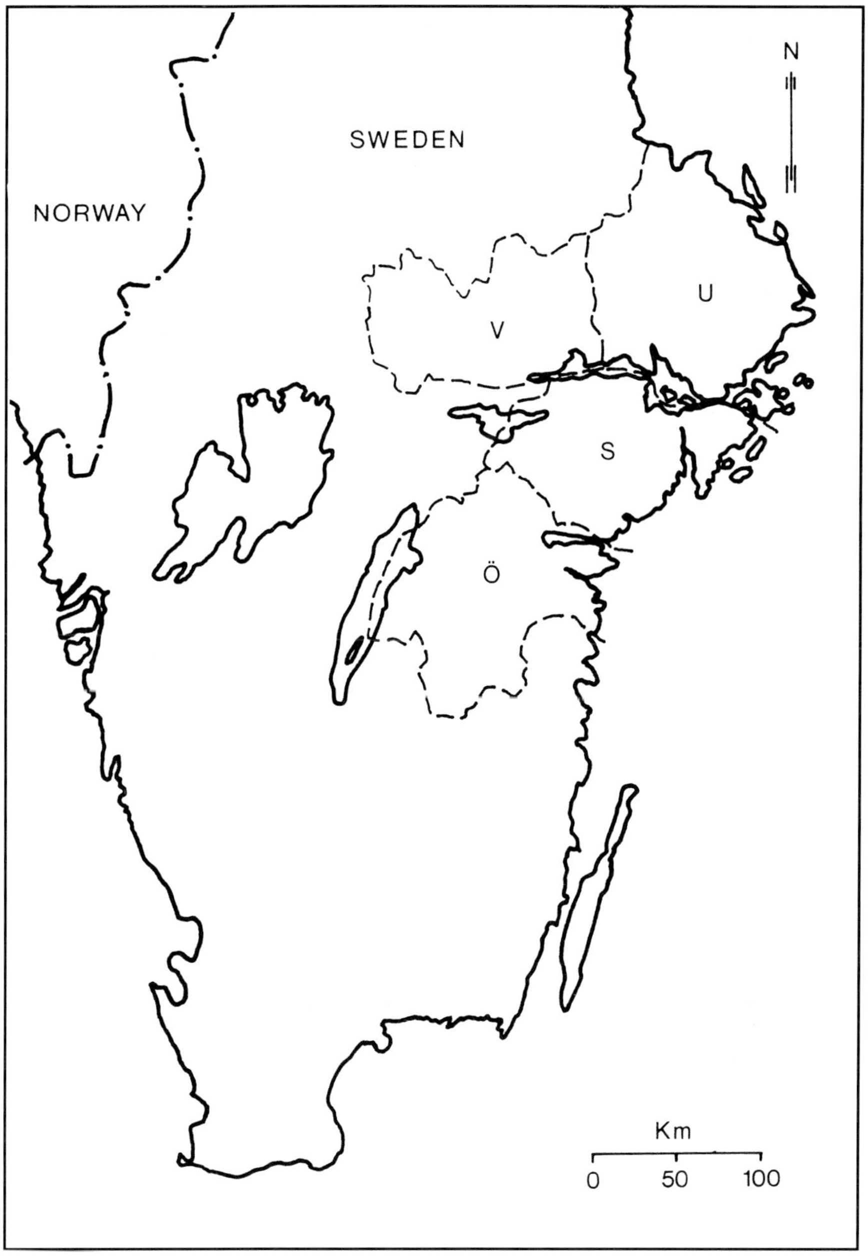

Fig. 62— Map of southern Sweden with the provinces of Västmanland (V), Uppland (U), Södermanland (S) and Östergötland (Ö) marked.

need for building mounds — collecting the fire-cracked stones and placing them at a particular spot in the village, finally resulting in a *skärvstenshög* — must be taken to be in proportion to the produced quantities of stones.

In this part of Sweden these heaps, consisting of a mixture of charcoal, sooty soil and burnt, fire-cracked stones, were noticed as early as the beginning of this century by Swedish archaeologists such as Arthur Nordén (1925) and Erik Bellander (1938). Nordén argued for an intimate relationship between the formation of *skärvstenshögar* and the making and ritual use of Bronze Age rock art. This assumption derives from the fact that he himself had noted some *skärvstenshögar* in the vicinity of one of the major rock-carving centres in the province of Östergötland, one of which he also excavated during the summer of 1921 (Nordén 1925, 64). The only find that came out of this 1921 excavation, which indeed strengthened the chronological links between *skärvstenshögar* and rock carvings, was a double stud of Late Bronze Age period IV/V type (Baudou 1960, 89, 294; Larsson 1986, 58–9). Nordén believed that the charcoal and fire-cracked stones, deposited next to the rock surfaces where the artists of the Late Bronze Age depicted their mysterious symbols, were the remains of great fires, lit for magical purposes in close intimacy with the ritual activities for which the rock carvings served as central places (Nordén 1925, 138).

143

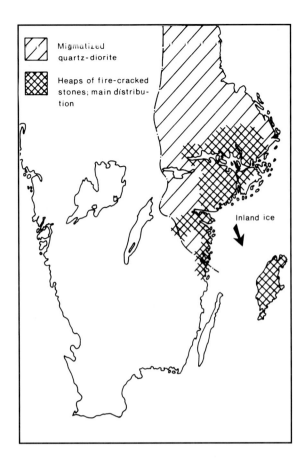

Inland ice

Fig. 63 —The distribution of migmatised
quartz–diorite and burnt
mounds in Sweden.

However, in the light of the recent survey of ancient monuments carried out by the Central Board of National Antiquities, it is perfectly clear that the spatial relationship between *skärvstenshögar* and rock art of Bronze Age type is not as direct and simple as one would have been tempted to believe in the 1920s. The survey has shown that *skärvstenshögar* have a much wider spatial distribution than rock art, and that the centres for rock art often tend to be located in rather limited and peripheral parts of the main agglomerations of *skärvstenshögar* in eastern central Sweden (Larsson 1986, 150). If the bulk of *skärvstenshögar* can be regarded as contemporary with the making and active use of rock art, which indeed is a likely hypothesis, the spatial relationship between the two features may also encompass information about a socio-religious system, in which particular areas and places had different status — a differentiation between the daily used and settled area and the sacred places. The societal aspects of the spatial configurations will not be pushed any further here, though it is an important issue for Bronze Age research in central Sweden (see Larsson 1986, 139–58, for a more elaborate discussion).

The general assumption that *skärvstenshögar* represent settlement sites of the Bronze Age can be accepted in the light of numerous excavations, particularly in the provinces of Västmanland, Uppland, Södermanland and, recently, also Östergötland.

The mounds regularly contain fragments of pottery, burnt clay (often with impressions of wooden branches and twigs), burnt animal bones, simple hammerstones, pieces of grinding stones, and in some cases also casting moulds and crucibles (Hyenstrand 1968; Larsson 1986, 153; Oldeberg 1960). All together, the archaeological indications point towards settlement activities, and that *skärvstenshögar* could be regarded as refuse dumps that were located some 10–30m away from the houses.

Where are these houses, and what did they look like? There are still too few excavations of both *skärvstenshögar* and the immediate area around them to enable us to make any general statements. Excavations have produced hearths, post-holes and great amounts of burnt clay, indicating houses with wattle-and-daub walls (Kjellén and Hyenstrand

144

1977), but sites where whole houses have been reconstructed are unfortunately very rare.

Another example of an excavated settlement site comes from the parish of Turinge in the province of Södermanland. Before excavation, the presence of nine *skärvstenshögar* were the main indicators of settlement. Out of a total of more than 400 post-holes and numerous cooking pits and hearths the excavator was able to distinguish ten different houses (Tesch 1983, 40–4), of which three could possibly be of Bronze Age date. The other houses were, according to ¹⁴C datings from charcoal in hearths (Tesch 1983, 41), of later date, *c.* AD 1–500. The most significant house from this site was a rectangular longhouse, 19m x 7.5m, aligned NW–SE. The house was of three-aisled type, with five pairs of inner posts supporting the roof, and with an entrance placed on the eastern long side. Only 4m from the western long side a *skärvstenshög* was deposited, and another one was situated just 1m from the NE corner of the house.

A longhouse of rather similar construction and proportions was found at the rich Bronze Age site at Hallunda in Södermanland (Jaanusson 1981). Hallunda is known for enormous amounts of Bronze Age pottery and also for Late Bronze Age metalworking activities. Together with these remains, huge banks of fire-cracked stones, which covered a large part of the site, were also found and excavated (Jaanusson 1981, 15f.). At all three sites the relationship between fire-cracked stones (deposited in the form of either banks or mounds) and rectangular houses is very distinct.

There is another site, in the province of Östergötland, where we also find a 'complete' settlement area with *skärvstenshögar* and a house. This was excavated in 1980–1 by the Central Board of National Antiquities and a total area of 16,000m² was uncovered. The site is named Tallboda, in the parish of Rystad. The house was indicated by eight very distinct stone-lined post-holes in two parallel rows, giving a three-aisled structure of 9m x 4m. Two hearths were also found inside the western part of the house. Large amounts of pieces of burnt clay with twig impressions were also found, indicating a wattle-and-daub wall. Carbonised material from the post-holes have been radiocarbon-dated to the Late Bronze Age. Unfortunately, the complete report of this excavation has not been published yet, so a more precise dating is not available to the author at present.

DATING

Figure 64 shows the ¹⁴C datings of *skärvstenshögar* from central Sweden that are available at present; with some exceptions the chronological sequence that can be established indicates that these are mainly a Bronze Age feature. For the Lake Mälaren Valley it must also be noted that the great majority of the dates are of the Early Bronze Age. Nearly 60% of the samples are dated earlier than 1000 BC, using calibrated figures. The sequence for the province of Östergötland, with samples from my own excavations (Larsson 1986, 152f.), clearly belongs to a period before 1000 BC, mainly 1100–600 BC. These samples were analysed by the accelerator technique at the Tandem Accelerator Laboratory in Uppsala by Dr Göran Possnert (Possnert and Olsson 1986), while the samples from the Lake Mälaren Valley are dated by conventional ¹⁴C method. Whether this difference in the dating techniques used is of any significance for the obvious difference in date of *skärvstenshögar* from the Lake Mälaren Valley and Östergötland (Jensen 1986) is difficult to say at the moment. However, the difference in dating seems rather clear.

Analyses of stones from *skärvstenshögar* in the province of Södermanland using the TL technique (thermoluminescence dating) have given a mean of 1020 ± 75–180 BC, based on nine samples (Wigren 1987, 102). A mean dating of 1020 BC could, however, indicate that the *skärvstenshögar* from which the nine samples were taken were deposited during both the early and the late phases of the Bronze Age.

As can be seen from this short presentation of the dates from

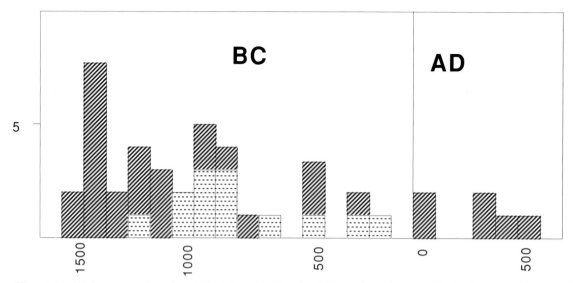

Fig. 64—Histogram showing ¹⁴C dates (calibrated) from burnt mounds in the provinces of Uppland (diagonal shading) and Östergötland (dotted shading).

skärvstenshögar, they should be regarded as Bronze Age remains, naturally with some exceptions, even if it is far from clear today whether there are chronological differences between various regions of eastern central Sweden. According to the ¹⁴C datings presented in Fig. 64 the *skärvstenshögar* of the Mälaren basin might represent a longer chronological sequence with a peak in the Early Bronze Age, while those monuments in Östergötland are the remains of human settlement activities mainly during the Late Bronze Age.

An adaptive settlement strategy has recently been suggested for the Bronze Age in the Lake Mälaren basin by Jensen (1986), in which the changing physical environment, owing to the isostatic land-uplift processes, is thought to be an important factor when studying the settlement pattern from a diachronic perspective. The distribution of *skärvstenshögar* in one of the rather dense areas of the Lake Mälaren Valley (Broby, north-west of Uppsala) serves as an example of the adaptive model put forward by Jensen. The more or less continuous growth of available land for settlement and economic use that was 'created' by the isostatic processes did most certainly affect the settlement pattern and the socio-economic territories in this part of Sweden during the Bronze Age.

Expansion and colonisation of land that had risen from the sea might have been an important socio-environmental factor for prehistoric development particularly in parts of Sweden where a few metres of vertical land-uplift during some 500 years resulted in thousands of acres of 'new' land. Following this model, the earliest *skärvstenshögar*, deposited around 1500 BC, should be located at higher levels in the terrain than the younger ones; a high positive correlation between increasing age and increasing altitude above the present sea level is to be expected if the settlement expansion has followed closely in the footsteps of the shore displacement.

Whether or not the chronological sequence of ¹⁴C dates presented by Jensen is highly correlated with a gradual change in altitude of the dated *skärvstenshögar* is not made explicit in his paper; however, it is most likely.

MORPHOLOGY

During the summer of 1983 the author carried out a series of sample excavations of 20 *skärvstenshögar* in the province of Östergötland. The objective of this sample test, in which *c.* 1m³ of each *skärvstenshög* was dug out and collected, was twofold: (1) to find carbonised organic material for ¹⁴C datings and (2) to use the collected carbonised material for macrofossil analysis. The latter task is still in progress, and so far only a small report has been published about the organic content in one of the partly excavated *skärvstenshögar* (Ekroth 1986).

The sample excavations and the sections drawn when digging the 1m² trenches brought a new question into focus: why are some *skärvstenshögar* very homogeneous, with a compact mixture of charcoal, fire-cracked stones and organic soil, from bottom to top, while others only consist (more or less) of fire-cracked stones and light, sandy soil, without the black charcoal filling? After putting together information from the 20 *skärvstenshögar*, and looking at the section drawings, it was quite clear that the partly excavated 'heaps' could be classified into three general types (Fig. 65):

(i) *type A*, which has a very homogeneous mixture of fire-cracked stones, pieces of charcoal and black, sooty soil from bottom to top;

(ii) *type B*, which comprises *skärvstenshögar* with a *c.* 30–50cm-thick top layer of fire-cracked stones mixed with rather sterile material of a sand/gravel fraction, covering a 'core' of the same consistency as type A;

(iii) *type C*, representing 'heaps' that consist of fire-cracked stones and sand/gravel, with only small lenses of darker, charcoal-mixed material.

Irrespective of whether the *skärvstenshögar* were of type A, B or C, the quantitative relationship between the amount of stones and soil in 1m³ was very similar. Out of 1000 litres approximately 500 litres were fire-cracked stones and the other 500 litres were black charcoal-mixed soil or sand/gravel.

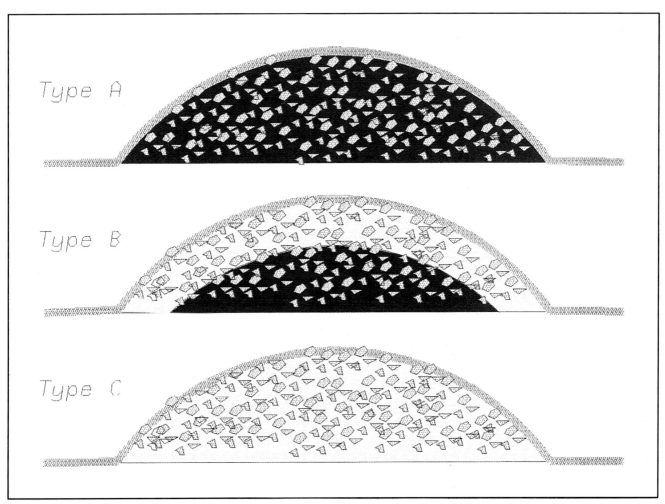

Fig. 65 —Schematic section drawings showing three types of burnt mound stratigraphy found in southern Sweden. Black — charcoal mixture; shaded — sand/gravel; surface shade — grass/turf.

147

This noted difference in stratigraphy relates either to formation processes or to post-depositional factors. The first alternative could encompass functional differences; the three types represent the accumulated remains of different activities (e.g. cooking, heating of houses, metalworking etc.). This differentiated use of heating stones, visible in the stratigraphy of the *skärvstenshögar,* could then relate to sites with a slightly different function in the Bronze Age socio-economic system. Type A, with a lot of charcoal and carbonised organic material, might indicate the 'normal' refuse dump from a 'normal' dwelling site. The removal from cooking pits and hearths of heating stones, ash and charcoal, that must have been regularly undertaken at a Bronze Age settlement, resulted in the formation of *skärvstenshögar* of type A.

On sites where 'heaps' of type C were deposited it is obvious that almost no charcoal or other carbonised materials were dumped together with the cracked heating stones. The stones were separated from the charcoal that must have been produced when heating the stones. The activities on sites where the C types are deposited must have differed from those where the A types were formed.

The question is whether the separation of fire-cracked stones from charcoal and other organic remains, where only the stones are thrown together on a 'heap', indicate sites with other activities than those that took place at sites where all the products from the heating/cooking process were dumped together. Because this question has come up very recently, after my own sample excavations, there is no certain answer for the moment.

The existence of an 'intermediate' type (type B), with a core of A type and a covering 'mantle' of B type, makes it quite possible that the three types represent a chronological sequence: A–B–C. The B phase could then indicate a period of the Bronze Age during which the custom of depositing ash, charcoal and heating stones changed from mixed to separated deposition. The accelerator datings from the province of Östergötland tend to support this hypothesis, even if eleven samples are perhaps too few to form a good statistical basis. The mean dating of type A is 980 BC, type B 950 BC, and type C 400 BC (Larsson 1986, 153). For future research on Bronze Age settlement and society in eastern central Sweden the questions concerning the three types of *skärvstenshögar* must be given a high priority.

Turning to other morphological aspects, the Swedish *skärvstenshögar* can be subdivided into a number of different types (Löthman 1986, 11), but a classification into four broad categories is enough to cover the bulk of them. In Fig. 66 I have schematically illustrated the four types in section and plan. A type that is known in certain parts of Uppland (but mostly relates to Late Stone Age sites in north Sweden; Spång 1986) is the wall-formed type (66a). The shape of the low wall of fire-cracked stones can be round or oval, ranging in size from 3m to 10m in diameter. While some of these forms can be the result of later destruction by digging, some might also be classified as hut circles. This type resembles the burnt mounds and fulachta fiadh of northern Britain and Ireland as regards morphological traits, even if the Swedish ones tend to be smaller in size. The distinct horseshoe shape of many west European mounds is not very common among the central Swedish *skärvstenshögar*. In northern Sweden, however, this form is not uncommon for Stone Age hut circles (Löthman 1986; Spång 1986).

The forms most typical of the Bronze Age settlement sites in central Sweden are the round and oval *skärvstenshögar*, usually 3–15m in diameter and 0.3–2.5m high. One extreme is 80m x 10m and 1m high, giving a total volume of *c.* 715,430m^3 (Anderson 1984, 66). A more 'normal' and representative round *skärvstenshög* of 10m in diameter and 0.7m in height contains a volume of *c.* 25,000m^3 of fire-cracked stones and soil (*op. cit.*).

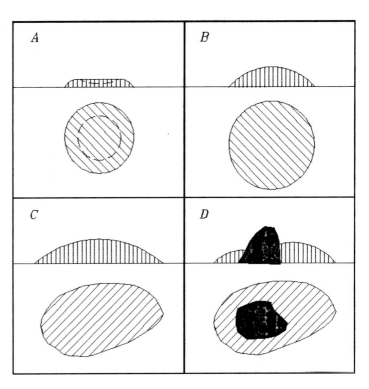

Fig. 66 —The most common types of burnt mounds in southern Sweden. A – wall-formed or horseshoe-shaped; B – round; C– elongated; D – mound around a boulder.

This kind of size–volume calculation has shown that the amount of deposited heating stones varies a great deal from site to site, reflecting differences in population density and/or differences in the time during which the settlements have been used (Anderson 1984; 1986). When trying to discuss the settlement structure and the Bronze Age socio-economic pattern in central Sweden in greater detail, the differences between sites with 700,000m³ of settlement debris and those with only 20,000m³ must of course be highlighted and included in the discussion.

A fourth type of *skärvstenshög* that is rather common, particularly in Uppland, is the one which is built around a boulder (Fig. 66d). The form is often irregular. A major difference between type A and types B–D is the fact that A might be the remains of the hut/house (comparable with the reconstruction of Ballyvourney I made by O'Kelly (1954, pl. IX)), while the other types only indicate the presence of settlement and houses in the immediate surroundings.

SOCIO-ECONOMIC PATTERNS AND CHANGE

The most significant relationship in Late Bronze Age central Sweden is to be found between the settlement clusters and damp clay basins (Bertilsson and Larsson 1985; Larsson 1986, 155f.). This is very noticeable in the province of East Götaland. The economic potential of these wetlands must have been related to an economy based on extensive cattle-rearing — a pastoral mode of production. This general hypothesis fits well with the observations made when excavating burnt mounds. They contain rather large amounts of animal bones, mainly cattle and sheep (Hyenstrand 1968; Kjellén and Hyenstrand 1977).

The great importance of the natural wetlands, fertilised by the nutritious spring floods, as the earliest type of pasture and meadow in Sweden has for long been advocated by human geographers (e.g. Aronsson 1979). Access to highly-productive natural grass vegetation and water — prerequisites for a pastoral mode of production — was most readily available in the specific areas where we find the clusters of burnt mounds. This is surely no coincidence.

The pattern evident from Fig. 67 is therefore dependent on both the physical landscape (the best ecological zones for extensive grazing) and social organisation (giving each group enough land for living and moving the herds). In some cases the rather large zones without settlements

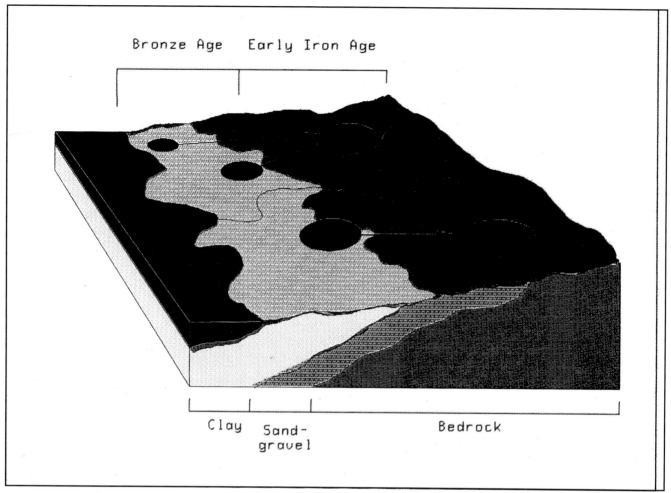

Fig. 67 —Block diagram illustrating the shift in settlement location (arrows) occurring between the Late Bronze Age and the Early Iron Age, in relation to topography and geology.

between the clusters shown in Fig. 67 are as suitable for grazing as the areas within the clusters, which might be an indication of the strong need for quite large buffer zones between the different communities — something rather typical of pastoralists (cf. Orme 1981, 109; Sherratt 1981, 298).

Because of the total lack of evidence for regulated land use, like enclosures or boundary walls, the Late Bronze Age production system must have been very open and extensive. Cattle and sheep might have been allowed to move around in large herds.

In contrast to the Late Bronze Age, the Early Iron Age economy was based more on division of land and, consequently, a more differentiated land use. The growing importance of arable farming is one cause of this development, requiring fences to keep the animals away from the crops. Also, the climatic deterioration that occurs in Scandinavia around 500 BC (Berglund 1983; Jensen 1982, 136) brings two new elements into the picture: the need for meadows and winter fodder, and the need to stall the cattle during the cold months of the year. The archaeological evidence of stalling in Scandinavia dates from the middle of the first millennium AD (Myrdal 1984), showing a good correlation with the change to wetter and cooler conditions.

The last observation that must be added when discussing the difference between Late Bronze Age and Early Iron Age socio-economic structures is directly linked to the change in land use and the increased importance of arable farming. When mapping burnt mounds and boundary walls, it is noticeable that the two types seldom appear in the same physiographic setting. Generally, the Bronze Age settlements are situated at lower levels than the settlements from the Early Iron Age. There is a

Plate 19— A burnt mound (skärvstenshög in Swedish) from the province of Östergötland during excavation (photo: the Central Board of National Antiquities).

shift in location between the two periods — a movement from the damp clay zone to the drier upland moraines (Fig. 67).

An economy largely based upon cereal production (and farming) requires rather well-drained soils, while the primary requirement for the pastoral economy is land with a high rate of grass production, in this case the clay basins near lakes and shallow bays. The change in settlement location is therefore a result of economic changes relating to food production.

REFERENCES

ANDERSON, PH. 1984 Frequency diagrams and size–volume calculations. In Å. Hyenstrand (ed.), *Bronsåldersforskning — kring aktuella projekt*, 61–75. Stockholm Archaeological Reports 17.

ANDERSON, PH. 1986 Frequency diagrams and size–volume calculations — one way of approaching the study of the ancient monuments category heaps of fire-cracked stones. In T.B. Larsson (ed.), *Skärvstenshög och skärvstensvall*, 46–9. Rapport 8, Södermanlands Museum.

ARONSSON, M. 1979 Slåtter — och betesmark i det äldre odlingslandskapet. Odlingslandskap och livsform. *Bygd och Natur*, 72–96.

BAUDOU, E. 1960 *Die regionale und chronologische Einteilung der jüngeren Bronzezeit im Nordischen Kreis.* Stockholm.

BELLANDER, E. 1938 Bålrösen — offerrösen. *Kulturhistoriska studier tillägnade Nils Åberg*. Stockholm.

BERGLUND, B. 1983 *Paleoclimatic changes in Scandinavia and on Greenland — a tentative correlation based on lake and bog stratigraphic studies*. Quaternal Studies in Poland 4.

BERTILSSON, U. and LARSSON, T.B. 1985 Economy and ideology in the Swedish Bronze Age. *Cambridge Archaeol. Rev.* **4** (2), 215–26.

BINFORD, L.R. 1972 *An archaeological perspective*. New York.

EKROTH, H. 1986 Förkolnat botaniskt material från en skärvstenshög i Östergötland. In T.B. Larsson (ed.), *Skärvstenshög och skärvstensvall*, 24–9. Rapport 8, Södermanlands Museum.

HYENSTRAND, Å. 1968 Skärvstenshögar och bronsåldersmiljöer. *TOR* **XII**, 61–80.

JAANUSSON, H. 1981 *Hallunda. A study of pottery from a Late Bronze Age settlement in central Sweden*. Stockholm.

JENSEN, J. 1982 *The prehistory of Denmark*. London.

JENSEN, R. 1986 Skärvstenshögar och bosätningsmönster i Mälardalen under bronsåldern. In K.-G. Selinge (ed.), *Fornlämningar och bebyggelsehistoria*, 17–34. Bebyggelsehistorisk tidskrift 11. Stockholm. (Engl. summary)

KJELLÉN, E. and HYENSTRAND, Å. 1977 *Hällristningar och bronsålderssamhälle i sydvästra Uppland*. Upplands fornminnesförenings tidskrift 49. Uppsala.

LARSSON, T. B. 1986 *The Bronze Age metalwork in southern Sweden. Aspects of social and spatial organization 1800–500 BC*. Archaeology and Environment 6. University of Umeå.

LERCHE, G. 1969 Kogegruber i New Guineas Højland. *Kuml*, 195–209.

LÖTHMAN, L. 1986 Från Stalon till Fole —skärvstensanläggningarnas utbredning, morfologi och ekologi i tre regioner. In T.B. Larsson (ed.), *Skärvstenshög och skärvstensvall*, 10–15. Rapport 8, Södermanlands Museum.

MYRDAL, J. 1984 Elisenhof och järnålderns boskapsskötsel i Nordvästeuropa. *Fornvännen* **79**, 73–92.

NORDÉN, A. 1925 *Östergötlands bronsålder*. Linköping.

O'KELLY, M. 1954 Excavations and experiments in ancient Irish cooking-places. *J. R. Soc. Antiq. Ir.* **84**, 105–55.

OLDEBERG, A. 1960 *Skälbyfyndet. En boplatslämning från den yngre bronsåldern*. Antikvariskt arkiv 15. Stockholm.

ORME, B. 1981 *Anthropology for archaeologists*. London.

POSSNERT, G. and OLSSON, I.U. 1986 The radiocarbon dating of samples from heaps of fire-cracked stones found in the county of Östergötland. In T.B. Larsson (ed.), *The Bronze Age metalwork in southern Sweden. Aspects of social and spatial organization 1800–500 B.C.*, appendix 1, pp 198–200. Archaeology and Environment 6. University of Umeå.

SHERRATT, A. 1981 Plough and pastoralism: aspects of the secondary products revolution. In I. Hodder *et al.* (eds), *Patterns of the past*, 261–305. Cambridge.

SPÅNG, L. G. 1986 Vad säger skärvstensvallar om stenåldersbostäder. In T.B. Larsson (ed.), *Skärvstenshög och skärvstensvall*, 65–72. Rapport 8, Södermanlands Museum.

TESCH, S. 1983 Ett par bronsåldersmiljöer med huslämningar i Skåne och Södermanland. *Arkeologi i Sverige 1980.* Riksantikvarieämbetet. Stockholm.

WIGREN, S. 1987 *Sörmländsk bronsåldersbygd.* Theses and Papers in North-European Archaeology 16. Stockholm. (Engl. summary)

14. ANTHROPOLOGY

An anthropologist's tale

Declan Hurl

In examining the subject of fulachta fiadh/burnt mounds/*skärvstenshögar* most archaeologists have some particular area of interest — geology, dendrochronology, or perhaps a regional approach. My own view is tainted with the smoke of anthropological campfires.

How is anthropology relevant to archaeology in general and the study of fulachta fiadh in particular? If you ask this of anthropologists, they will assert that their chosen discipline has relevance in every field of human experience, from marriage ceremonies to practices in the heavy engineering industry — if not a cure-all for society's ills, then a diagnostic tool of daunting potential. Whilst practitioners may be forgiven for an element of overstatement, in practice anthropology is, if not always a problem-solver, an instrument with which to approach and tease and, indeed, threaten those problems.

Anthropologists study diverse societies and cultures, and are thus *au fait* with the 'hardware' and 'software' of different peoples, giving them opportunities to examine problems from an extra-cultural vantage point, as well as providing rich sources of information on a range of technologies.

Archaeology, like all disciplines, has problematic areas. Items can be disguised under the title 'ritual object' or couched in a language in which people may be embarrassed to admit a lack of fluency. For example, an elbow-shaped object was often portrayed being held in an upraised manner in the tomb paintings of Egypt. Some ritual lauding of the gods and/or their physical aspect represented by the pharaoh utilising the artifact was obviously in progress. That is, until it was pointed out that the farmers of the area were adopting a similar pose with an identical item — mattocking in nearby fields!

The physical remains under scrutiny in this case are pits surrounded by mounds of stones which have been exposed to intense heat, usually in close proximity to a water source such as a stream, river or lake. What were they? How were they used? Because we do not use similar artifacts, it is left to our imaginations and enigmatic literary sources to unravel the mysteries of such sites. However, could we not ask one more question: are there any peoples who do use such artifacts and leave similar traces?

The anthropologist, in this case, would look to that Happy Hunting Ground of ethnographers, Papua–New Guinea. The people are, or were until recently, both horticulturalists and hunter-gatherers. They grow bananas, yams, taros and green vegetables, and keep pigs and chickens. They also collect wild fruit and vegetables and hunt feral pig, cassowary, various marsupials and rats. They live in light timber-framed houses thatched with leaves, and use polished stone axes and digging sticks, with bamboo tubes and gourds as containers.

It is these peoples we find utilising earth ovens of similar construction to the fulachta fiadh. On certain occasions, such as marriages and semi-ritualised combats, they dig large cooking pits, up to 130m2 and 0.3m deep, though smaller versions, c. 1m^2, are used on a daily basis. They build two fires, one in the pit, which they sometimes line with wood, and one beside the pit, both of which are used to heat stones. A layer of banana and kapiak leaves and ferns is laid across the hot stones in the pit and covered with vegetables, such as yam and taro, as well as greens. Hot stones from the neighbouring fire, wrapped in more leaves, form the next layer mixed with meat from butchered pigs and more greens. Finally, the whole pit is covered again by leaves and sealed with a capping of earth, retaining the heat and steam generated by the stones in proximity to the vegetables and meat.

I should point out that the stones utilised by these people come from a nearby stream or river. The latter provide a ready supply of accessible stones which would also be water-smoothed, thus resisting flaking and burning through their leafy envelopes. They are also clean owing to the water action.

When the oven, or *mu-mu*, has been several hours in operation, with a makeshift shelter over it if it has been raining, the earth cap is removed and the top leaves thrown off, leaving the contents to cool before being distributed, with a split branch acting as a pair of tongs. Afterwards, all that remains is a charred pit, a hearth and a pile of cracked or charred stones.

Obviously, I'm not suggesting a cultural link between the Irish fulachta fiadh and the New Guinean *mu-mu*. However, we are presented with enigmatic features in excavations which resemble items paralleled in use elsewhere at the present time. I cannot say that such features do or did not exist elsewhere, involved in a different process. Then again, can we say that all fulachta fiadh were used in the same way, given the diverse features exhibited on the sites bound together by the title? What we can say is that roasting pits do belong in the European context — in Viking Age Denmark, there was a tradition of pit roasting alongside the boiling of food in vessels.

This is a cautionary tale. If the function of a feature is in doubt, check the historical references, though these tend to give very tangential mention to the more mundane practices which are and should remain the mainstay of archaeological enquiry. If they fail to give satisfactory explanation, address the ethnographic sources. If people live in a society with a material culture more similar to that of our ancestors than is our own, *maybe* they can give us a few clues and therefore point us in certain directions that we might otherwise overlook or dismiss through our own ignorance. If this leads nowhere, *then* we are left with rational speculation — or another ritual item!

REFERENCES

RAPPAPORT, R.A. 1968 *Pigs for the ancestors*. London. Yale University Press.

STEENSBERG, A. 1980 *New Guinea gardens*. London. Academic Press.

PART 6

SPECIALIST CONTRIBUTIONS

15. IRISH LITERATURE

Fulachta fiadh: the value of early Irish literature

Diarmuid A. Ó Drisceóil

Passages in early Irish literature have frequently been used by antiquarians and archaeologists in interpreting archaeological evidence. Attempts, not always successful, have been made to give a cultural and temporal context to monuments and artifacts in addition to interpreting their function. Fulachta fiadh have figured in these attempts from as early as the middle of the nineteenth century. Two antiquarians, 'Eirionnach' and 'Anglicus', writing in the *Ulster Journal of Archaeology* of 1858 (101, 185), used the famous passage in Geoffrey Keating's *Foras Feasa ar Éirinn* to explain the cooking process carried out at a fulacht fiadh. Other writers have also had recourse to this body of material in seeking supporting evidence for their suggestions regarding the function of these monuments (e.g. Cooke 1849–51, 216; Trench 1885–6; Wood-Martin 1902; Macalister 1949, 172f.). It was the late Professor M.J. O'Kelly in his discussion of the excavated evidence from the fulachta fiadh at Ballyvourney and Killeens who convinced many of the value of these early accounts. He based experiments and reconstructions on these accounts and also used them as dating evidence (O'Kelly 1954). Some of the conclusions drawn by O'Kelly from his enquiry into these early references are not convincing. Since the publication of his paper archaeologists have not looked closely at this early material and have accepted tentative suggestions as established facts in some instances. It would be wrong to uncritically accept the early Irish literary evidence in an interpretation of the cultural, social and economic contexts of fulachta fiadh, in dating them and in ascribing a function to them.

As part of a postgraduate thesis on fulachta fiadh (Ó Drisceóil 1980) the author examined many early texts and isolated instances of the term *fulacht* and references to activities that may have taken place at such sites. An attempt was made to look more critically at a greater body of evidence to see what, if anything, it might contribute to a greater understanding of fulachta fiadh. This paper is a summary account of that study of the early Irish literary material.

The range of material in which these references occur is very varied. It can date from as early as the ninth century AD, if not indeed earlier, to the eighteenth century. All the texts are in the Irish language — Old, Middle, Early Modern and Modern. The texts include early Irish law tracts, glossaries, saints' lives, tales of the Rúraíocht and Fiannaíocht (i.e. Ulster and Finn cycles), histories, annals and poetry. There are many difficulties in dealing with this type of evidence. Many of the tales, for example, are amalgams of earlier tales and may have had a very long life of oral transmission before they were first written down. A number of written transmissions may have followed. The language is frequently difficult to interpret and translate. Descriptions of cooking methods, and indeed other activities, can be very fanciful and may not describe contemporary conditions or activities of the real world. The corpus of early Irish law is very complex and even an expert linguist can fall prey to its many pitfalls. If one is to use material such as this in dating archaeological monuments, for example, is the language itself the means of dating, or is it the date at which the material was first written down, or does one add some hundreds of years to the suggested date to allow for an unknown period of oral tramsmission? Even if the references, or apparent references, to fulachta fiadh were clear and precise, these difficulties would demand great caution on the part of the archaeologist.

The complete term *fulacht fiadh* does not appear in any of the early material examined. It appears to be a nineteenth- or twentieth-century invention. *Fulacht* appears on its own with variations in spelling — *fulucht, fulocht, folucht. Inadh fulachta* (cooking place) occurs, as do *fulucht fianachta, fulacht fiansae, folach fiann, Fulacht Fian* and *Fulacht na bhFian.*

The word *fulacht* can have a variety of meanings. Originally it may have meant 'recess' or 'cavity'. It is used in this sense in a text on the privileges and responsibilities of poets, where the path of the voice from the lungs through the various recesses and cavities of the throat and mouth to its final expression in poetry is described (Gwynn 1942, 36, 37).

The possible original meaning of 'recess' or 'cavity' may have been extended to mean 'pit', subsequently 'cooking pit' or 'cooking place', and eventually the act of cooking or indeed the cooked food. It is only by examining the context of the use of the term *fulacht* that the precise meaning can be determined, and frequently the context offers little or no supplementary information. Even when a cooking place is clearly implied in the use of the term it is not necessarily a fulacht fiadh or burnt mound as known in archaeology. A cooking on a spit, in a cauldron or on a griddle can be the activity described, and this cannot necessarily be interpreted as a description of a method that would use the features of fulachta fiadh as excavated, or produce the type of debris associated with fulachta fiadh.

Fulachta fiadh have been traditionally viewed as the field kitchens or base camps of roving hunters and it is claimed that early Irish literature supports this view. Again Geoffrey Keating's description is the main evidence produced from this source. However, Keating, writing in the early seventeenth century, was almost as far removed in time from the period in which the sites were used as we are today. His understanding of the cultural context of the sites has no sound basis. He was obviously aware of the sites in the landscape of his time and he attributed them to the Fianna of Fionn Mac Cumhail, a group of men whose life-style and exploits, frequently involving hunting, are probably no more than the invention of earlier storytellers. One is tempted to ask if the hunting hypothesis would have been postulated and so readily and uncritically accepted if Keating's account had never been written. While some other passages in the early literature in which the term *fulacht* appears apparently suggest an association with hunting, we cannot be sure that a fulacht fiadh or burnt mound was the type of site referred to.

While the problems of language and interpretation added to the paucity of detail in most of the early texts limit their archaeological value, the time gap, of up to two thousand years or more, between the period of use of the fulachta fiadh and the date of even the earliest texts is a difficulty well-nigh insurmountable.

In the survey of published editions of the early texts, fifty-nine passages in which the term *fulacht* appears were considered in addition to a small number where the word *fulacht* is not used but where the cooking described matches that postulated for a fulacht fiadh. Space does not permit here an examination of all the relevant passages, and the following are offered as a representative sample. The full discussion of all references can be consulted in *Fulachta fiadh: a study* (Ó Drisceoil 1980, 90–177).

1. From 'Sanas Chormaic' (Bergin *et al.* 1912, 46)
        'Esnad... for *esnad* was the name of the music the *fianae*
        used to make at their *fulacht fiansae.'*
There is no information as to the nature of the *fulacht*. The text from which the lines come, 'Cormac's Glossary', dates to the beginning of the ninth century. *Fianae*, the plural of *fian*, at this time meant 'A band of men whose principal occupations were hunting and was also a troop of professional fighting men under a leader' (*RIA Contributions, fian*). This would seem to suggest a hunting context for the site, but given the lack of

detail one cannot regard the *fulacht fiansae* as a fulacht fiadh.

2. From 'The Cain Domnaig' (Bergin *et al.* 1910, 22)
> '...the seeking of a *folucht* with a return journey from it
> to a house without digression/delay of supporting
> *indainiul.*'

The lines refer to a journey permitted on a Sunday. No details are given of the *folucht* itself, except that it was apparently located away from the house, presumably a permanent dwelling. If it were a fulacht fiadh then the lines might suggest an asociation with permanent habitation and a location some distance from the habitation, possibly adjacent to a water source.

3. From *Ancient laws of Ireland*, vol. I (1865, 200–I, 206)
> (i) 'Recovery (i.e. by distraint)... for wrongfully
> exploring a *folach fiann*...'
> (ii) 'For a *folach fiann* i.e. a cooking-hut i.e. for every
> *set* i.e. for food or for livestock which is brought
> out of the hut.'

The first quotation comes from the original text of the law tract and the term *fiann* would seem to associate the *folach* with hunters or warriors. The second quotation is a later gloss on *folach fiann* and attempts to explain the nature of the 'wrongful exploring' — the taking of food or livestock from the site. The glossator, rightly or wrongly, understood the site to consist wholly or partly of a hut and the temptation is to regard it as the type of hut found associated with sites such as Ballyvourney I and II, for example (O'Kelly 1954, 139), and which are seen by some as meat-stores at these fulachta fiadh.

4. From *Ancient laws of Ireland,* vol. V (1901, 482, 484)
> (i) 'How much would be drawn in by pledge to every *tuath,*
> mutual surety fitting for every law? Everyone's due:... the
> *fulacht* of every wood.'
> (ii) '... the *fulacht* of every wood i.e. the thing in which a
> cooking is made in the wood i.e. a griddle.'

The suggestion in this tract is that once a *fulacht* had been set up everyone had the right to use it. The original text, (i), gives the *fulacht* a location in a wood and the glossator understood the site to consist of a griddle. This is not what one traditionally regards as the type of cooking principally carried on at a fulacht fiadh.

5. From *Táin Bó Cuailnge* (O'Rahilly 1976, 139)
> ' "Well", said Conchobar, "if I now had a roast pig (*mucc
> fhonaithe*), I shall live."
> "I will go and fetch one," said Cu Chulainn. He went off then
> and saw a man at a *fulacht* in the middle of the wood, with
> one hand holding his weapons, the other cooking (*oc funi*) a
> pig. Great was the fearsomeness of the man.
> Nevertheless he attacked him and carried off his head and his
> pig.
> Afterwards Conchobar ate the pig.'

The man at the *fulacht* is 'cooking a pig', *oc funi in tuircc* in the original. *Oc funi* (the verbal noun of *fo-noi*) is more correctly rendered as 'roasting' or 'baking' rather than the less specific 'cooking', and accordingly an association with the fulacht fiadh of archaeology is less convincing, boiling in a pit being the more likely form of cooking at such a site.

6. From 'Cúchulainn's death' (Stokes 1876–8, 176–7)
> 'Then he saw somewhat, three crones, blind of the left eye,
> before him on the road. They had cooked on spits of
> rowantree a dog with poisons and spells. And one of the

159

> things that Cuchulainn was bound not to do, was going to a
> *fulacht* and consuming the food...
> "The food is (only) a hound," quoth she. "Were this a great
> *fulocht* thou wouldst have visited us. But because what is here
> is little, thou comest not." '

The cooking at the *fulacht* was a roasting of meat on spits. *Fo-noí* is again the verb used to describe the nature of the cooking. Though a great *fulocht* is mentioned also, no indication is given of whether a different type of site or cooking activity is implied.

7. From 'Aideadh Ferghusa' (O'Grady 1892, vol. I, 249; vol. II, 282)
> 'Twelve doors there are to that house of roomy beds and
> (window) lighted sides,
> 'tis of best marble (blocks),
> and in every doorway doors of gold.
> Of red of yellow and green, of azure and of blue its bedcloths
> are;
> Its authority is of ancient date: *fulachta fian* it includes and
> baths...'

These lines form part of a very fanciful description of a house. The *fulachta fian* are located within this house but no details are furnished about the type of cooking associated with them.

8. From 'The cooking of the Great Queen (*Fulacht na Mórrigna*)' (Hyde 1916, 339, 345)
> 'Because it was they themselves who had to make a bothy for
> themselves that night, and a broiling of food was made by
> them. And Caoilte and Finnachaidh go down to the stream to
> wash their hands.
> "This is a cooking-place (*inadh fulachta*)", said Finnachaidh,
> "and it is a long time since it was made."
> "That is true," said Caoilte, "and this is the cooking-place (*fulacht*)
> of the Great Queen. And it is not to be worked without water." '

This quotation is among the more interesting. The characters seem to be discussing a fulacht fiadh. The cooking place (*inadh fulachta*) is located by a stream (a typical location for fulachta fiadh), water was needed in its operation and it is regarded as ancient. Were Caoilte and Finnachaidh looking at what was an ancient monument at the time the tale was composed, probably the twelfth century?

Fulacht na Mórrigna occurs elsewhere in the early literature and does not seem to be an example of the fulacht fiadh of archaeology. The following quotations illustrate the point.
> 'The *Fulacht* of the great Queen here. Its wheel was of wood;
> and of wood its shaft (axle?) between fire and water; its frame
> was of iron. Twice nine pulleys (?) were in that shaft.
> Smoothly and swiftly it revolved. Thirty spits projected from it,
> thirty hooks, and thirty spindles. It had a sail, and wonderful it
> looked when its hooks and pulleys were in motion. The
> *Fulacht* of the great Queen always had a fresh... of a smith'
> (Mackinnon 1912).

> '*Fulacht na Mórrigna*. Three kinds of victuals in it i.e. dressed
> victuals, and raw victuals, and butter; and the dressed food
> was not burned, and the raw food was dressed, and the butter
> was not dissolved, but as was proper' (Petrie 1935–9, 214).

9. From *The history of Ireland (Foras Feasa ar Éirinn)* by G. Keating, vol. II (Dinneen 1908, 326–9)
> 'However, from Bealltaine until Samhain, the Fian were
> obliged to depend solely on the products of their hunting and
> of the chase as maintenance and wages from the kings of

160

Ireland; thus, they were to have the flesh for food, and the skins of the wild animals as pay. But they took only one meal in the day-and-night, and that was in the afternoon. And it was their custom to send their attendants about noon with whatever they had killed in the morning's hunt to an appointed hill, having wood and moorland in the neighbourhood, and to kindle raging fires thereon, and put into them a large number of emery stones; and to dig two pits in the yellow clay of the moorland, and put some of the meat on spits to roast before the fire; and to bind another portion of it with sugans in dry bundles, and set it to boil in the larger of the two pits, and keep plying them with stones that were in the fire, making them seethe often until they were cooked. And these fires were so large that their sites are today in Ireland burnt to blackness, and these are now called Fulacht Fian by the peasantry.

As to the Fian, when they assembled on the hill on which was the fire, each of them stripped off, and tied his shirt round his waist, and they ranged themselves round the second pit we have mentioned above, bathing their hair and washing their limbs, and removing their sweat, and then exercising their joints and muscles, thus ridding themselves of their fatigue; and after this they took their meal; and when they had taken their meal, they proceeded to build their hunting tents, and so prepare themselves for sleep.'

This is the most detailed account in the early literature of the use of a *fulacht*, and one of the latest. Much of the detail regarding the location and features of the site match what we know of fulachta fiadh today and the cooking process described formed the basis for many successful experiments. A hunting context is given to the sites and they are said to have been constructed and used by the mythical Fianna. Washing and bathing at the site are also described and this is of interest in the discussion of whether fulachta fiadh were primarily cooking or bathing places (Barfield and Hodder 1987; Ó Drisceoil 1988). The passage cannot be used to date the fulachta fiadh to as late as the seventeenth century, when Keating wrote his history. It is clear in his discussion of the monuments that he regarded them as antiquities. In offering an explanation for these sites, which must have been even more common than they are today, Keating was probably drawing on contemporary folk knowledge of the relevant cooking method or possibly on information in what he terms 'na sein leabhraibh' (the old books), many of which are not extant today and of whose contents we are ignorant. While the principle of the cooking method, the heating of liquid by the immersion of hot stones, was known and practised in Keating's time, open-air cooking on a large scale in pits and resulting in a fulacht fiadh was probably not carried out.

10. From 'The romance of Mis and Dubh Ruis' (Ó Cuív 1954)

'When he reached the mountain he sat where he thought she might pass and he spread his cloak on the ground and spread his gold and silver around its edges. He lay on the cloak and took up his harp. He opened his trews and bared himself for he thought that if he could lie and have intercourse with her that it would be a good way to bring her to sanity again. Not long after that she came to where he was on hearing the harp-music and she stood there in all her wildness listening and looking at him and waiting.

"Are you not a person?" she said.

"Yes," he said.

"What is this?" she said, putting her hand on the harp.

"A harp," he said.

"Ho," she said, "I remember the harp. My father used to play

161

one. Play it for me."

"I wlll, he said, "but please do not harm me."

"I will not," she said.

She saw the gold and silver and said:

"What is this?"

"Gold and silver," he said.

"I remember," she said, "my father used to have gold."

She glanced at him and saw his nakedness and his playful members and said:

"What are these?", pointing to his bag or testicles. And he told her.

"What is this?" she said pointing to the other thing she saw.

"That is my magic wand/staff of play."

"I do not remember that," she said, "my father did not have anything like that. A magic wand," she said, "What tricks can it do?"

"Sit near me and I will do the trick for you."

"I will," she said, "but stay with me."

"I will," he said, and he lay with her and had intercourse.

"Ha," she said, "that was a good trick. Do it again."

"I will," he said, "but I will play the harp first."

"Don't bother with the harp," she said, "but do the trick."

"Well," he said, "I would like some food first. I am hungry."

"I will get you a deer," she said...

She was not long gone from him when she returned carrying a deer under her arm. She was about to tear it apart and eat it as it was when Dubh Ruis said to her:

"Wait until I slaughter the deer and boil the meat."

With that he cut the deer's throat and skinned it. Then he made a large fire of dead wood from the forest and he gathered a heap of granite stones, and put them in the fire. He made a pit, square all round in the ground, and he filled it with water. He cut up his meat and wrapped it in marsh grass, with a well-turned sugan around it, and he put it in the hole and he was supplying and continuously putting the well-reddened, long-heated stones in the water, and he kept it constantly boiling until his meat was cooked...

He then took her to the hole in which was the cold broth with the fat of the deer melted on it, and he put her standing in it, and he took a piece of the deer's skin and he rubbed and massaged the joints of her body and all her bones, and he took to smearing her, rubbing her, and spreading her with the grease of the deer and with the broth until he had cleaned much of her, and until he brought streams of sweat out of her like that.'

The text from which this passage is taken came from a manuscript written in 1769. The editor of the text believes that the original tale may have perished in the sixteenth or seventeenth century. The tale itself dates to a few centuries, at least, before the date of the manuscript. The word *fulacht* does not appear in the text, but the cooking method described is what is suggested for a fulacht fiadh and closely resembles Keating's account in many details. This account differs, however, in that the composer of the tale did not set out to explain a field monument, but rather incorporated the account of the cooking in the narrative. It is not possible to say whether the cooking episode was part of the original tale, whenever it was composed, or whether it was added later by someone borrowing from Keating's account. Washing and bathing form part of the activity at the site, as with Keating, and in this latter text it has a curative purpose in that it forms part of the cure for Mis's insanity.

The archaeologist must be wary of using a body of evidence gleaned from such wide and varied material as the corpus of early Irish literature in explaining monuments and the activities associated with them that appear to date to some two thousand years or more before much of that literature was composed, let alone written down. The Irish literary tradition, both oral and written, is very ancient and doubtless has roots in prehistoric times, but to use its conservatism and archaism to bridge an apparent two-thousand-year gap would, in the present state of knowledge, be somewhat reckless. The survey of the early literature as it relates to fulachta fiadh does throw up some interesting associations. The cooking and eating of food, washing and bathing, music and sex are activities very basic to man and the combination of some of these, and in one case all four, in some of the passages quoted in this paper may hint at a significance for fulachta fiadh, the definition of which as yet eludes us. Joseph Falaky Nagy, in a paper delivered to the International Folk Epic Conference in 1985, 'Fenian heroes and their rites of passage', looks at this question from a non-archaeological perspective (Almquist *et al.* 1987, 161–82).

ACKNOWLEDGEMENTS

The author would like to thank the following: the late Professor M. J. O'Kelly who gave me the initial direction; the late Dr A. T. Lucas who assisted me in collecting references in the early literature; Diarmaid and Ger Ó Catháin and Miriam O'Sullivan who were always available for discussion.

REFERENCES

ALMQVIST, B., Ó CATHÁIN, S. and Ó HÉALAÍ, P. (eds) 1987 *The heroic process: form, function and fantasy in folk epic.* Dun Laoghaire.

'ANGLICUS' 1858 Note. *Ulster Journal of Archaeology* **6**,101.

Ancient laws of Ireland , vol. I (Dublin, 1965); vol. V (Dublin, 1901).

BARFIELD, L. and HODDER, M. 1987 Burnt mounds as saunas, and the prehistory of bathing. *Antiquity* **61**, 370–9.

BERGIN, O.J. *et al.* (eds) 1910 *Anecdota from Irish manuscripts* 3. Dublin.

BERGIN, O.J. *et al.* (eds) 1912 *Anecdota from Irish manuscripts* 4. Dublin.

COOKE, T.L. 1849–51 Discovery in the ruins of Killyon. *J. Roy. Soc. Antiq. Ir.***1**, 215–16.

DINNEEN, P.S. (ed.) 1908 *The history of Ireland. Foras Feasa ar Éirinn by G. Keating,* 2. London.

'EIRIONNACH' 1858 Ancient Irish cookery. *Ulster J. Archaeol.* **6**, 185.

GWYNN, E.J. 1942 An Old Irish tract on the privileges and responsibilities of poets. *Ériu* **13**, 13–60, 220–32.

HYDE, D. (ed.) 1916 The cooking of the Great Queen. *Celtic Review* **10**, 335–50.

MACALISTER, R.A.S. 1949 *The archaeology of Ireland.* London.

MACKINNON, P. 1912 Fulacht na Mórrigna. *Celtic Review* **8**, 74–6.

Ó CUÍV, B. 1954 The romance of Mis and Dubh Ruis. *Celtica* **2**, 325–33.

Ó DRISCEOIL, D.A. 1980 Fulachta fiadh: a study. Unpublished M.A. thesis, University College, Cork.

Ó DRISCEOIL, D.A. 1988 Burnt mounds: cooking or bathing? *Antiquity* **62**, 671–80.

O'GRADY, S.H. (ed.) 1892 Agallamh na Senorach. *Silva Gadelica* (2 vols). London.

O'KELLY, M.J. 1954 Excavations and experiments in ancient Irish cooking-places. *J. Roy. Soc. Antiq. Ir.* **84.** 105–55.

O'RAHILLY, C. (ed.) 1976 *Táin Bó Cuailnge, Recension*. Dublin.

PETRIE, G. 1835–9 On the history and antiquities of Tara Hill. *Trans. Roy. Ir. Acad.* **18**, 25–232.

R.I.A. Contrib. Royal Irish Academy, Contributions to a dictionary of the Irish language. Fasc. 3 and 4. Dublin. Royal Irish Academy

STOKES, W. (ed.) 1876–8 Cúchulainn's death. Abridged from the Book of Leinster. *Revue Celtique* **3**, 175–85.

TRENCH, M.L. 1885–6 Ancient cooking-places. *J. Roy. Soc. Antiq. Ir.* **17**, 663–4.

WOOD-MARTIN, W.G. 1902 *Traces of the elder faiths of Ireland*, 1. London.

16. DATES

Provision of dates for fulachta fiadh

M. G. L. Baillie

Jan Lanting's contribution of a significant body of radiocarbon dates for fulachts has helped considerably in answering the question of their chronology (see Brindley and Lanting, this volume). It has long been clear that these sites represented an excellent opportunity for radiocarbon analysis. This was because, like dug-out boats or wooden bowls, the chronological questions being asked were essentially blunt.

The fulacht sites turn up little in the way of datable material, nor do they offer much in the way of typology. As a result the underlying chronological questions being asked of the sites are at the level of 'Are they Bronze Age or medieval?'. When chronological questions are as blunt as this, radiocarbon is without doubt the correct tool for the job. This applies equally well to the subsidiary question, 'Are fulachts (broadly) all of a similar date, or are they spread significantly through time?'. It was clear from the first excursions into their dating that the majority were likely to be Bronze Age simply because a random sample gave every appearance of tending to cluster there. The dates now available confirm the basic Bronze Age character of these sites beyond doubt.

Now why is a dendrochronologist advocating the use of radiocarbon dating rather than his own chronologically more refined technique? There are several answers to this question and these relate just as well to the other objects cited above. I will discuss them in turn.

LIMITED APPLICABILITY

Dendrochronology inevitably suffers from limited applicability. In Ireland, Britain and most of northern Europe it works successfully as a dating method only on oak. It requires long-lived and preferably replicated ring-patterns.

Its success rate is best illustrated by comparing its performance in dating horizontal mills and dug-out boats. Horizontal mills are multiple-component structures using substantial oak timbers. It is therefore possible in many cases to build long, well-replicated site chronologies. Such chronologies maximise the tree-ring 'signal' and hence have a high chance of successful dating against a relevant master chronology. Dug-outs on the other hand are, almost by definition, single timbers. Only examples with very long ring-records tend to date successfully. In these cases the *length* of tree-ring record tends to 'maximise' the tree-ring signal and effectively makes up for the lack of replication.

Further discussion brings in two additional factors which relate to 'time depth' and geographical spread.

TIME DEPTH AND GEOGRAPHICAL SPREAD

If a dendrochronologist is dealing with, say, a medieval timber drawn from an area where a master chronology was constructed, he knows that he can expect cross-dating, because the master is relevant to the sample. In addition he can reasonably expect that he should find the best cross-matching position somewhere broadly in the medieval period.

The problems are rather different where the sample under investigation could have been drawn from a very wide window in time. For example, a solitary bog oak could date from anywhere from the second millennium AD to the sixth millennium BC or beyond. An isolated dug-out could be anything from Mesolithic to post-medieval.

There are additional complications where the single sample is not from

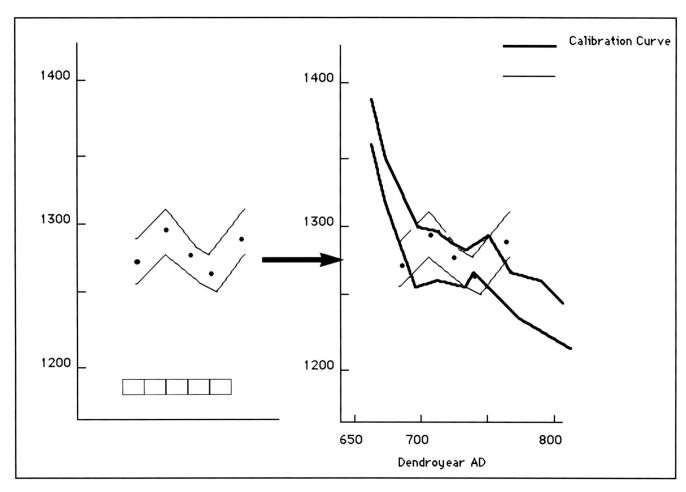

Fig. 68—An oak sample from Ardnagross horizontal mill was divided into five consecutive blocks of rings. High-precision radiocarbon dates yield a short section of calibration which is 'fixed' in the radiocarbon time-scale. It can only fit the calibration curve at one position as indicated. Allowing for missing sapwood the timber must have been felled within two decades of AD 809.

the same immediate area as the master chronology (against which it is to be dated). It has been shown elsewhere that oaks throughout Ireland and Britain (Baillie 1982, 107) and indeed throughout northern Europe (Baillie 1983) behave as though responding to some common 'signal'. However, that work related to the observation of common signals between well-replicated *site* chronologies. The situation is inevitably less clear for single samples where 'noise' tends to dilute the 'signal'. The ability to reliably date individual samples decreases when the sample is from an area well away from the master area.

In Ireland the basic reference chronology was constructed in the north of Ireland (Baillie 1985; Baillie and Pilcher 1987). So, although there has been good success in dating site chronologies from throughout Ireland against the Belfast master, single timbers have proved to be more of a problem. One consequence of this finding is that if the ring-pattern from a dug-out boat is at all marginal, say less than 150 rings, then in order to back up anything other than the most certain dating it is essential to have some independent 'order of magnitude' dating. Normally this will mean obtaining a radiocarbon date for the sample to establish that any suggested tree-ring date is in the correct half-millennium. Because such an exercise is inherently dubious, this author has in the past tended to state the case for dating dug-outs as follows: 'Any isolated sample which is marginal from a tree-ring viewpoint will require a supporting radiocarbon date. Since a radiocarbon date is in itself sufficient to answer the broad dating question — (therefore) — use radiocarbon rather than dendrochronology in these marginal cases'.

166

DATING FULACHTS

It is quite clear that fulachts suffer from most if not all of the possible limitations which could affect samples for dendrochronology. Even if the timber from a fulacht is oak, it is likely to represent a single tree or a very small number of trees (probably replicates from a single tree). It is likely to have a ring-pattern of only marginal length (on the basis of observed specimens) and it is most likely to derive from an area outside the north of Ireland (on the basis of current distributions).

All these considerations have tended to force the conclusion that, in the first instance, routine radiocarbon analysis is the most appropriate dating method for these sites.

However, there comes a point where it may no longer be appropriate to abandon more refined chronology. This becomes clear from the initial run of radiocarbon dates produced for fulachts. It appears that the main group of these sites fall chronologically in the middle/late Bronze Age and show some depletion broadly around the twelfth century BC (calibrated radiocarbon years). This of course raises the question of whether or not this apparent drop-off in the frequency of fulachts is related to the environmental effects associated with the Hekla 3 eruption in Iceland. It appears that a protracted 'narrowest ring' event in Irish bog oaks was one result of the climatic effects of this major volcanic eruption. The beginning of the event is precisely dated to 1159 BC and it has been suggested elsewhere that this event might be expected to show up in the archaeological record (Baillie and Munro 1988; Baillie 1988; 1989).

The coincidence in broad terms between a depletion in the construction of fulachts, as observed from the radiocarbon dates, and an environmental downturn in the mid twelfth century BC, postulated from tree-rings, poses a new question. Are the two observations connected and did some environmental catastrophy actually cause the reduction in fulacht construction — as might be expected in the event of a population collapse of the type suggested by Burgess (1985)? Here immediately we have a question which requires more refined dating. We want to know the relation of fulacht construction to 1159 BC — for example, is there a real fall-off? Is the fall-off significantly earlier? Now clearly routine radiocarbon analysis is not capable of answering such a question. The only available methods which can offer sufficiently accurate dating are dendrochronology and the application of radiocarbon in the form of high-precision wiggle-matching. The purpose of this article is to note how these techniques could be applied to the question of fulacht depletion.

DENDROCHRONOLOGY

We have already noted how fulachts form less than ideal subjects for tree-ring dating, with problems relating to the use of non-oak timbers, single samples, short ring-patterns and geographical isolation.

However, with many sites dating to the Bronze Age, some of the imponderables which might have severely limited tree-ring analysis have been removed. We can now imagine that cross-dating might be *expected* between timbers from some local groups of contemporary fulachts. If cross-dating was established between sites it would provide at least a relative chronology.

It might eventually become possible, over time, to construct replicated local chronologies which could be dated against the existing long oak chronologies. If such a stage could be reached, the exact chronological relationship between the sites and dated events, such as the Hekla 3 eruption, could be investigated.

HIGH-PRECISION RADIOCARBON

It has to be recognised that many of the fulachts which produce timber will not produce oak or will produce undatable oak. In these cases the possibility exists of applying high-precision radiocarbon dating. Conventional or routine radiocarbon analysis produces date ranges, for single samples, which are seldom better than three to four centuries — after calibration at 95% confidence limits (Baillie 1985). Such ranges are not useful when making comparison with the precise dates produced by dendrochronology. By comparison, high-precision radiocarbon dates are defined as those with *realistic* errors of about ± 40 years at 2-sigma (95% confidence) limits. When radiocarbon dates of this quality are calibrated they produce date ranges of around one to two centuries depending on the detailed shape of the calibration curve (except in the mid first millennium BC when, because of a major calibration 'wiggle', no single radiocarbon date can be interpreted to better than the range 800–400 BC (Baillie and Pilcher 1983)).

Clearly, date ranges of one to two centuries still limit interpretation against tree-ring dated events. However, it has now been demonstrated that multiple high-precision radiocarbon measurements on consecutive samples from a single piece of wood can be tied down with a very high level of accuracy. This involves splitting a wood sample with 40–100 growth rings into four or five consecutive blocks of 10–20 rings. Since these samples are in fixed chronological order, their high-precision measurement effectively reproduces a short section of the original Belfast high-precision calibration curve (Pearson *et al.* 1986). This short section of calibration can be fitted to the complete calibration curve with a high level of certainty and allows the estimation of the true age of the sample to within a few decades (Pearson 1986). Figure 68 illustrates the technique for a wood sample from a horizontal mill at Ardnagross, Co. Westmeath. In this case the estimated date for the end of the consecutive samples is within two decades of AD 777 and, allowing for missing sapwood, the felling date for the timber should be within two decades of AD 809. Similar examples have produced similarly accurate results. With dates of this quality it would be possible to establish whether or not fulachts were being constructed before or after specific events such as that at 1159 BC. In particular, this high-precision radiocarbon approach does not require oak but can operate on samples of any species with more than about 40 growth rings.

It is clear that the technology now exists to answer more refined chronological questions than has been possible hitherto. Conventional radiocarbon analyses and dendrochronology have provided the broad framework within which the more detailed chronological questions can be couched. Although this discussion has been applied to fulachts and the 1159 BC event, it could be generalised to apply to any type of site which produces marginal wood samples and to any dated event.

REFERENCES

BAILLIE, M.G.L. 1982 *Tree-ring dating and archaeology.* London. Croom Helm.

BAILLIE, M.G.L. 1983 Is there a single British Isles oak tree-ring signal? *Proceedings of the 22nd Symposium on Archaeometry, Bradford 1982,* 73–82. University of Bradford.

BAILLIE, M.G.L. 1985 Irish dendrochronology and radiocarbon calibration. *Ulster J. Archaeol.* **48**, 11–23.

BAILLIE, M.G.L. 1988 Irish oaks record prehistoric dust-veils drama. *Archaeology Ireland* **2**(2), 71–4.

BAILLIE, M.G.L. 1989 Hekla 3 — Just how big was it? *Endeavour* (forthcoming).

BAILLIE, M.G.L. and MUNRO, M.A.R. 1988 Irish tree-rings, Santorini and volcanic dust veils. *Nature* **332**, 344–6.

BAILLIE, M.G.L. and PILCHER, J.R. 1983 Some observations on the high precision calibration of routine dates. In B.S. Ottaway (ed.), *Archaeology, dendrochronology and the radiocarbon calibration curve,* 51–63. University of Edinburgh Occasuional Paper No.9.

BAILLIE, M.G.L. and PILCHER, J.R 1987 T*he Belfast 'long chronology' project*, 203–14. British Archaeological Reports (International Series) 333.

BURGESS, C. 1985 *Population, climate and upland settlement*. British Archaeological Reports (British Series) 143, 195–229.

PEARSON, G.W. 1986 Precise calendrical dating of known growth-period samples using a 'curve fitting' technique. *Radiocarbon* **28**, 292–9.

PEARSON, G.W., PILCHER, J.R., BAILLIE, M.G.L., CORBETT, D.M. and QUA, F. 1986 High-precision ^{14}C measurement of Irish oaks to show the natural ^{14}C variations from AD 1840 to 5210 BC. Radiocarbon 28, 911–34.

17. EXPERIMENTATION

Experiments using a reconstructed fulacht with a variety of rock types: implications for the petro-morphology of fulachta fiadh

Victor M. Buckley

The classic fulacht fiadh is often described as a kidney-shaped or horseshoe-shaped mound, formed to some degree or other by a mixture of burnt stone, charcoal and 'blackened soil'. However, increasing numbers of sites are being discovered in Ireland merely as patches of blackened soil and a spread of fire-cracked stones. Are these all sites which were levelled at some time in the past, or smaller sites which may have been used less frequently, producing less geological detritus, and which may therefore have been of a more transient nature? Also, does the predominant rock type in an area have any bearing on their morphology and, more importantly, on the national distribution pattern of fulachta fiadh?

O'Kelly (1954, 144–5) suggested that the absence of fulachta fiadh in counties Clare, Galway and Limerick was due to the limestone substrata, because limestone on contact with heat and water would turn to calcium hydroxide. His explanation for the paucity of sites in the midland limestone belt was that they existed only where small patches of drift allowed a supply of sufficient sedimentary rocks. Evidence from recent field survey has shown these gaps in the distribution to be due to the lack of detailed field survey in the 1950s rather than to the geological explanation. Examples have been found throughout County Galway (Gosling *et al.* 1987) and even in remote parts of Connemara and the offshore islands (M. Gibbons, pers. comm.), while in County Clare over 400 examples have been found by the diligent work of Tom Coffey, many in the heart of the Burren limestone plateau. Field survey in the midland counties has also increased their numbers, so that by 1985 there were just over 4000 recorded examples in Ireland (Buckley 1985). The bulk of these are found in County Cork, with over 2000 sites (Power, this volume), and large concentrations also in counties Kilkenny, Clare, Mayo and Waterford. Examples have now been located in every county in Ireland.

EXPERIMENTAL FIRING

In 1988, with the aid of a Royal Irish Academy Archaeological Research Grant, experiments were carried out with different rock types from various parts of the country, in order to record the number of heatings/dowsings it took to completely shatter the stone. In order to give some degree of control and to make the experiments as authentic as possible, a wooden trough was constructed (L 1.9m, W 0.9m, D 0.9m, which would appear from excavated sites in Ireland to be the standard size of trough for a fulacht fiadh). An open hearth was built adjacent to the trough. The stones were heated for 15 minutes each and the water pre-heated using a Le Chatelier element. Measurement of the water temperature was taken using a maximum/minimum thermometer. The water temperature reached 28° C after 5 minutes. An average stone diameter of 15cm was used as it was logically decided that, in the past, three or four of these could be carried more easily by one person from any nearby source and also heated more quickly than larger blocks. This also permitted the keeping of a control on the shatter variations and sizes of the gradually disintegrating rocks. Declan Hurl (this volume) noted that in the ethnographic parallel of the *mu-mu*, the nearby stream-bed provided the source for much of the stone used in the cooking process, not only because the stones were in portable proximity but also because they had been naturally washed clean

170

— why contaminate your food with dirty stone? Certainly this source of stone must be borne in mind when considering the percentage of Irish fulachta fiadh situated beside streams or former stream-beds.

The types of stone which were used in the experiment were Micaceous Sandstone, Arkose (a coarse angular sandstone, mainly composed of quartz), Gabbro, Agglomerate, a mixture of Basaltic types, Vesiculated Basalt and Limestone. These rock types broke down into fragments less than 5cm in size (which was when they were deemed un-reusable) after the following number of heatings/dowsings.

Table 1

Rock type	No. of heatings/dowsings	Nature of clasts
Micaceous Sandstone	5	Rect./square, angular
Limestone	6	Rounded, friable
Agglomerate	10	Rounded
Arkose	12	Rect./square, angular
Basaltic	20	Rounded, slight cracking
Vesiculated Basalt	>25*	Rounded, slight cracking
Gabbro	>25*	Square, slight cracking

*Experiments discontinued owing to no visible upper limit being foreseeable.

It should be noted from these results that the sedimentary rocks produced more waste product for the same number of heatings/dowsings than the igneous and metamorphosed rocks. This may account for the more easily recognisable upstanding 'classic' types found in County Cork. The relatively small number of fulachta fiadh in the north of Ireland may be partially explained by the use of igneous rocks which could be frequently reused and therefore may only have left a slight trace behind despite the same number of uses. An example of this can be given from Ballyremon Commons, Co. Wicklow, at the western foot of the Sugar Loaf Mountain, excavated by the writer in 1983, which produced a ^{14}C date of 3410 ± 40 BP (GrN-12617) (Ó Drisceoil 1988, 672). In this townland a group of 'classic' horseshoe-shaped fulachta fiadh appear to be mostly composed of sandstones, while the excavated example, visible as a slight spread of stone, was composed mostly of an igneous rock which, though fire-cracked, barely appeared burnt. One can only postulate multiple reuse of the same stones for its uncharacteristic nature.

COMPARATIVE ANALYSIS

At the same time as the experiments were being conducted, the opportunity to carry out the random analysis of two previously unrecorded destroyed sites arose. These were in different parts of the country with different subsurface geology. It was hoped by taking a random sample and analysing the rock types found to determine the preferential rock types. These two sites were at Muingbaun td, Co. Galway (OS 6" sheet Galway 117), discovered during land reclamation, and Castlebellingham td, Co. Louth (OS 6" sheet Louth 12), found during trenching for the North-Eastern gas pipeline. Muingbaun is located in the Limestone Belt, while Castlebellingham is in a greywacke area (Buckley *et al.* 1987). In both cases there is a marked preference for sedimentary rocks, though the naturally occurring bedrock is also used in both cases (almost 25% in the case of Muingbaun and 5% in the case of Castlebellingham). It must be seen from these two breakdowns that the preferential rock type was drift-derived material. Also notable is that 40% of all stone at the Castlebellingham site was igneous in origin.

The breakdown of rock types is as follows:

Table 2

MUINGBAUN		CASTLEBELLINGHAM	
Rock type	*No.*	*Rock type*	*No.*
Sandstone	87	Arkose	108
Sandstone (unburnt)	32	Vesiculated Basalt	41
Limestone (pure)	13	Granitoid	14
Limestone (shaley)	22	Volcanic Agglomerate	14
Chert	12	Greywacke	11
Shale/Mudstone	7	Gabbro	11
		Metamorphic	1
TOTAL	173	TOTAL	200

CONCLUSIONS

A number of tentative conclusions can be drawn from the combined evidence gleaned from the experimental testing of shatter variation in different rock types and the random analysis of samples from two sites in different geological areas.

Firstly, drift-derived material was most commonly used and, though the type of drift material was different, sedimentary rocks were preferred. Secondly, igneous and some metamorphosed rocks are very reusable and may present a problem for archaeologists, particularly in northern areas, who may find a different morphology for fulachta fiadh owing to this lithic longevity.

ACKNOWLEDGEMENTS

The writer wishes to thank the Royal Irish Academy for a research grant into shatter variation by experimental means; the project's referees Mr D. Sweetman and Professor J. Brindley; Professor Brindley for his analysis of the Muingbaun sample; Alan Vaughan for analysing the Castlebellingham clasts; and Tom Condit and Kieran Campbell for assistance in sampling these sites.

REFERENCES

BUCKLEY, V.M. 1985 Curraghtarsna. *Current Archaeol.* **98**, 70–1.

BUCKLEY, V.M., GOWEN, M. and VAUGHAN, A. 1987 Analysis of the petro-morphology of a destroyed fulacht fiadh at Castlebellingham, Co. Louth. *Co. Louth Archaeol. J.* **21** (3), 294–6.

GOSLING, P. *et al.* 1987 Sites and Monuments Record for Co. Galway. UCG/OPW (limited distribution).

Ó DRISCEÓIL, D.A. 1988 Burnt mounds; cooking or bathing? *Antiquity* **62**, 671–80.

O'KELLY, M.J. 1954 Excavations and experiments in ancient Irish cooking-places. *J. Roy. Soc. Antiq. Ir.* **84**, 105–55.

APPENDICES

APPENDIX 1

Soil analysis of the burnt mounds of the East Rhins

I. D. Máté

INTRODUCTION
The samples from the burnt mounds were analysed for qualitative 'available' phosphate (P), pH and low-temperature loss on ignition (LOI) as part of the routine analysis carried out by the CEU. The phosphate determinations were repeated using longer than standard development time to check on the appreciably higher levels of phosphate in the samples from the site at Dervaird (mound 1). The significance of the result is discussed. The references for this section will be found in the main Scottish bibliography on pp 103–4

METHODS
All the samples were air-dried and the >2mm fraction removed by sieving. Phosphate determinations were made using Eidt's method (Eidt 1973) wherein the strength of developed blue colouration (assumed to be proportionate to the available phosphate content) was assessed after two minutes. The blue colour development results from the application of two drops of a solution 'A' (HCl in an ammonium molybdate solution) followed 30 seconds later by two drops of solution 'B' (an ascorbic acid solution) (Bethell and Máté 1989). The results ('P2') were marked as high, medium or low. A second set of determinations were made on the same air-dried samples one year later, using a ten-minute development period. The results ('P10') were scored on a five-point scale (low, low to medium, medium, medium to high, and high).

The pH measurements were made with 1:2.5 w/v suspensions (i) in water ('pHw') and (ii) in 0.01M CaC12 ('pHc').

LOI was determined by heating at 390°C for 4 hours (Davies 1974). A separate sample was heated at 105°C to determine soil water. The weight loss is given as a percentage of the oven-dried <2mm fraction.

RESULTS

Site/FNo.	Context	P2	P10 pH	pHw	pHc	LOI %
Dervaird						
1		med	low–medium	3.6	n.d.	24
2		med	low–medium	4.3	n.d.	16
3		med	medium–high	4.8	n.d.	14
4		med	medium–high	5.2	n.d.	18
5		high	high	4.8	n.d.	19
7		med	medium–high	4.8	n.d.	8
8		med	low–medium	4.7	n.d.	15
9		med	high	5.1	n.d.	22
10		med	high	5.4	n.d.	14
11		med	medium	5.0	n.d.	13
Auld Taggart 2						
1000	topsoil	low	low	5.1	4.2	93
1002	mound	low	low–medium	4.9	4.4	37
1003	sub-mound	low	low	4.4	3.9	25
1005	natural	low	low	5.2	4.3	6
1006	sub-mound	low	low	4.7	3.8	n.d.

Auld Taggart 4

4000	topsoil	low	low	4.9	4.0	35
4001	mound	low	low–medium	4.6	3.5	47
4008	mound	low	low–medium	4.6	3.6	54
4009	mound	low	low	4.6	3.6	47
4010	mound	low	low	5.0	4.2	12
4011	natural	low	low	5.1	4.2	6
4012	mound	low	low	5.3	4.4	11
4015	mound	low	low–medium	4.8	3.8	40
4019	sub-mound	low	low	5.7	4.7	12

Cruise 1

2000	topsoil	low	low	4.3	3.9	33
2001	mound	low	medium–high	4.7	4.4	43
2003	mound	low	low–medium	4.4	4.2	13
2005	mound	low	high	5.0	4.8	31
2013	natural	low	low	5.0	4.6	6

Stair Lodge

3000	topsoil	low	low	4.0	3.6	n.d.
3001	peat	low	low	4.0	3.8	n.d.
3002	peat	low	low	4.4	4.1	n.d.
3003	peat	low	low	4.3	4.0	n.d.
3004	mound	low	medium–high	4.3	4.0	29
3005	mound	low	medium	4.5	4.1	26
3006	natural	low	low	4.9	4.3	7
3007	natural	low	low	5.0	4.6	41
3008	peat	low	low	4.6	4.3	n.d.

Gabsnout Burn

5000	topsoil	low	low–medium	4.8	4.1	4
5001	mound	low	medium	4.7	4.3	44

Claddy House Burn

6000	topsoil	low	low	4.2	3.7	26
6001	mound	low	medium	5.2	4.8	16
6002	mound	low	medium–high	5.0	4.5	27
6003	natural	low	low	5.1	4.5	n.d.

DISCUSSION

Using a two-minute development time, the samples from Dervaird burnt mound had medium and high available-phosphate scores, while all the other samples had low scores. The higher levels could not be explained by reference to soil type since all these burnt mounds are on soils dominated by Ettrick Association parent materials (Bown and Heslop 1979; Bown et al. 1982). It was felt that this discrepancy needed further examination, not only to check the results but also to throw more light on the use of burnt mounds. Therefore a second set of determinations were carried out.

The '2-minute' result confirmed the original findings, with the sample from context 5 at Dervaird having, relatively, a very positive result. However, the samples were left to develop over a ten-minute period and a more complicated pattern emerged. The results show that all the intra-mound samples had higher phosphate levels than the topsoils and subsoils. The results from Dervaird were higher than those from the other sites and this distinction was more pronounced after two minutes than after ten minutes. This suggests that the Dervaird phosphates were not only present in higher concentrations but were also more readily available with this extraction method. The site of Auld Taggart 4 (mound 3) had the lowest levels of easily-available phosphates.

Doubt has been cast on the quality of the spot-test results (Keeley 1981; 1983; Bethell and Máté 1989). These results indicate their lack of definition, using a standard two-minute development time. Standardisation has been necessary in the interests of inter-site comparability, while generally intra-site comparability is the most which should be attempted.

It therefore seems acceptable to allow development to carry on until the results are most discriminating. It is felt that the apparent increased phosphate levels of the mounds are real.

Increased phosphates on archaeological sites are caused by concentrations of organic material (generally), which includes not only bone but also ash (Sanchez and Salinas 1981) and animal and human excreta (Cook and Heizer 1965). The levels of phosphate cannot resolve unambiguously between the proposed functions of burnt mounds since they can be derived from wood ash.

It was thought that the sites would show an enhanced pH owing to mineral increases associated with the concentrating, by burning, of wood debris. This is not the case. There is no intra-mound enhancement nor general enhancement over those values found for Ettrick Association soils generally (Bown and Heslop 1979, appendix II).

The LOI mound results are generally high. This perhaps indicates that organic material is being actively moved around the environment of the mound, most notably from the surface downwards, in response to enhanced nutrient levels within the mound. This explanation is preferred to the alternative that the high organic levels result from original organic matter. The 'natural' samples include a variety of soil layers including organic-rich Ah horizons.

APPENDIX 2

A gazetteer of burnt mounds in Scotland

Lesley Ferguson

This gazetteer comprises details of the burnt mounds recorded in the National Monuments Record of Scotland up to May 1989. The information in the NMRS has been gathered from a variety of sources, including the record cards of the former OS archaeological division, the publications and fieldwork of the Royal Commission, and other bibliographic sources. Because of the diverse nature and purpose of the sources, the information available for each site varies considerably. Every entry has at least a national grid reference (NGR) and a site name, but without a detailed programme of fieldwork the site specifications cannot be fully verified and hence are not included here. Descriptions have been standardised and the term crescentic includes sites which have been described in the original reports as U-shaped, C-shaped, horseshoe-shaped, penannular or kidney-shaped.

    The sites are arranged in regions and districts and, within these, alphabetically by place name. The format of the entries is as follows.

—The site name. Sites with the sign # after the name no longer exist.

—The NGR and the NMRS site number.

—The shape and measurements (if recorded). If three measurements are given these are respectively length, breadth and height. If fewer measurements were available these are identified by l (length), b (breadth) or h (height).

—'Possible' is used to indicate the uncertainty of the burnt mound classification.

— Bibliographic references

ACKNOWLEDGEMENTS
I would like to thank my colleagues for their assistance in the preparation of this gazetteer, in particular S. P. Halliday for his help and advice and C. Allan for preparing the typescript.

BORDERS REGION

Berwickshire District

1. Edington Castle
    NT894 561   NT85NE 11
    13m x 12m x 1.5m
    RCAHMS 1915, 21, no. 41; C. Stuart
    1872, 349–50; Craw 1922, 178;
    RCAHMS 1980a, 67, no. 590

Ettrick and Lauderdale

2. Lauder Common
    NT496 463   NT44NE 14
    Oval, 10m x 7m x 1m

Roxburgh District

3. Cocklawfoot Burn
    NT85941913   NT81NE 52
    Possible

4. Rubers Law
    NT57271543   NT51NE 44

DUMFRIES AND GALLOWAY

Annandale and Eskdale District

5. Green Burn
    NT05460028   NT00SE 40
    Crescentic, 6.5m x 6.5m x 0.6m

Stewartry District

6. Abbey Burn
    NX74178639   NX78NW 6
    Crescentic, 8m x 7m x 0.6m

7. Barskeoch Mains#
    NX60878319   NX68SW 6
    Crescentic, 10.6m(l) x 1m(h)
    DES (1961), 28, 34

8. Round Craigs
    NX64679343   NX69SW 27
    Crescentic, 9m x 9m x 1.1m

9. Snab Hill
    NX562 832   NX58SE 3.1
    DES (1961), 34

10. Snab Hill
    NX563 833   NX58SE 3.2
    DES (1961), 34

Wigtown District

11. Airyhemming
    NX16895966   NX15NE 57
    8.7m x 5.3m x 0.5m
    RCAHMS 1987, 49, no. 230

12 Auchie
    NX14956481   NX16SW 76
    Triangular, 6m x 5m x 0.5m
    RCAHMS 1987, 49, no. 231

13. Auchie
    NX14786447   NX16SW 77
    5.5m x 4.2m x 0.6m
    RCAHMS 1987, 49, no. 232

14. Auchie
    NX14806439   NX16SW 78
    22m x 5.5m x 0.5m
    RCAHMS 1987, 49, no. 233

15. Auld Taggart
    NX14876671   NX16NW 52
    Crescentic, 11.8m x 9m x 0.9m
    RCAHMS 1987, 49, no. 234

16. Auld Taggart
    NX15166700   NX16NE 54
    RCAHMS 1987, 49, no. 235;
    DES (1987), 8; Russell-White
    (this volume)

17. Auld Taggart
    NX15296705   NX16NE 55
    3.8m x 2m x 0.4m
    RCAHMS 1987, 49, no. 236

18. Auld Taggart
    NX15136696   NX16NE 56
    Crescentic, 4.8m x 3.2m x 0.5m
    RCAHMS 1987, 49, no. 237;
    DES (1987), 8; Russell-White
    (this volume)

19. Balker#
    NX10 63   NX16SW 33.1
    Stair 1874, 701; RCAHMS 1987,
    49, no. 238

20. Balker#
    NX10 63   NX16SW 33.2
    Stair 1874, 701; RCAHMS 1987,
    49, no. 238

21. Balker#
    NX10 63   NX16SW 33.3
    Stair 1874, 701; RCAHMS 1987,
    49, no. 238

22. Balneil
    NX18516391   NX16SE 91
    Crescentic, 12.5m x 8.5m x 0.6m
    RCAHMS 1987, 49, no. 239

23. Balneil
    NX18846392   NX16SE 87
    6.5m x 4.5m x 0.4m
    RCAHMS 1987, 50, no. 240

24. Barlure
    NX17206719   NX16NE 80
    Crescentic, 4.5m x 2.5m x 0.3m
    RCAHMS 1987, 50, no. 241

25. Barlure
    NX16376731   NX16NE 64
    7m x 3.5m x 0.3m
    RCAHMS 1987, 50, no. 242

26. Broody Burn
    NX18346237   NX16SE 90.1
    Circular, 9m x 0.7m(h)
    RCAHMS 1987, 50, no. 243

27. Breedy Burn
    NX18366236   NX16SE 90.2
    12m x 6.5m x 0.8m
    RCAHMS 1987, 50, no. 243

28. Brown Hill Plantation
    NX15446666   NX16NE 52
    Crescentic, 5.5m x 3.7m x 0.3m
    RCAHMS 1987, 50, no. 244

29. Brown Hill Plantation
    NX15666675   NX16NE 53
    Oval, 6.5m x 4.7m x 0.6m
    RCAHMS 1987, 50, no. 245

30. Carscreugh Fell
    NX22726152   NX26SW 34
    Crescentic, 10m x 8m x 1m

31. Claddy House Burn
    NX08006849   NX06NE 55
    4m x 2.8m x 0.6m
    RCAHMS 1987, 50, no. 246;
    DES (1987), 8; Russell-White
    (this volume)

32. Coburn Burn
    NX14056281   NX16SW 75
    Crescentic, 4.5m x 4m x 0.6m
    RCAHMS 1987, 50, no. 247

33. Craigbirnoch
    NX16566920   NX16NE 57
    6.5m x 4.5m x 0.5m
    RCAHMS 1987, 50, no. 248

34. Craigbirnoch
    NX16216895   NX16NE 73
    7.4m x 6.4m x 0.4m
    Possible
    RCAHMS 1987, 50, no. 249

35. Craigbirnoch, Altigoukie Burn
    NX16606879   NX16NE 58
    10.5m x 6.5m x 0.6m
    RCAHMS 1987, 51, no. 251

36. Craigbirnoch, Altigoukie Burn
    NX16476820   NX16NE 59
    10m x 7m x 0.7m
    RCAHMS 1987, 51, no. 252

37. Craigbirnoch, Altigoukie Burn
    NX16336810   NX16NE 60
    7m x 4.5m x 0.6m
    RCAHMS 1987, 51, no. 253

38. Craigbirnoch, Altigoukie Burn
    NX16726846   NX16NE 74
    Circular, 11.5m x 0.5m(h)
    RCAHMS 1987, 51, no. 250

39. Craigbirnoch, Altigoukie Burn
    NX16596896   NX16NE 62
    Crescentic, 11.3m x 6.7m x 0.6m
    RCAHMS 1987, 51, no. 254

40. Craigencor, Markdhu
    NX18937458   NX17SE 52.1
    10m x 5m x 0.9m
    RCAHMS 1987, 51, no. 255

41. Craigencor, Markdhu
    NX18937458   NX17SE 52.2
    8m x 4.5m x 0.9m
    RCAHMS 1987, 51, no. 255

42. Cruise
    NX18816314   NX16SE 102
    11m x 3m x 0.4m
    RCAHMS 1987, 51, no. 256;
    DES (1987), 8; Russell-White
    (this volume)

43. Cruise
    NX19056308   NX16SE 101
    15.5m x 11m x 0.8m
    RCAHMS 1987, 51, no. 257

44. Cruise
    NX19116290   NX16SE 117
    Crescentic, 6m x 0.4m(h)
    RCAHMS 1987, 51, no. 258

45. Cruise Bridge
    NX17306334   NX16SE 118
    Crescentic, 7m x 6m x 0.2m
    RCAHMS 1987, 51, no. 259

46. Cruise Burn
    NX17986347   NX16SE 88
    7.6m x 6.4m x 0.7m
    RCAHMS 1987, 51, no. 260

47. Dervaird
    NX22465830   NX25NW 46
    14.5m x 12m x 0.8m
    DES (1987), 8–9;
    Russell-White (this volume)

48. Dunnerum
    NX13796957   NX16NW 54.1
    9.3m x 7.8m x 0.4m
    RCAHMS 1987, 52, no. 261

49. Dunnerum
    NX13766958   NX16NW 54.2
    Crescentic, 8m x 5.8m x 0.4m
    RCAHMS 1987, 52, no. 261

50. Eggerness
    NX487 487   NX44NE 44
    Circular, 15m
    Possible
    DES (1988), 11

51. Falhar
    NX470 387   NX43NE 36
    Circular, 15m
    Possible
    DES (1988), 11

52. Fauldinchie
    NX19286497   NX16SE 119
    Circular, 10.5m x 0.7m(h)
    RCAHMS 1987, 52, no. 262

53. Fauldinchie
    NX19406496   NX16SE 120
    Crescentic, 4.7m x 3.5m x 0.4m
    RCAHMS 1987, 52, no. 263

54. Gabsnout Burn
    NX19686103   NX16SE 83
    12m x 7.7m x 1m
    RCAHMS 1987, 52, no. 264;
    DES (1987), 8; Russell-White
    (this volume)

55. Gabsnout Burn
    NX19316091   NX16SE 84
    6m x 4.5m x 0.5m
    RCAHMS 1987, 52, no. 265

56. Gabsnout Burn
    NX19216078   NX16SE 85
    Crescentic, 6.5m x 4m x 0.5m
    RCAHMS 1987, 52, no. 266

57. Gleniron Fell
    NX18986195   NX16SE 86
    13m x 7.5m x 0.7m
    RCAHMS 1987, 52, no. 267

179

58. Gleniron Fell
NX18826186   NX16SE 92
Crescentic, 6.5m x 3.6m x 0.4m
RCAHMS 1987, 52, no. 268

59. Glenwhilly
NX16497224   NX17SE 81
Circular, 5m x 0.6m(h)
RCAHMS 1987, 52, no. 269

60. Glenwhilly
NX16587234   NX17SE 82
Oval, 7m x 5.7m x 0.6m
RCAHMS 1987, 52, no. 270

61. High Airyolland
NX15386196   NX16SE 109
Crescentic, 10.3m x 6.7m x 0.6m
RCAHMS 1987, 53, no. 273

62. High Airyolland
NX15416227   NX16SE 114.1
15m x 7m x 0.4m
RCAHMS 1987, 53, no. 271

63. High Airyolland
NX15426225   NX16SE 114.2
Crescentic, 9m x 4.2m x 0.4m
RCAHMS 1987, 53, no. 271

64. High Airyolland
NX15416240   NX16SE 116
9.5m x 6.5m x 0.6m
Possible
RCAHMS 1987, 53, no. 272

65. High Eldrig
NX24676908   NX26NW 25.1
12m x 11.5m x 0.6m

66. High Eldrig
NX24676908   NX26NW 25.2
11m x 9m x 0.5m

67. High Eldrig
NX24326958   NX26NW 26
Crescentic, 12.7m x 9.4m x 0.8m

68. High Eldrig
NX24306970   NX26NW 27
10.6m x 7.8m x 0.8m

69. Inchbread
NX15476395   NX16SE 79
10.4m x 3m x 0.3m
RCAHMS 1987, 53, no. 274

70. Inchbread
NX15686438   NX16SE 80
Crescentic, 9.5m x 7m x 0.4m
RCAHMS 1987, 53, no. 275

71. Kilfeddar, Tongue Glen Burn
NX15906868   NX16NE 61
7.5m x 6.5m x 0.7m
RCAHMS 1987, 53, no. 276

72. Kilfeddar, Tongue Glen Burn
NX15936899   NX16NE 63
9m x 7.5m x 0.9m
RCAHMS 1987, 53, no. 277

73. Kilhern
NX19276406   NX16SE 95
8.8m x 5.2m x 0.7m
RCAHMS 1987, 53, no. 279

74. Kilhern
NX19056370   NX16SE 96
11.5m x 5.5m x 0.6m
RCAHMS 1987, 53, no. 278

75. Kilhern
NX19516351   NX16SE 110
Crescentic, 14m x 9m x 0.8m
RCAHMS 1987, 54, no. 282

76. Kilhern
NX19686348   NX16SE 111.1
Crescentic, 8.5m x 6.5m x 0.7m
RCAHMS 1987, 53, no. 280

77. Kilhern
NX19686348   NX16SE 111.2
Crescentic, 9m x 5m x 0.5m
RCAHMS 1987, 53, no. 280

78. Kilhern
NX19666352   NX16SE 112
Crescentic, 9m x 6.5m x 0.7m
RCAHMS 1987, 54, no. 281

79. Kilhern
NX20356361   NX26SW 36
Oval, 7m x 5m x 0.8m

80. Kilhern
NX20276362   NX26SW 37
Crescentic, 6m(l) x 3.5m(b)

81. Kilhern Loch
NX200 646   NX26SW 38
10.5m x 9.5m x 1m

82. Knockiebae
NX17396601   NX16NE 51
6.3m x 4m x 0.4m
RCAHMS 1987, 54, no. 284

83. Knockiebae
NX18086634   NX16NE 77
7.8m x 6.6m x 0.4m
RCAHMS 1987, 54, no. 283

84. Knockiebae, Glen of the Dubloch
NX18276664   NX16NE 78.1
Crescentic, 9m x 6.8m x 0.6m
RCAHMS 1987, 54, no. 285

85. Knockiebae, Glen of the Dubloch
NX18286662   NX16NE 78.2
Crescentic, 9.5m x 6.2m x 0.4m
RCAHMS 1987, 54, no. 285

86. Knockiebae, Glen of the Dubloch
NX18236675   NX16NE 79
13m x 7.9m x 0.8m
RCAHMS 1987, 54, no. 286

87. Lochinch Castle#
NX10 61   NX16SW 32
19.5m x 15m x 1m
Stair 1874; RCAHMS 1987, 54,
no. 287

88. Marklach
NX17267237   NX17SE 57
10m x 8.5m x 0.4m
RCAHMS 1987, 54, no. 288

89. Miltonise
NX19527475   NX17SE 66
Crescentic, 9m x 8m x 0.6m
RCAHMS 1987, 54, no. 289

90. Pularyan
NX13976852   NX16NW 53
Crescentic, 10.4m x 9.2m x 0.2m
RCAHMS 1987, 54, no. 290

91. Pultadie
NX18616940   NX16NE 75
RCAHMS 1987, 55, no. 292

92. Pultadie
NX18416936   NX16NE 76
Crescentic, 9.5m x 7.5m x 0.6m
RCAHMS 1987, 55, no. 291

93. Quarter
NX18976840   NX16NE 67
Crescentic, 8.8m x 6m x 0.6m
RCAHMS 1987, 55, no. 293

94. Quarter
NX19106860   NX16NE 72
6.5m(l) x 3m(b)
RCAHMS 1987, 55, no. 294

95. Quarter Fell
NX19996856   NX16NE 68
Crescentic, 6.6m x 4.8m x 0.5m
RCAHMS 1987, 55, no. 295

96. Quarter Fell
NX19506920   NX16NE 69
9.5m x 5m x 0.5m
RCAHMS 1987, 55, no. 296

97. Quarter Fell
NX19146928   NX16NE 70
10.5m x 8m x 0.7m
RCAHMS 1987, 55, no. 297

98. Quarter Fell
NX19506864   NX16NE 71
Crescentic, 9.5m x 5m x 0.4m
RCAHMS 1987, 55, no. 298

99. Quarter Fell
NX20016853   NX26NW 24
Crescentic, 5.5m(l) x 0.3m(h)
Possible

100. Slickconerie
NX15977132   NX17SE 58

7.5m x 5.5m x 0.4m
RCAHMS 1987, 55, no. 299

101. Stair Lodge
NX17716686   NX16NE 124
2.5m(l) x 0.3m(h)
RCAHMS 1987, 55, no. 300;
DES (1987), 8

102. Trycock Burn
NX17887172   NX17SE 79
Crescentic, 5.3m x 3.5m x 0.4m
RCAHMS 1987, 55, no. 301

103. Trycock Burn
NX18177154   NX17SE 80
Crescentic, 6.3m x 3.3m x 0.4m
RCAHMS 1987, 56, no. 302

104. Ward Burn
NX17026605   NX16NE 50
3.5m(l) x 2m(b)
RCAHMS 1987, 56, no. 303

GRAMPIAN REGION

Banff and Buchan District

105. Burreldales#
NJ74 39   NJ73NW 20
Unknown number
Chalmers 1862, 429; J. Stuart 1866,
218

Kincardine and Deeside District

106. West Brachmont
NO81489507   NO89NW 22
Oval, 11m x 6.5m x 0.5m
RCAHMS 1984a, 42, no. 283

Moray District

107. Culbin Sands, 'MacBeth's Hillock'
NJ021 644   NJ06SW 3
Circular, 21.3m x 6.1m(h)
Linton 1876, 546; Black 1891,
487–8; Bain 1893, 58

108. Kennieshillock
NJ302 607   NJ36SW 10
PSAS 21 (1887), 286

109. Urquhart
Unlocated   NJ26SE 57
Unknown number
J. Morrison 1883, 46–7

HIGHLAND REGION

Caithness District

110. Achlibster
ND10085276   ND15SW 30
Crescentic, 9m x 9m x 0.4m

111. Achrasker
NC99286328   NC96SE 36
Circular, 8.0m x 0.7m(h)

112. Ackergill Links
ND34035674   ND35NW 9
Oval, 36m(l) x 24m(b)
Possible
Batey 1984, no. 122

113. Allt Torigil
ND03225881   ND05NW 24
Oval, 12.5m x 5.5m x 1.3m

114. Borag Knowe
NC97306302   NC96SE 40
Crescentic, 9m x 8m x 0.5m

115. Borlum Rock
NC97406375   NC96SE 41
Crescentic, 9.5m x 8m x 0.8m

116. Bouilag
ND09773286   ND03SE 10
9.5m x 7m x 0.8m

117. Bouilag Hill
ND09123290   ND03SE 11
Circular, 9m x 1m(h)

118. Bouilag Hill
ND09783298   ND03SE 15
Crescentic, 9m x 7.5m x 0.8m

180

119. Broubster
ND02986013   ND06SW 30
11m x 6m x 0.9m

120. Broubster Cottage
ND02006246   ND06SW 40
Circular, 8.5m x 0.6m(h)
Possible

121. Broubster,"Torr An T-Sniombe'
ND02846103   ND06SW 15
17m x 9.5m x 1.3m
RCAHMS 1911b, 107, no. 396

122. Brounaban
ND323 434   ND34SW 35
Circular, 9.1m x 1.2m(h)
Anderson 1873, 295–6;
Calder 1965, 79

123. Clashmore
NC99996314   NC96SE 27
14m x 12m x 1.3m
Possible

124. Cnoc Sheangan
ND16413314   ND13SE 48
Crescentic, 12m(l) x 1.2m(h)

125. Creag Bhuidhe
ND05777075   ND07SE 3
Circular, 24m x 2m(h)
Mercer 1981, 142

126. Forse
ND223 352   ND23NW 35
Circular, 5m x 0.4m(h)
Possible
Mercer (forthcoming), Area 6,
Mon. 18, 1984

127. Forse House
ND20573500   ND23NW 13.1
Crescentic, 20m(l) x 10m(b)

128. Forse House
ND20583501   ND23NW 13.2
Crescentic, 20m(l) x 10m(b)

129. Forse House
ND20593500   ND23NW 13.3
11m(l) x 5m(b)

130. Forse House
ND20403484   ND23SW 21
13m(l) x 11m(b)
Possible
Mercer (forthcoming), Area 7,
Mon. 38, 1984

131. Forse House
ND201 348   ND23SW 23
Crescentic, 12m x 9m x 1.5m
Possible
Mercer (forthcoming), Area 8,
Mon. 31, 1984

132. Hill of Forss
ND07146771   ND06NE 3
14m x 7m x 1m
RCAHMS 1911b, 125, no. 452;
Name Book (Caithness), 11,
1872, 157; Mercer 1981, 146

133. Hill of Yarrows
ND30164333   ND34SW 89
Crescentic, 8.5m(l) x 7.5m(b)
Mercer 1985, 225

134. Knockinnon
ND17533104   ND13SE 52
Oval, 8m x 7m x 1m

135. North Bilbster
ND27505442   ND25SE 19
28m x 14m x 1.5m
Possible
Mercer (forthcoming), Area 5,
1987

136. Sibster Farm
ND31295224   ND35SW 9.1
13m x 12m x 0.9m
Rhind 1857, 372–6

137. Sibster Farm
ND31645205   ND35SW 9.2
20m x 14m x 1.4m
Rhind 1857, 372–6

138. Strath Beag
ND14464891   ND14NW 3

10.8m x 14.3m x 1.1m
RCAHMS 1911b, 43, no. 153

139. 'Thorny Hillock', Barrock Mill
ND29606243   ND26SE 5
Crescentic
RCAHMS 1911b, 191, no. 591

140. Tobar Bhuirn
ND20593496   ND23SW 22
16.5m x 10m x 1m
Mercer (forthcoming), Area 7,
Mon. 65, 1984

141. Torran Dubh
ND05466989   ND06NE 6
Crescentic, 15m x 13m x 2m
RCAHMS 1911b, 124, no. 447;
Mercer 1981, 143

142. Torranreach
ND28763615   ND23NE 14
13m(l) x 12.5m(b)
Possible
Batey 1984, no. 229

143. Tulloch Turnal
ND09162288   ND02SE 30
Circular , 7m x 1m(h)

144. Uppertown, Stroma
ND35837691   ND37NE 1
Crescentic, 17m x 9.5m x 1.2m

145. Wag of Forse
ND20473518   ND23NW 17
Circular, 8m x 7m(h)
Possible

146. West Shebster
ND01886306   ND06SW 38
13.5m x 8.5m x 0.7m

147. Yarrows
ND308 434   ND34SW 34
Circular, 9m x 1.2m(h)
Anderson 1873, 295–6

Inverness District

148. Culnakirk Burn
NH503 319   NH53SW 21
Crescentic

149. Garbeg
NH513 318   NH53SW 20
Oval, 16m(l) x 1m(h)

150. Loch Ashie
NH62193362   NH63SW 69.1
Crescentic

151. Loch Ashie
NH62193362   NH63SW 69.2
Crescentic

152. Loch Ashie
NH62193367   NH63SW 69.3

Ross and Cromarty District
153. Ardvannie
NH69258752   NH68NE 40
Crescentic, 9.5m(l) x 0.5m(h)

154. Ardvannie
NH69758777   NH68NE 41.1
Oval, 6m x 4.5m x 0.8m

155. Ardvannie
NH69758777   NH68NE 41.2

156. Aultanfearn
NH59147571   NH57NE 4
Circular, 10.5m x 1.2m(h)

157. Balnacraig
NH64507070   NH67SW 24
Circular, 11.3m x 1m(h)
RCAHMS 1979, 22, no. 178

158. Balnacraig
NH64607073   NH67SW 25
Oval, 11m x 9m x 1m
RCAHMS 1979, 22, no. 179

159. Loch Achilty
NH44195656   NH45NW 8
10.8m x 7m x 0.6m

160. Loch Ussie
NH49845767   NH45NE 65
Circular, 13.5m x 12.5m x 0.8m

161. Loch Ussie#
NH49655723   NH45NE 66.1

162. Loch Ussie#
NH49855725   NH45NE 66.2

163. Loch Ussie
NH49555702   NH45NE 67
10m(l) x 6m(b)

164. Loch Ussie
NH49945660   NH45NE 68
Oval, 16m x 11.5m x 1.2m

165. Newhouse
NH49716063   NH46SE 3
Crescentic, 10m x 9m x 0.9m

Skye and Lochalsh District

166. Ashaig
NG69122408   NG62SE 8
9m(l) x 8m(b)
Possible

Sutherland District

167. Achamore
NC73955777   NC75NW 44
8m(l) x 0.7m(h)

168. Achamore
NC74045770   NC75NW 59
Crescentic, 9.5m x 9m x 1.2m

169. Achamore
NC73965786   NC75NW 60
Crescentic, 9.5m x 8.5m x 1.3m

170. Achargary
NC72925474   NC75SW 23
Crescentic, 10m x 7.5m x 1m

171. Achargary
NC72295493   NC75SW 27
Crescentic, 11m x 10m x 1m

172. Achargary
NC72715461   NC75SW 29
7m x 4m x 1.1m

173. Achargary
NC72515471   NC75SW 30
Crescentic, 12m(l) x 1.5m(h)

174. Achargary
NC72785499   NC75SW 32
Circular, 10m x 1m(h)

175. Achargary
NC72695496   NC75SW 64
Crescentic, 11m x 9m x 0.9m

176. Achargary
NC72915451   NC75SW 66
Crescentic, 11m x 7m x 0.6m

177. Ach'Na H-Uai
NC83223208   NC83SW 14
9m x 8m x 0.9m

178. Ach'Na H-Uai
NC83033215   NC83SW 15
Crescentic, 9m x 7.5m x 1m

179. Achnidale
NC83012051   NC82SW 5
Crescentic, 9.5m x 8.5m x 0.9m

180. Achrimsdale Hill
NC77892685   NC72NE 5
Crescentic, 10.5m x 8m x 0.8m

181. Allt a'Chnoic Leith
NC63443980   NC63NW 25
Crescentic, 10m x 7.5m x 1.2m

182. Allt A' Choire Mhoir
NC91571840   NC91NW 28
Crescentic, 11m x 8m x 1m

183. Allt a Mhuilleir
NC45896051   NC46SE 8
Crescentic, 13m(l) x 0.8m(h)

184. Allt Badaidh Bhraid
NC63975818   NC65NW 14
Crescentic, 8.5m(l) x 5.5m(b)

185. Allt Coire Nam Mang
NC83164232   NC84SW 5
10m x 8m x 0.9m

186. Allt Eriboll
NC42615616   NC45NW 12
Crescentic, 12.5m(l) x 9m(b)

187. Allt Meall a Bhreac-Leathaid
NC65924691   NC64NE 12
Crescentic, 9m x 7m x 1m

188. Alltnacaillich
NC45924580   NC44NE 1
Oval, 9.5m x 9m x 1.2m

189. Allt Poll a Choire
NC77580863   NC70NE 17
17m x 14m x 1.3m

190. Am Breac Leathad
NC46055989   NC45NE 21
Circular, 11.5m x 0.9m(h)

191. An Cnoc Buidhe
NC87402780   NC82NE 30
Crescentic, 15m x 2.2m x 1.8m

192. An Cnoc Buidhe
NC87542786   NC82NE 34
Crescentic, 9m(l) x 0.2m(h)

193. Armadale Burn
NC79596239   NC76SE 10
Crescentic, 9m x 8m x 0.8m

194. Baledigle
NC91354193   NC94SW 6
Crescentic, 9.5m x 7.5m x 0.8m

195. Beinn Dubhain
NC94482037   NC92SW 30
Circular, 11m x 1.3m

196. Braemore
NC55240303   NC50SE 56
Crescentic, 15m x 13m x 1.2m

197. Breton Rock, Grudie
NC74860906   NC70NW 70
Oval, 11m x 10m x 1.2m

198. Bunahoun
NC89105195   NC85SE 9
Crescentic, 13m x 9.5m x 1.6m

199. Caen Burn
ND01201825   ND01NW 32
8m x 5m x 1.2m
RCAHMS 1911a, 109, no. 317

200. Ceannabhaid
NC82962598   NC82NW 17
Crescentic, 11.5m x 9.5m x 1m

201. Clachan Burn
NC72916113   NC76SW 30
Crescentic, 7m(l) x 1m(h)

202. Claisfearn
NC19774609   NC14NE 5
Crescentic, 8m(l) x 7m(b)

203. Cnoc Airigh an Leathaid
NC70283286   NC73SW 9
Crescentic, 10.5m(l) x 1.2m(h)

204. Cnoc Airigh An Leathaid
NC70273329   NC73SW 14
Oval, 9m x 7m x 0.5m

205. Cnoc an Achaidh Mhoir
NC58300236   NC50SE 40
Circular, 8.5m x 0.7m(h)
RCAHMS 1911a, 22, no. 56

206. Cnoc an Liath-Bhaid
NC73560988   NC70NW 21
Crescentic, 10m x 5m x 0.9m

207. Cnoc an Ruidhean Chruaidh
NC76610719   NC70NE 12
Crescentic, 16m x 14m x 1.4m
RCAHMS 1911a, 175, no. 502

208. Cnoc Bad A' Chlair
NC75593270   NC73SE 10
Crescentic, 9m x 7m x 1m

209. Cnoc Garbh
NC23255617   NC25NW 4
Crescentic, 7m x 6m x 0.8m

210. Cnoc Moine na Cailinn

NC61520619   NC60NW 35
Crescentic, 11m x 7m x 0.9m

211. Cnoc Moloch
NC78193567   NC73NE 9
Circular, 10m x 1.2m(h)

212. Cnoc na Gamhna
NC69073620   NC63NE 48
11m x 10m x 1.3m
RCAHMS 1911a, 67, no. 204

213. Cnoc Olasdail
NC55221746   NC51NE 5
Crescentic, 10m x 8m x 0.6m
Mercer 1980, 109, no. 44a

214. Coillelyal
NC71355989   NC75NW 61
4.5m(l) x 0.6m(h)

215. Coire Buidhe
NC67784406   NC64SE 44
12m x 9m x 1.2m

216. Coire Buidhe
NC66554368   NC64SE 48
Oval, 7.5m x 6m x 0.4m

217. Coriefeuran Hill
NC66303298   NC63SE 14
Circular, 8.5m x 0.6m(h)

218. Corienamfeuran
NC65653478   NC63SE 17
Crescentic, 13m x 11m x 0.7m

219. Craggie Burn
NC88214996   NC84NE 7
Crescentic, 12m x 10m x 1.2m

220. Creag Bhlarach
NC69050467   NC60SE 21
11m x 10m x 0.9m

221. Creag Dhubh
NC64100986   NC60NW 49
Oval, 10m x 9m x 0.9m

222. Cromsac Hill
NC78926308   NC76SE 9
Crescentic, 11m x 9m x 1m

223. Dail na Drochaide
NC72255734   NC75NW 73.1
12m x 10m x 1.2m

224. Dail na Drochaide
NC72275731   NC75NW 73.2
Crescentic, 10m x 7m x 0.8m

225. Dalhalvaig
NC89725460   NC85SE 14
Circular, 10.5m x 0.6m(h)

226. Dalveghouse
NC71725559   NC75NW 74
9m x 6m x 1.1m

227. Dola
NC61390721   NC60NW 21
9m x 6m x 0.9m

228. Dremergid
NC73880655   NC70NW 35
Crescentic, 9.5m x 6.5m x 0.8m

229. Dremergid
NC73940642   NC70NW 36
Crescentic, 9.5m x 6.5m x 1m

230. Dunviden
NC72515148   NC75SW 39
16m x 9m x 1m

231. Fastly
NC73875961   NC75NW 55
Oval, 11m x 10m x 1m

232. Fastly
NC73406035   NC76SW 27
Crescentic, 7m(l) x 0.8m(h)

233. Forsinain
NC89884905   NC84NE 10
Crescentic, 9m x 6.5m x 1.1m

234. Forsinain Burn
NC92844826   NC94NW 4
9.5m x 8.5m x 0.8m

235. Forsinard

NC90344520   NC94NW 2
Crescentic, 0m x 7m x 0.5m

236. Forsinard
NC90334485   NC94SW 7
Crescentic, 6.5m x 5.5m x 0.5m
Mercer 1980, 142, no. 149

237. Gailiable
NC95111820   NC91NE 48
Circular, 12m x 1.3m(h)

238. Garbh-Allt
NC73040557   NC70NW 66
10m x 8m x 1m

239. Garvault Hotel
NC78533850   NC73NE 7
Circular, 10.5m x 0.9m(h)

240. Golual
NC90036214   NC96SW 10
9m x 8m x 0.5m

241. Grummore
NC60653726   NC63NW 21
8.7m x 6.5m x 0.9m
Possible

242. Henman's Burn
NH58739649   NH59NE 23
Oval, 12m x 7m x 0.9m

243. Invershin
NH57879681   NH59NE 22
Crescentic, 13m x 13m x 1m

244. Kilearnan
NC94901815   NC91NW 33.1
Oval, 3.5m x 2.5m x 0.3m
Haggarty (this volume)

245. Kilearnan
NC94901815   NC91NW 33.2
Circular, 5m x 0.5m(h)
Haggarty (this volume)

246. Kilearnan
NGR not available
Crescentic
Haggarty (this volume)

247. Kinbrace Burn
NC87532828   NC82NE 29
12m x 11m x 0.8m

248. Lairg Muir
NC58690753   NC50NE 58
Crescentic, 13m x 11m x 0.8m

249. Leadoch
NC85630499   NC80SE 27
Crescentic, 12m x 11m x 1.5m

250. Leathad Bad Na Crubaig
NC74083220   NC73SW 20
Crescentic, 8.5m(l) x 0.8m(h)

251. Leathad Bad Na Crubaig
NC73823206   NC73SW 21
7.5m(l) x 6m(b)

252. Leathad Bad Na Crubaig
NC73933188   NC73SW 22
Crescentic, 10m x 8m x 1.1m

253. Leathad Carnaich
NC89495527   NC85NE 7
11m x 9.5m x 1m

254. Leitir Chaggie
NC61990623   NC60NW 33
Crescentic, 9m x 6.5m x 1m

255. Loch Crocach
NC63955965   NC65NW 9
Crescentic, 8.5m(l) x 1m(h)

256. Loch Dola
NC61580817   NC60NW 19
Crescentic, 8.5m x 6m x 0.5m

257. Loch Dola
NC61260797   NC60NW 20
10.5m x 8.5m x 1.1m

258. Loch Farlary
NC77530496   NC70SE 41
12.5m x 11.5m x 1.2m

259. Loch Leathad nan Cruineachd
NC16284414   NC14SE 9
Crescentic, 9.5m x 7.5m x 1.2m

260. Loch Leathad nan Cruineachd
NC16574402   NC14SE 15
Crescentic, 9m(l) x 1.1m(h)

261. Loch Ma Naire
NC72925394   NC75SW 35
Crescentic, 11m x 8m x 1.5m

262. Loch nam Faoileag
NC72855511   NC75NW 67
Crescentic, 9.5m x 7.5m x 0.5m

263. Loch nan Coinean
NC66484661   NC64NE 7
Circular, 5.5m x 0.8m(h)

264. Loch Side
NC47605858   NC45NE 14
8m x 3.5m x 0.9m

265. Loch Tarbhaidh
NC64023583   NC63NW 30
10.5m x 7.5m x 0.7m

266. Market Stance
NH62009173   NH69SW 54
Crescentic, 11.5m x 9.5m x 1.3m

267. Meall a Gob Mor
NC57893614   NC53NE 4
Crescentic, 9m x 6m x 0.7m
RCAHMS 1911a, 65, no. 197

268. Oulmsdale Burn
NC95341747   NC91NE 55
Oval, 14m x 12m x 1.5m

269. Rhaoine
NC64540512   NC60NW 40
Oval, 12.5m x 10m x 1.2m

270. River Naver
NC72524815   NC74NW 12
Crescentic, 10.5m x 8.5m x 1.1m

271. Rivershin
NC57460226   NC50SE 62.1
Crescentic, 15.5m x 11m x 0.8m

272. Rivershin
NC57480229   NC50SE 62.2
8m x 6m x 0.5m

273. Rossal
NC68610326   NC60SE 15
9m x 7m x 0.6m

274. Savalbeg
NC60070755   NC60NW 39
Crescentic, 17m x 12m x 1.5m

275. Savalmore
NC58350881   NC50NE 69
Circular, 12m x 0.8m(h)

276. Shinness Hall
NC55131371   NC51SE 12
10m x 9m x 1.1m

277. Strath Brora
NC65351429   NC61SE 3
Crescentic, 8m x 5m x 0.9m

278. Strath na Frithe
NC78672622   NC72NE 7
9m x 3.4m x 0.7m

279. Strath na Frithe
NC85302711   NC82NE 33
6.5m x 5.5m x 1m

280. Strathseasgaich
NC30271019   NC31SW 1
Crescentic, 14.5m(l) x 1.5m(h)

281. Stronechrubie
NC24901870   NC21NW 3
12m x 11m x 1m

282. Syre
NC68984409   NC64SE 52
10.5m x 10m x 0.8m

283. The Ord
NC57560572   NC50NE 80
Oval, 14.5m x 11.5m x 1.6m

284. Tom Apigill
NC70515696   NC75NW 76
8.5m x 7.5m x 0.6m

285. Torr Adhaimh
NC74390746   NC70NW 43
Crescentic, 11.5m x 9.5m x 1.1m

286. Torr Liath
NC43795713   NC45NW 11
Oval, 8.5m x 5m x 1.5m

287. Torroble Burn, North
NC59940406   NC50SE 29
Circular ,12m x 1m(h)

289. Trantlebeg
NC899 535   NC85SE 7
Circular, 4.5m x 0.6m(h)

289. Trantlebeg
NC90265355   NC95SW 2
Crescentic, 10.5m x 10.5m x 1.2m

290. Trantlebeg
NC90185352   NC95SW 4
Crescentic, 9m x 7.5m x 0.6m

291. Truderscaig
NC70183463   NC73SW 15
Oval, 8m x 6m x 1m

292. Tuarie Burn
NC82232033   NC82SW 8
Crescentic, 10m x 7m x 0.8m

LOTHIAN REGION

Midlothian District

293. Side Plantation, Fountainside
NT28425603   NT25NE 6
6m x 4.3m x 0.5m
Possible
RCAHMS 1988, 33, no. 178

ORKNEY ISLANDS

Eday

294. Bay of Doomy#
HY55773481   HY53SE 9
Circular, 6m x 0.6m(h)
RCAHMS 1946, ii, 63, no. 228;
RCAHMS 1984b, 11, no. 20

295. Dale
HY52973311   HY53SW 1
Crescentic, 10.7m(l) x 1.4m(h)
RCAHMS 1946, ii, 62–3, no. 227;
RCAHMS 1984b, 12, no. 22

296. Fersness
HY52903375   HY53SW 6
RCAHMS 1984b, 11, no. 21

297. Greentoft#
HY55392878   HY52NE 7
RCAHMS 1946, ii, 62, no. 226;
RCAHMS 1984b, 12, no. 23

298. Knoll of Merrigarth
HY55282887   HY52NE 4
Name Book (Orkney),1880, no. 4,
137; RCAHMS 1946, ii, 63, no. 233;
RCAHMS 1984b, 12, no. 24

299. Skaill
HY56583293   HY53SE 10
Crescentic, 2m(h)
RCAHMS 1946, ii, 63, no. 230;
RCAHMS 1984b, 12, no. 25

300. Stenaquoy
HY56443080   HY53SE 11
RCAHMS 1946, ii, 63, no. 231;
RCAHMS 1984b, 12, no. 26

301. War Ness
HY55332845   HY52NE 3
14m(l) x 1m(h)
RCAHMS 1946, ii, 63, no. 232;
RCAHMS 1984b, 12, no. 27

302. Warrenhall#
HY530 322   HY53SW 2
RCAHMS 1946, ii, 63, no. 229;
RCAHMS 1984b, 12, no. 28

Hoy, Walls and Flotta

303. Blackawall, Flotta
ND35539415   ND39SE 9
Crescentic, 17m x 12m x 0.8m

304. Cantick, South Walls
ND33948929   ND38NW 4
1.4m(h)

305. Green Hill, South Walls
ND30998910   ND38NW 7
Crescentic, 3m(h)
Name Book (Orkney), 1880, no. 25;
RCAHMS 1946, ii, 341, no. 1017;
RCAHMS 1989, no. 44

306. Hillock of Salwick, Brims, Hoy
ND28768869   ND28NE 1
Triangular, 11m x 11m x 2m
RCAHMS 1946, 341, no. 1013;
RCAHMS 1989, no. 6

307. Kirbuster, South Walls#
ND32229070   ND39SW 2
RCAHMS 1946, ii, 341, no. 1014;
RCAHMS 1989, no. 43

308. Laurie's Knowe, South Walls
ND32259081   ND39SW 4
1m(h)
Name Book (Orkney), 1880,
no. 25, 50; RCAHMS 1946, ii,
340, no. 1011; RCAHMS 1989,
no. 45

309. Newbigging, South Walls#
ND331 901   ND39SW 3
RCAHMS 1946, ii, 341, no. 1015;
RCAHMS 1989, no. 46

Mainland

310. Ballarat House
HY30111634   HY31NW 22
RCAHMS 1946, ii, 35, no. 112

311. Ballarat House
HY30331640   HY31NW 26
Crescentic, 17m(l) x 1m(h)

312. Beaquoy#
HY30102198   HY32SW 11
RCAHMS 1946, ii, 35, no. 107;
DES (1974), 85; Hedges 1977,
39-98

313. Benziaroth
HY36781488   HY31SE 15
Oval, 22m x 17m x 1.7m
RCAHMS 1946, ii, 98, no. 342

314. Bigswell
HY33141045   HY31SW 29
RCAHMS 1946, ii, 319, no. 900

315. Braebuster
HY55010573   HY50NE 43
18m x 16m x 1.5m
Steedman 1980, no. 32

316. Breck
HY51470604   HY50NW 11
10m x 0.8m x 1.5m
RCAHMS 1946, ii, 246, no. 639

317. Breckness
HY29802173   HY22SE 7.1
Possible
Name Book (Orkney), 1880,
no.1, 207; RCAHMS 1946,
ii, 38, no. 144

318. Breckness
HY29802174   HY22SE 7.2
Possible
Name Book (Orkney), 1880,
no.1, 207; RCAHMS 1946, ii,
38, no. 144

319. Brettavale, Knarston
HY30582080   HY32SW 15
Circular, 13.7m x 1.5m(h)
RCAHMS 1946, ii, 34, no. 99

320. Bryameadow Farm
HY25822257   HY22SE 33.1
Name Book (Orkney), 1880, no. 17,
13

321. Bryameadow Farm
HY25822257   HY22SE 33.2
Name Book (Orkney), 1880, no. 17,
13

322. Bu of Orphir
HY33310469   HY30SW 5.1
18m(l) x 6.5m(b)
RCAHMS 1946, ii, 177, no. 492

323. Bu of Orphir
HY33350467   HY30SW 5.2
Circular, 7.5m x 1.2m(h)
Possible
RCAHMS 1946, ii, 177, no. 492

324. Burn of Gangsta
HY45730350   HY40SE 21
0.8m(h)

325. Burn of Geo
HY36251575   HY31NE 17
Circular, 5m x 0.8m(h)
Possible

326. Burn of Pow
HY33402867   HY32NW 3
11m(l) x 1.8m(h)

327. Burn of Una, Quholm
HY26301269   HY21SE 36.1
1.7m(h)
Name Book (Orkney),1880, no. 22,
48; RCAHMS 1946, ii, 326, no. 932

328. Burn of Una, Quholm
HY26301268   HY21SE 36.2
1m(h)
Name Book (Orkney),1880, no. 22,
45; RCAHMS 1946, ii, 326, no. 932

329. Burn of Una, Quholm
HY24841254   HY21SW 3
2.5m(h)
Name Book (Orkney),1880, no. 22,
45; RCAHMS 1946, ii, 326, no. 931

330. Burness Bridge
HY38861636   HY31NE 4.1
12m x 4m x 1.3m
RCAHMS 1946, ii, 98, no. 341

331. Burness Bridge
HY38851636   HY31NE 4.2
8m x 7m x 1.3m
RCAHMS 1946, ii, 98, no. 341

332. Campston
HY53420428   HY50SW 5
11m x 9m x 0.8m

333. Chrismo
HY31492890   HY32NW 8
Possible
RCAHMS 1946, ii, 84, no. 289

334. Copinsay Farm, Copinsay
HY60900150   HY60SW 2
RCAHMS 1946, ii, 249, no. 670

335. Crearhowe
HY49300235   HY40SE 7
24m x 18m x 1.1m
RCAHMS 1946, ii, 106, no. 371

336. Don
HY22701029   HY21SW 5
34m x 9m x 1.7m
Name Book (Orkney), 1880, no. 22,
63; RCAHMS 1946, ii, 326, no. 933

337. Durka Dale
HY30222495   HY32SW 20
Circular, 7.5m x 0.7m(h)
RCAHMS 1946, ii, 35, no. 105

338. Durkadale, Dounby
HY29902507   HY22NE 25
Crescentic, 10m(l) x 1m(h)
RCAHMS 1946, ii, 35, no. 104

339. East Bigging
HY226 150   HY21NW 3.1
Name Book (Orkney), 1880,
no. 17, 152; Petrie 1890, 94;
RCAHMS 1946, ii, 267, no. 715

340. East Bigging
HY22601496   HY21NW 3.2
8.5m x 7m x 1.3m
Name Book (Orkney), 1880,
no. 17, 152; Petrie 1890, 94;
RCAHMS 1946, ii, 267, no. 715

341. East House
HY28952059   HY22SE 18
Circular, 24m x 1m(h)
RCAHMS 1946, ii, 268, no. 723

342. Ellibister
HY38 21   HY32SE 3.1
RCAHMS 1946, ii, 84, no. 292

343. Ellibister

344. Ellibister
HY38 21   HY32SE 3.3
RCAHMS 1946, ii, 84, no. 292

345. Ellibister
HY38 21   HY32SE 4
RCAHMS 1946, ii, 84, no. 292

346. Esgar
HY29582106   HY22SE 11.1
0.8m(h)
RCAHMS 1946, ii, 35, no. 108

347. Esgar
HY29582107   HY22SE 11.2
0.8m(h)
RCAHMS 1946, ii, 35, no. 108

348. Fan Knowe, Hyval Cottage
HY29991975   HY21NE 31
23m x 16m x 1.8m
Possible

349. Finstown
HY35451400   HY31SE 16
Circular, 15m x 1.2m(h)
RCAHMS 1946, ii, 98, 343;
M. Hedges 1979, 154

350. Green Knowe, Braeside
HY28552471   HY22SE 37
Circular, 19m x 1.2m(h)
RCAHMS
1946, ii, 35, no. 10324;

351. Greentoft
HY56860698   HY50NE 3.1
10m x 7m x 0.4m
Name Book (Orkney)
1880, no. 3, 24; RCAHMS 1946, ii,
246, no. 644

352. Greentoft
HY56920698   HY50NE 3.2 10m x
7m x 0.4m Name Book (Orkney)
1880, no. 3, 24; RCAHMS 1946, ii, 246,
no. 644

353. Greentoft
HY56700682   HY50NE 41
50m x 17m x 2m
Steedman 1980, no. 25

354. Grimsquoy
HY47290846   HY40NE 9
Possible
RCAHMS 1946, ii, 161, no. 416

355. Grind
HY50300665   HY50NW 20
2m(h)

356. Hawell
HY51230651   HY50NW 10.1
16m x 10m x 1.7m
RCAHMS 1946, ii, 245–6, no. 637

357. Hawell#
HY51230651   HY50NW 10.2
RCAHMS 1946, ii, 245–6, no. 637

358. Holland
HY47931120   HY41SE 13
Circular, 15m
Possible
Neil 1981, 39

359. Howana Gruna#
HY32192305   HY32SW 12
RCAHMS 1946, ii, 38, no. 143

360. Howans#
HY25231755   HY21NE 44
RCAHMS 1946, ii, 271, no. 746

361. Howe of Langskaill
HY51471048   HY51SW 1
1.4m(h)
RCAHMS 1946, ii, 245–6, no. 638

362. Kingsdale
HY315 211   HY32SW 16
RCAHMS 1946, ii, 35, no. 110

363. Kirbister Farm
HY28222537   HY22NE 12
Name Book (Orkney), 1880, no. 1
107; RCAHMS 1946, ii, 35, no. 102

364. Knowe of Bea
HY297 096   HY20NE 7
RCAHMS 1946, ii, 319, no. 901

365. Knowe of Brenda, Downatown
HY26612381   HY22SE 40.1
Crescentic, 1.2m(h)
RCAHMS 1946, ii, 35, no. 114

366. Knowe of Brenda, Downatown
HY26602376   HY22SE 40.2
RCAHMS 1946, ii, 35, no. 114

367. Knowe of Dale#
HY24942434   HY22SW 22
27m x 18m x 1.6m
RCAHMS 1946, ii, 32-3, no. 89;
M. Hedges 1979, 153

368. Knowe of Eversti
HY23002288   HY22SW
3 1.7m(h)
RCAHMS 1946, ii, 35, no. 115

369. Knowe of Flaws
HY23132434   HY22SW 21
RCAHMS 1946, ii, 35, no. 118

370. Knowe of Forsakelda
HY28302314   HY22SE 49
Possible
Name Book (Orkney), 1880, No. 1,
161; RCAHMS 1946, ii, 35, no. 113

371. Knowe of Garraquoy
HY23742370   HY22SW 20
Crescentic, 1.2m(h)
RCAHMS 1946, ii, 35, no. 116

372. Knowe of Makerhouse
HY29352114   HY22SE 6
Circular, 24m x 1.7m(h)
RCAHMS 1946, ii, 35, no. 109

373. Knowe of Netherskaill
HY23412423   HY22SW 25
RCAHMS 1946, ii, 35, no. 117

374. Koffer Howe#
HY50SW 6.1
Unlocated
RCAHMS 1946, ii, 246, no. 644

375. Koffer Howe#
Unlocated   HY50SW 6.2
RCAHMS 1946, ii, 246, no. 644

376. Kokna - Cumming#
HY303 127   HY31SW 28
RCAHMS 1946, ii, 319, no. 899

377. Leequoy
HY23972502   HY22NW 2
Crescentic
RCAHMS 1946, ii, 35, no. 119

378. Loch of Tankerness
HY52190928   HY50NW 23
DES (1979), 20

379. Loch of Tronston
HY26172082   HY22SE 21
RCAHMS 1946, ii, 268, no. 721

380. Lower Gritley
HY56580444   HY50SE 2.1
RCAHMS 1946, ii, 246, no. 645

381. Lower Gritley
HY56600443   HY50SE 2.2
RCAHMS 1946, ii, 246, no. 645

382. Lower Gritley
HY56610441   HY50SE 2.3
RCAHMS 1946, ii, 246, no. 645

383. Lower Gritley
HY56630442   HY50SE 2.4
RCAHMS 1946, ii, 246, no. 645

384. Lower Gritley#
HY566 044   HY50SE 2.5
RCAHMS 1946, ii, 246, no. 645

385. Millbrae
HY51310530   HY50NW 12.1
RCAHMS 1946, ii, 246, no. 640

386. Millbrae
HY51310536   HY50NW 12.2
RCAHMS 1946, ii, 246, no. 640

387. Mussaquoy
HY56600369   HY50SE 1
Crescentic, 12m x 10m x 1.2m
RCAHMS 1946, ii, 246, no. 646

388. Ness
HY54360936   HY50NW 35

389. Overabist
HY331 238   HY32SW 7
RCAHMS 1946, ii, 35, no. 106

390. Oyce of Isbister
HY39001808   HY31NE 8.1
Possible
RCAHMS 1946, ii, 83–4, no. 285;
Petrie 1868, 414–18; M. Hedges 1979,
153, no. 10

391. Oyce of Isbister
HY39001811   HY31NE 8.2
Possible
RCAHMS 1946, ii, 83–4, no. 285;
Petrie 1868, 414–18; M. Hedges 1979,
153, no. 10

392. Oyce of Isbister
HY39001813   HY31NE 8.3
Possible
RCAHMS 1946, ii, 83–4, no. 285;
Petrie 1868, 414–18; M. Hedges 1979,
153, no. 10

393. Peerie Howe, Dingyshowe Bay
HY54750324   HY50SW 12
2m(h)
Possible

394. Pickaquoy
HY44071116   HY41SW 13
RCAHMS 1946, ii, 162, no. 419;
Petrie 1857, 61; Henshall 1963,
1, 225, no. 40; Renfrew 1979, 201
Morris 1981, 153; Simpson 1866

395. Quinni Moan
HY27642105   HY22SE 20.1
1.5m(h)
RCAHMS 1946, ii, 268, no. 722

396. Quinni Moan
HY27672103   HY22SE 20.2
1.5m(h)
RCAHMS 1946, ii, 268, no. 722

397. Redland
HY26721389   HY21SE 33
Name Book (Orkney), 1880, no. 22, 27;
RCAHMS 1946, ii, 326, no. 930

398. Redland
HY36631705   HY31NE 11.1
8m(l) x 6m(b)
RCAHMS 1946, ii, 94, no. 327

399. Redland
HY36661701   HY31NE 11.2
Possible
RCAHMS 1946, ii, 94, no. 327

400. Redland
HY36681701   HY31NE 11.3
Possible
RCAHMS 1946, ii, 94, no. 327

401. Redland
HY36691703   HY31NE 11.4
Possible
RCAHMS 1946, ii, 94, no. 327

402. Rennibister
HY39901293   HY31SE 2
Circular, 19m x 1m(h)
RCAHMS 1946, ii, 98, no. 344

403. Robie's Knowe
HY36202665   HY32NE 21
1m(h)
RCAHMS 1946, ii, 84, no. 291

404. St. Peter's Kirk
HY53680422   HY50SW 8
Circular, 0.5m(h)
RCAHMS 1946, ii, 246, no. 641

405. Saverock
HY43481280   HY41SW 6
2m(h)
RCAHMS 1946, ii, 162, no. 420

406. Seatter#
HY26811279   HY21SE 35
Name Book (Orkney), 1880, no. 22,
49; RCAHMS 1946, ii, 327, nos 944–5

407. Setter
HY34341560   HY31NW 12
Name Book (Orkney), 1880, no. 6,
23

408. Smoogro#
HY36 05   HY30NE 15
RCAHMS 1946, ii, 177, no. 493

409. Stembister
HY53840223   HY50SW 11
1m(h)

410. Swanbister House
HY35140531   HY30NE 11
10m x 6m x 0.8m
Possible
RCAHMS 1946, ii, 178, no. 508

411. Sweyn's Castle, Gairsay
HY45072195   HY42SE 1
Crescentic, 3m(h)
RCAHMS 1946, ii, 89, no. 314

412. Tower of Clett
HY49500165   HY40SE 10
1m(h)
RCAHMS 1946, ii, 106, no. 370

413. Upper Linklater
HY26012208   HY22SE 28.1
Crescentic
RCAHMS 1946, ii, 268, no. 720

414. Upper Linklater#
HY26012208   HY22SE 28.2
RCAHMS 1946, ii, 268, no. 720

415. Upper Stove
HY58030774   HY50NE 40
14m x 9m x 2m
Steedman 1980, no. 19

416. Voy
HY25351497   HY21SE 26
1m(h)
RCAHMS 1946, ii, 268, no. 726

417. The Ward
HY56890739   HY50NE 7
23m x 14m x 2m

418. Wasbister
HY28961378   HY21SE 20
Circular, 6m(l) x 0.3m(h)
Possible
RCAHMS 1946, ii, 268, no. 725

419. Windbreck#
HY55 05   HY50NE 23
RCAHMS 1946, ii, 246, no. 642

420. Winksetter
HY340 162   HY31NW 21
RCAHMS 1946, ii, 35, no. 111

North Ronaldsay

421. Ancum Loch
HY76235425   HY75SE 7
Crescentic, 1m(h)
RCAHMS 1946, ii, 51, no. 198;
RCAHMS 1980b, 15, no. 53

422. Ancumtoun
HY76775479   HY75SE 14.1
Circular, 12.5m x 1m(h)
RCAHMS 1980b, 15, no. 54

423. Ancumtoun
HY767 548   HY75SE 14.2
Crescentic, 15m(l) x 0.7m(h)
RCAHMS 1980b, 15, no. 54

424. Dennis Loch
HY78755547   HY75NE 13
5m x 4m x 0.4m
Possible
RCAHMS 1980b, 25, no. 163

425. Knowe O'Samilands
HY76575305   HY75SE 8
2.3m(h)
RCAHMS 1946, ii, 51, no. 199;
RCAHMS 1980b, 15, no. 56

426. Viggay
HY76875237   HY75SE 9
Crescentic, 2m(h)
RCAHMS 1946, ii, 51, no. 200;
RCAHMS 1980b, 15, no. 55

Rousay

427. Bleaching Knowe, Wasbister
HY39573316   HY33SE 6
RCAHMS 1946, ii, 226, no. 587;
RCAHMS 1982, 20, no. 53

428. Brendale
HY430 314   HY43SW 4
RCAHMS 1946, ii, 226, no. 592

429. Cogar, Wasbister
HY39433273   HY33SE 4
Circular, 8.5m x 0.7m(h)
RCAHMS 1946, ii, 226, no. 590

430. Corse#
HY391 281   HY32NE 20
RCAHMS 1946, ii, 226, no. 593

431. Cruar
HY44702891   HY42NW 31
24m x 10m x 1.5m

432. Kirbist, Egilsay
HY47552890   HY42NE 5
26m x 16m x 1m

433. Knowe of Dale, Quandale
HY37413217   HY33SE 15
Crescentic, 21.3m x 18.3m x 2.3m
RCAHMS 1946, ii, 225, no. 584

434. 'Knowe of Gorn'
HY38693341   HY33SE 3
15m x 14m x 1.6m
RCAHMS 1946, ii, 225, no. 586

435. 'Knowe of Hammar', Innister
HY38943351   HY33SE 9
Crescentic, 14m x 13m x 1.5m
RCAHMS 1946, ii, 226, no. 588

436. Knowe of Oro, Knarston
HY44402951   HY42NW 30
Crescentic, 18m x 13m x 1.8m

437. Langskaill
HY40203310   HY43SW 3
Triangular, 14m x 12m x 1.1m
RCAHMS 1946, ii, 226, no. 589

438. Lower Quandale
HY36823191   HY33SE 7
Circular, 15m x 1m(h)
RCAHMS 1946, ii, 226, no. 595; RCAHMS
1982, 21, no. 65

439. North Howe
HY37063098   HY33SE 25
17.5m x 13m x 0.8m
RCAHMS 1946, ii, 226, no. 594;
RCAHMS 1982, 21, no. 67

440. North Howe
HY36893077   HY33SE 42
9m x 7m x 1.5m
RCAHMS 1982, 21, no. 66

441. Quoynalonga Ness
HY36473200   HY33SE 5
Crescentic, 18.5m x 13m x 1.2m
RCAHMS 1946, ii, 225, no. 585

442. Skirmie Clett, Wyre
HY45552622   HY42NE
1 4.5m(l) x 2.1m(b)
Possible
RCAHMS 1946, ii, 239, no. 620

443. Suso Burn
HY42253085   HY43SW 37
M. Hedges 1979, 153

444. Tafts, Quendal
HY37123249   HY33SE 8
Crescentic, 16m x 12m x 1m
RCAHMS 1946, ii, 226, no. 596

445. Testaquoy, Wyre
HY43672580   HY42NW 35.1
Circular, 6m x 0.4m(h)

446. Testaquoy, Wyre
HY43692580   HY42NW 35.2

447. Woo
HY43463113   HY43SW 2
Circular, 17m x 0.8m(h)
RCAHMS 1946, ii, 226, no. 591

448. Woo
HY43363092   HY43SW 25

Sanday

449. Annabrake
HY66374424   HY64SE 34
RCAHMS 1980b, 13, no. 32

450. Butter Knowe
HY70964315   HY74SW 3
Circular, 14m x 0.8m(h)
RCAHMS 1946, ii, 170, no. 453;
RCAHMS 1980b, 13, no. 34

451. Cleat
HY70554263   HY74SW 4
0.7m(h)
RCAHMS 1946, ii, 170, no. 453;
RCAHMS 1980b, 14, no. 36

452. Cleat
HY70344258   HY74SW 5
1.2m(h)
RCAHMS 1946, ii, 170, no. 453;
RCAHMS 1980b, 14, no. 35

453. Colligarth
HY68964168   HY64SE 3.1
0.8m(h)
RCAHMS 1946, ii, 167, no. 442;
NSA, xv (Orkney), 140;
RCAHMS 1980b, 14, no. 38

454. Colligarth
HY68924165   HY64SE 3.2
0.5m(h)
RCAHMS 1946, ii, 167, no. 442;
NSA, xv (Orkney), 140;
RCAHMS 1980b, 14, no. 38

455. Colligarth
HY689 416   HY64SE 3.3
0.9m(h)
RCAHMS 1946, ii, 167, no. 442;
NSA, xv (Orkney), 140;
RCAHMS 1980b, 14, no. 38

456. Colligarth#
HY69164153   HY64SE 4
0.9m(h)
RCAHMS 1946, ii, 173, no. 480;
RCAHMS 1980b, 14, no. 37

457. Hoosie Mound
HY62 37   HY63NW 6
Possible
RCAHMS 1946, ii, 43, no. 169;
RCAHMS 1980b, 14, no. 39

458. Ivar's Knowe
HY71584335   HY74SW 10
26m(l) x 22m(b)
RCAHMS 1946, ii, 173, no. 478;
Name Book (Orkney), 1879, no.2,
147; Petrie 1890, 94; *NSA*, xv
(Orkney), 139; RCAHMS 1980b, 14,
no. 41

459. Knowe
HY67864418   HY64SE 11
RCAHMS 1946, ii, 43, no. 168;
RCAHMS 1980b, 14, no. 42

460. The Knowes
HY63423880   HY63NW 3
Oval, 20m x 10m x 0.6m
Possible
RCAHMS 1946, ii, 41, no. 162

461. Leavisgarth
HY70014145   HY74SW 12.1
RCAHMS 1980b, 14, no. 44

462. Leavisgarth#
HY70094172   HY74SW 12.2
RCAHMS 1980b, 14, no. 43

463. Newbiggings
HY65994179   HY64SE 9
RCAHMS 1946, ii, 42, no. 166;
RCAHMS 1980b, 13, no. 33

464. Northskaill
HY68144453   HY64SE 10
1m(h)
RCAHMS 1946, ii, 43, no. 168;
RCAHMS 1980b, 14, no. 46

465. Northwall#
HY75 44   HY74SE 5

RCAHMS 1946, ii, 170, no. 454;
RCAHMS 1980b, 14, no. 45

466. Ortie
HY68534505   HY64NE 2
1m(h)
RCAHMS 1946, ii, 42, no. 167;
RCAHMS 1980b, 14, no. 47

467. Park
HY77274371   HY74SE 1
RCAHMS 1946, ii, 170, no. 455;
RCAHMS 1980, 14, no. 48

468. Pincod
HY66314397   HY64SE 35
1.5m(h)
RCAHMS 1946, ii, 15, no. 49

469. Quivals Loch
HY67034186   HY64SE 40
1.3m(h)
RCAHMS 1946, ii, 15, no. 50

470. Scarrigarth#
HY62903862   HY63NW 26
RCAHMS 1980b, 14, no. 40

471. Spur Ness
HY60603479   HY63SW 6
Crescentic, 23m x 14m x 2m
RCAHMS 1980b, 15, no. 51

472. Stove
HY60993582   HY63NW 7
1m(h)
RCAHMS 1946, ii, 43, no. 170;
RCAHMS 1980b, 15, no. 52

473. Tofts Ness, 'Shelly Knowe'
HY75994652   HY74NE 1
Crescentic, 1.8m(h)

Shapinsay

474. Garth, Shapinsay
HY48662016   HY42SE 2
7m(l) x 5m(b)
RCAHMS 1946, ii, 278, no. 791

475. Hanna Toft
HY50421684   HY51NW 9
RCAHMS 1946, ii, 279, no. 794

476. Haroldsgarth#
HY51981591   HY51NW 8
RCAHMS 1946, ii, 278, no. 792

477. 'Hillock of Homrie', Waltness
HY47781938   HY41NE 11
Circular, 20m x 0.6m(h)
RCAHMS 1946, ii, 278, no. 790

478. Steaquoy
HY51901638   HY51NW 13
RCAHMS 1946, ii, 279, no. 793

479. Strathore
HY49001933   HY41NE 7
RCAHMS 1946, ii, 278, no. 789

South Ronaldsay

480. Barswick, South Ronaldsay
ND43098606   ND48NW 9
16m x 11m x 1m
RCAHMS 1946, ii, 289, no. 836

481. Brecks, South Ronaldsay
ND47819336   ND49SE 10
Oval, 24m x 16m x 1m
RCAHMS 1946, ii, 288, no. 830

482. Clouduhall
ND43518940   ND48NW 13
Circular, 15m x 2m(h)

483. Dyke-End, South Ronaldsay
ND47589227   ND49SE 9.1
Circular, 10.5m x 1m(h)
Possible
RCAHMS 1946, ii, 288, no. 831

484. Dyke-End, South Ronaldsay
ND47589227   ND49SE 9.2
Circular, 7.5m x 1m(h)
Possible
RCAHMS 1946, ii, 288, no. 831

485. Dyke-End, South Ronaldsay
ND47589227   ND49SE 9.3
Circular, 4m x 0.5m(h)
Possible

RCAHMS 1946, ii, 288, no. 831

486. Greenquoy,   South Ronaldsay
ND43468627   ND48NW 11
21m x 14m x 1.5m

487. Hall of Cara, South Ronaldsay
ND47999465   ND49SE 11
RCAHMS 1946, ii, 288, no. 829

488. Honeysgeo, South Ronaldsay
ND48689317   ND49SE 2
Name Book (Orkney) 1879, no. 20,
115; RCAHMS 1946, ii, 291, no. 856

489. Hune Bay, South Ronaldsay
ND43508828   ND48NW 7.1
Circular, 15m x 0.7m(h)
RCAHMS 1946, ii, 289, no. 837

490. Hune Bay, South Ronaldsay
ND43508828   ND48NW 7.2
Circular, 15m x 0.7m(h)
RCAHMS 1946, ii, 289, no. 837

491. The Kiln, Muckle Skerry
ND46387844   ND47NE 3
13m x 11m x 1m
Possible
Longworth 1963, 354

492. Kirkhouse, South Ronaldsay
ND47169119   ND49SE 15

493. Liddel, South Ronaldsay
ND46468411   ND48SE 2
Circular, 22m x 1.8m(h)
RCAHMS 1946, ii, 289, no. 834;
Hedges 1974 251–3; Hedges 1977 39–98;
DES (1975), 34–5;
DES (1974), 85; Renfrew 1979, 5,
195, 197

494. Liddel, South Ronaldsay
ND46498416   ND48SE 5
Hedges 1977, 39, 78–9, 83, 88

495. Little Myre, South Ronaldsay
ND43399117   ND49SW 17
12m(l)

496. Mossetter, South Ronaldsay
ND449 863   ND48NW 8
RCAHMS 1946, ii, 289, no. 833

497. Mucklehouse, South Ronaldsay
ND43868891   ND48NW 12
Circular, 16m x 0.3m(h)

498. Mucklehouse, South Ronaldsay
ND43578883   ND48NW 18
Possible
Name Book (Orkney), 1879,
no. 20, 222

499. Newbigging Farm
ND43289066   ND49SW 16
26m x 22m x 2m
DES (1983), 20

500. Newhouse, South Ronaldsay
ND43678939   ND48NW 6
RCAHMS 1946, ii, 288, no. 832

501. Oyce of Herston, South Ronaldsay
ND42059072   ND49SW 15
Circular, 16m x 1.6m(h)

502. South Cara, South Ronaldsay
ND478 930   ND49SE 14
RCAHMS 1946, ii, 288, no. 830

Stronsay

503. Banks, 'The Navsy'
HY65142373   HY62SE 5.1
RCAHMS 1946, ii, 311, no. 958;
RCAHMS 1984 b, 23, no. 107

504. Banks, 'The Waspy'#
HY652 238   HY62SE 5.2
Marwick 1927, 64;
RCAHMS 1946, ii, 311, no. 958;
RCAHMS 1984b, 24, no. 113

505. Bleaching Knowe
HY65352804   HY62NE 3.1
Oval, 1.2m(h)
Name Book (Orkney), 1879, no. 24,
33; *PSAS* 44 (1909–10), 103;
RCAHMS 1946, ii, 330, no. 962;
Marwick 1927, 62; Petrie 1890, 94;
RCAHMS 1984b, 22, no. 99

186

506. Bleaching Knowe
HY65352804   HY62NE 3.2
Name Book (Orkney), 1879, no. 24,
33; *PSAS*, 44 (1909–10), 103;
RCAHMS 1946, ii, 330, no. 962;
Marwick 1927, 62; Petrie 1890, 94;
RCAHMS 1984b, 22, no. 99

507. Dale#
HY64962516   HY62NW 6
RCAHMS 1946, ii, 335, no. 986;
RCAHMS 1984b, 23, no. 100

508. Easthouse Knowe, Papa Stronsay
HY66752944   HY62NE 11
17m(l) x 2m(h)
RCAHMS 1946, ii, 336, no. 996;
Marwick 1927, 62;
RCAHMS 1984b, ii, 38, no. 225

509. Grobister#
HY65622400   HY62SE 2.1
Marwick 1927, 82–3;
RCAHMS 1946, ii, 330, no. 953;
RCAHMS 1984b, 23, no. 101

510. Grobister#
HY65812382   HY62SE 2.2
Marwick 1927, 82–3;
RCAHMS 1946, ii, 330, no. 953;
RCAHMS 1984b, 23, no. 101

511. 'The Hillocks'
HY63192992   HY62NW 15.1
RCAHMS 1946, ii, 328, no. 948;
RCAHMS 1984b, 23, no. 102

512. 'The Hillocks'#
HY63192992   HY62NW 15.2
RCAHMS 1946, ii, 328, no. 948;
RCAHMS 1984b, 23, no. 102

513. Kirbister
HY68582356   HY62SE
3 29m x 22m x 2.5m
RCAHMS 1946, ii, 331, no. 956;
RCAHMS 1984b, 23, no. 102

514. Lodge Farm
HY64592413   HY62SW 3
RCAHMS 1946, ii, 331, no. 959;
RCAHMS 1984b, 23, no. 104

515. 'Mells Kirk'
HY656 219   HY62SE 4
RCAHMS 1946, ii, 331, no. 957;
RCAHMS 1984b, 23, no. 105

516. Mid Garth#
HY63012832   HY62NW 2
RCAHMS 1946, ii, 331, no. 955;
RCAHMS 1984b, 23, no. 106

517. Mid Garth, 'Stursy'
HY634 286   HY62NW 3
Marwick 1927, 82;
RCAHMS 1946, ii, 331, no. 955;
RCAHMS 1984b, 24, no. 111

518. 'Monkhouses', Auskerry
HY67291634   HY61NE 2
Crescentic, 22.3m x 15.8m x 1.3m
RCAHMS 1946, ii, 337, no. 1001

519. Odness#
HY68292523   HY62NE 8
Name Book (Orkney), 1879, no. 24,
83; RCAHMS 1946, ii, 335, no. 990;
RCAHMS 1984b, 23, no. 108

520. Odness
HY68682544   HY62NE 24
Oval, 2m(h)
Possible
RCAHMS 1984b, 23, no. 109

521. Sands of Rothleshulm
HY62692433   HY62SW 2
Marwick 1927, 62;
RCAHMS 1946, ii, 330, no. 954;
RCAHMS 1984b, 23, 110

522. Yearnasetter
HY64202692   HY62NW 30
17m x 11.5m x 1.2m
RCAHMS 1984b, 24, no. 114

Westray

523. Benziecott#
HY49973923   HY43NE 1.1

RCAHMS 1946b, ii, 359, no. 1062

524. Benziecott#
HY49973923   HY43NE 1.2
Circular, 15.2m x 1.5m(h)
RCAHMS 1946, ii, 359, no. 1062

525. Claybraes#
HY50594014   HY54SW 5.1
RCAHMS 1946, ii, 359, no. 1061;
RCAHMS 1983, 27, no. 84

526. Claybraes#
HY50594014   HY54SW 5.2
RCAHMS 1946, ii, 359, no. 1061;
RCAHMS 1983, 27, no. 84

527. Garth
HY46614525   HY44NE 4
RCAHMS 1946, ii, 359, no. 1056;
RCAHMS 1983, 27, no. 85

528. Gill Pier
HY45024923   HY44NE 10
13m x 5m x 0.6m
RCAHMS 1983, 27, no. 86

529. Hilldavale
HY42614788   HY44NW 37
Possible
RCAHMS 1983, 27, no. 87

530. Holland, Papa Westray
HY48725123   HY45SE 6
RCAHMS 1946, ii, 185, no. 531;
RCAHMS 1983, 13, no. 5

531. Kirk of Howe, Papa Westray
HY493 530   HY45SE 8
RCAHMS 1946, ii, 185, no. 533;
RCAHMS 1983, 13, no. 6

532. Knowe of Backiskaill, Papa Westray
HY48535090   HY45SE 2
Crescentic, 2.9m(h)
Marwick 1925, 40; RCAHMS 1946,
ii, 185, no. 538; RCAHMS 1983,
14, no. 7

533. Knowe of Cotterchan
HY51144154   HY54SW 2
RCAHMS 1946, ii, 359, no. 1058;
RCAHMS 1983, 28, no. 90

534. Knowe of Goltoquoy
HY50934168   HY54SW 1
21.3m(l) x 1.5m(h)
RCAHMS 1946, ii, 359, no. 1058;
RCAHMS 1983, 28, no. 91

535. Knowe of Hamar
HY50394127   HY54SW 3
28m x 13m x 1.4m
RCAHMS 1946, ii, 359, no. 1059;
RCAHMS 1983, 28, no. 92

536. Knowes of Mayback, Papa Westray
HY49425228   HY45SE 9.1
Crescentic, 1.8m(h)
RCAHMS 1946, ii, 185, no. 534;
RCAHMS 1983, 14, no. 8

537. Knowes of Mayback, Papa Westray#
HY49425228   HY45SE 9.2
RCAHMS 1946, ii, 185, no. 534;
RCAHMS 1983, 14, no. 8

538. Langskaill
HY43634301   HY44SW 5
Circular, 11m x 1.3m(h)
RCAHMS 1946, ii, 359, no. 1063;
RCAHMS 1983, 27, no. 88

539. Loch of Burness
HY42684807   HY44NW 19
Circular, 12m x 0.6m(h)
RCAHMS 1983, 28, no. 93

540. Loch of Burness
HY429 481   HY44NW 20
RCAHMS 1946, ii, 358–9, no. 1055;
RCAHMS 1983, 28, no. 95

541. Loch of Burness
HY42 48   HY44NW 38
RCAHMS 1946, ii, 358–9, no. 1055;
RCAHMS 1983, 28, no. 94

542. Loch of Wastbist
HY48984263   HY44SE 4
Oval, 17m x 9m x 1.4m
RCAHMS 1946, ii, 359, no. 1057;
RCAHMS 1983, 28, no. 96

543. 'Milliemahoose', Papa Westray
HY48955167   HY45SE 10
Circular, 12m
RCAHMS 1946, ii, 185, no. 535;
RCAHMS 1983, 14, no. 9

544. Newbigging, Papa Westray
HY49135334   HY45SE 7.1
2.4m(h)
RCAHMS 1946, ii, 185, no. 532;
RCAHMS 1983, 14, no. 10

545. Newbigging, Papa Westray
HY49135334   HY45SE 7.2
1.1m(h)
RCAHMS 1946, ii, 185, no. 532;
RCAHMS 1983, 14, no. 10

546. Newbigging, Papa Westray
HY49135334   HY45SE 7.3
1.4m(h)
RCAHMS 1946, ii, 185, no. 532;
RCAHMS 1983, 14, no. 10

547. Noup
HY41684893   HY44NW 9
9.1m x 6.1m x 1.2m
RCAHMS 1946, ii, 352, no. 1040;
RCAHMS 1983, 28, no. 97

548. Pierowall
HY43 48   HY44NW 18
RCAHMS 1946, ii, 358, no. 1054;
RCAHMS 1983, 29, no. 99

SHETLAND ISLANDS

Bressay

549. Brough
HU51914121   HU54SW 3
2m(h)
Name Book (Shetland), 1878,
no. 39, 187; RCAHMS 1946, iii,
5, no. 1094

550. Cruester
HU48154232   HU44SE 8
Circular, 22m x 2m(h)
RCAHMS 1946, iii, 5, no. 1092

551. Cullingsburgh
HU52064213   HU54SW 7
RCAHMS 1946, iii, 5, no. 1093

552. Hellia Cluve, Isle of Noss
HU53944013   HU54SW 13
Crescentic, 10m(l) x 1m(h)
RCAHMS 1946, iii, 8, no. 1111

553. Loch of Beosetter
HU49054397   HU44SE 1
21m x 13.7m x 2.2m
Name Book (Shetland), 1878,
no. 39, 33; RCAHMS 1946, iii, 5,
no. 1090; *PSAS* 65 (1930–1), 10

556. Pettigarth
HU49944085   HU44SE 6
Circular, 14m x 2m(h)
Name Book (Shetland), 1878,
no. 39, 182; RCAHMS 1946, iii, 6,
no. 1098

555. Skeo Back
HU51733870   HU53NW 7
Crescentic, 11m x 8m x 0.6m

556. Ullins Water
HU520 409   HU54SW 10
RCAHMS 1946, iii, 6, no. 1095

557. Wadbister
HU51383945   HU53NW 2
Circular, 10m
RCAHMS 1946, iii, 6, no. 1096

558. Wadbister
HU51563937   HU53NW 3
Crescentic, 10m(l) x 6m(b)
RCAHMS 1946, iii, 6, no. 1097

559. Will Houll, Grindiscol
HU49294002   HU44SE 17
Circular, 16.5m x 2.3m(h)
Name Book (Shetland), 1878,
no. 39, 324; Hunt 1866;
Mitchell 1870, 127–8; RCAHMS
1946, iii, 5, no. 1091

Fair Isle

500. Fair Isle, site 65#
HZ19927042   HZ17SE 28
Circular, 2m(l)
Hunter 1984, 13, no.65

561. Fair Isle, site 134
HZ20087081   HZ27SW 85
1.5m(l) x 1m(b)
Possible
Hunter 1984, 4, 18, no. 134

562. Fair Isle, site 178
HZ20717148   HZ27SW 129
9m x 8m x 0.3m
Possible
Hunter 1984, 4, 21, no. 178

563. Fair Isle, site 179
HZ20707147   HZ27SW 130
3m x 3m x 0.3m
Possible
Hunter 1984, 4, 21, no. 179

564. Fair Isle, site 182
HZ20877154   HZ27SW 133
10m(l) x 8m(b)
Hunter 1984, 4, 22, no. 182

565. Fair Isle, site 183
HZ20857155   HZ27SW 134
5m(l) x 5m(b)
Hunter 1984, 4, 22, no. 183

566. Fair Isle, site 216
HZ20507157   HZ27SW 167
5m x 3m x 0.6m
Possible
Hunter 1984, 4, 24, no. 216

567. Fair Isle, site 230, Pund
HZ20707161   HZ27SW 8
RCAHMS 1946, iii, 47, no. 1200;
Hunter 1984, 4, 25, no. 230

568. Fair Isle, site 231, Vaasetter
HZ20747155   HZ27SW 4.1
42m x 37m x 3.7m
RCAHMS 1946, iii, 47, no. 1196;
Hunter 1984, 4, 25–6, no. 231

569. Fair Isle, site 232, Vaasetter
HZ20747155   HZ27SW 4.2
19m x 13m x 1.9m
RCAHMS 1946, iii, 47, no. 1196;
Hunter 1984, 4, 25–6, no. 232

570. Fair Isle, site 248, Sukka Moor
HZ20757206   HZ27SW 1
16m x 7m x 2m
RCAHMS 1946, iii, 47, no. 1199;
Hunter 1985, 12, no. 248

571. Fair Isle, site 295, Burn of Furse
HZ21727252   HZ27SW 3.2
Circular, 8m x 1.2m(h)
RCAHMS 1946, iii, 47, no. 1198;
Miller 1967; Hunter
1985, 18, no. 295

572. Fair Isle, site 296, Burn of Furse
HZ21807258   HZ27SW 3.1
Circular, 14m x 1.5m(h)
RCAHMS 1946, iii, 47, no. 1198;
Miller 1967 ; Hunter
1985, 18, no. 296

573. Fair Isle, site 297
HZ21417226   HZ27SW 188
12m x 10m x 2m
Hunter 1985, 18, no. 297

574. Fair Isle, site 314
HZ21297247   HZ27SW 189
13m x 5m x 1.5m
Hunter 1985, 20, no. 314

575. Fair Isle, site 337
HZ21807258   HZ27SW 190
7m x 3m x 0.7m
Hunter 1985, 23, no. 337

576. Fair Isle, site 351
HZ20757206   HZ27SW 191
5.5m x 2m x 0.4m
Hunter 1985, 24, no. 351

577. Fair Isle, site 408
HZ20377074   HZ27SW 192
Circular, 12m x 0.75m(h)
Hunter 1986, 11, no. 408

578. Fair Isle, site 410, The Houll
HZ20507070   HZ27SW 10
Crescentic, 11m(l) x 1.5m(h)
RCAHMS 1946, iii, 48, no. 1202;
Hunter 1986, 11, no. 410

579. Fair Isle, site 448
HZ20917072   HZ27SW 193
2m(l) x 1m(b)
Possible
Hunter 1986, 16, no. 448

580. Fair Isle, site 491, The Rippack
HZ20857038   HZ27SW 5.1
Circular, 15m x 1.2m(h)
RCAHMS 1946, 47, no. 1197;
PSAS 17(1882-3), 293;
Hunter 1986, 20, no. 491

581. Fair Isle, Site 491
HZ20857038   HZ27SW 5.2
Circular, 7m x 0.5m(h)
Hunter 1986, 20, no. 491

582. Fair Isle, Site 491
HZ20857038   HZ27SW 5.3
Circular, 6m x 0.5m(h)
Hunter 1986, 20, no. 491

583. Fair Isle, site 632
HZ21517153   HZ27SW 194
11m x 10m x 1m
Hunter 1987, 9, no. 632

584. Fair Isle, site 633
HZ21507154   HZ27SW 195
8m x 5m x 1m
Hunter 1987, 9, no. 633

585. Fair Isle, site 636
HZ21597161   HZ27SW 196
Circular, 9m x 1.2m(h)
Hunter 1987, 9–10, no. 636

586. Fair Isle, site 638, Gilsetter
HZ21267170   HZ27SW 7
9.1m x 7m x 1.1m
RCAHMS 1946, iii, 47, no. 1195;
Hunter 1987, 10, no. 638

587. Fair Isle, site 667
HZ21847210   HZ27SW 197
Circular, 7m x 0.7m(h)
Possible
Hunter 1987, 13, no. 667

588. Fair Isle, site 744#
HZ21267180   HZ27SW 12
Possible
RCAHMS 1946, iii, 47, no. 1195;
Hunter 1987, 24, no. 744

589. Stonybreck#
HZ20527083   HZ27SW 9
RCAHMS 1946, iii, 48, no. 1201

Fetlar

590. Burn of Funzie
HU66078977   HU68NE 2
11m x 10m x 1m

591. Selli Geos, Lamb Hoga
HU613 874   HU68NW 3
RCAHMS 1946, iii, 59,
no. 1222

592. Swainkatofts
HU63339000   HU69SW 28
Crescentic, 6m x 4m x 0.8m
RCAHMS 1946, iii, 59, no. 1221

Foula

593. Biggines, Hametoun
HT96493705   HT93NE 2
RCAHMS 1946, iii, 154, no. 1686

594. South Harrier
HT95844038   HT94SE 3
14m x 3m x 1m
RCAHMS 1946, iii, 154, no. 1683

595. Whirly Knowe, Hametoun
HT96433721   HT93NE 1
14m x 10m x 1.7m
RCAHMS 1946, iii, 154, no. 1685

596. Wilse
HT96014026   HT94SE 4

Circular, 8m x 1m(h)
RCAHMS 1946, iii, 154, no. 1684

Mainland (includes Burra, Mousa and Noss)

597. Assater
HU29787937   HU27NE 11
0.7m(h)
RCAHMS 1946, iii, 97, no. 1371

598. Benston
HU46335418   HU45SE 5
15m x 5.5m x 1.2m
Calder 1965, 80, no. 4

599. Biggings, Papa Stour
HU17576021   HU16SE 8
Crescentic, 1.5m(h)
RCAHMS 1946, iii, 155, no. 1698

600. Bight of the Sandy Geos, West Burra
HU35882925   HU32NE 9
Crescentic, 11m x 8m x 2m
Hedges 1984, 41, M100

601. Bight of the Sandy Geos, West Burra
HU35902940   HU32NE 10
7m x 5m x 1.5m
Hedges 1984, 41, M100

602. Bottom of Clodisdale
HU22945089   HU25SW 13
Crescentic, 1.7m(h)
RCAHMS 1946, iii, 150, no. 1640

603. Braefield
HU40081823   HU41NW 8
0.6m(h)
RCAHMS 1946, iii, 42, no. 1168;
Calder 1965, 82

604. Branchiclett, West Burra
HU36923535   HU33NE 4
Crescentic, 1.3m(h)
RCAHMS 1946, iii, 76, no. 1272

605. Branchiclett, West Burra
HU36883547   HU33NE 6.1
Circular, 7m x 1.3m(h)
Hedges 1984, M110

606. Branchiclett, West Burra
HU36883549   HU33NE 6.2
Circular, 5m x 0.5m(h)
Hedges 1984, M110

607. Breckans
HU21075025   HU25SW 15.1
0.6m(h)
RCAHMS 1946, iii, 151, no. 1651

608. Breckans
HU21075025   HU25SW 15.2
0.6m(h)
RCAHMS 1946, iii, 151, no. 1651

609. Breibister
HU21834950   HU24NW 9
Crescentic, 1.3m(h)
RCAHMS 1946, iii, 151, no. 1644

610. Breibister
HU21934938   HU24NW 10
Crescentic, 1m(h)
RCAHMS 1946, iii, 151, no. 1645

611. Bretabister
HU48155738   HU45NE 19
12m x 6m x 1m
RCAHMS 1946, iii, 81, no. 1295;
Calder 1965, 84

612. Broch of Mousa, Mousa
HU45952371   HU42SE 3.1
12m x 11m x 1.2m
RCAHMS 1946, iii, 55, no. 1208;
Calder 1965, 83

613. Broch of Mousa, Mousa
HU45972368   HU42SE 3.2
Oval, 7.5m x 4m x 1m
RCAHMS 1946, iii, 55, no. 1208;
Calder 1965, 83

614. Brough
HU22334965   HU24NW 19
Crescentic, 1.3m(h)
RCAHMS 1946, iii, 150, no. 1641

615. Brouster
HU25905150   HU25SE 28
Oval, 1m(h)
RCAHMS 1946, iii, 150, no. 1629

616. Bruna Ness
HU38123658   HU33NE 3.1
RCAHMS 1946, iii, 76, no. 1271;
Calder 1965, 83; Hedges 1984,
M133

617. Bruna Ness
HU38163659   HU33NE 3.2
RCAHMS 1946, iii, 76, no. 1271;
Calder 1965, 83; Hedges 1984,
M133

618. Bruna Ness
HU38173661   HU33NE 3.3
RCAHMS 1946, iii, 76, no. 1271;
Calder 1965, 83; Hedges 1984,
M133

619. Bruna Ness
HU38193662   HU33NE 3.4
RCAHMS 1946, iii, 76, no. 1271;
Calder 1965, 83; Hedges 1984,
M133

620. Bruna Ness
HU38203660   HU33NE 3.5
RCAHMS 1946, iii, 76, no. 1271;
Calder 1965, 83; Hedges 1984,
M133

621. Brunatwatt
HU24865108   HU25SW 10.1
Crescentic, 1.7m(h)
RCAHMS 1946, iii, 150, no. 1630

622. Brunatwatt
HU24865100   HU25SW 10.2
1.4m(h)
RCAHMS 1946, iii, 150, no. 1630

623. Burn of Scudillswick
HU47455647   HU45NE 17
13m x 5m x 0.8m
RCAHMS 1946, iii, 81, no. 1296

624. Burn of Setter
HU21155038   HU25SW 14.1
Crescentic, 1.4m(h)
RCAHMS 1946, iii, 150, no. 1652

625. Burn of Setter
HU21185036   HU25SW 14.2
Circular, 0.7m(h)
RCAHMS 1946, iii, 150, no. 1652

626. Burn of Setter
HU21215049   HU25SW 16
Oval, 1.1m(h)
RCAHMS 1946, iii, 151, no. 1653

627. Burnside
HU28057842   HU27NE 10
Crescentic, 11m x 8m x 1m
RCAHMS 1946, iii, 97, no. 1369

628. Burn, Wester Skeld
HU29844370   HU24SE 8
12m x 10.4m x 1.7m
RCAHMS 1946, iii, 110–11, no. 1449

629. Burrastow
HU22234780   HU24NW 12
RCAHMS 1946, iii, 151, no. 1647

630. Burwick
HU39514116   HU34SE 5.1
Crescentic, 14m x 11m x 1.3m
RCAHMS 1946, iii, 123, no. 1513

631. Burwick
HU39524116   HU34SE 5.2
10m x 8m x 1m
RCAHMS 1946, iii, 123, no. 1513

632. Churchton
HU39004765   HU34NE 3
Crescentic, 1.5m(h)
RCAHMS 1946, iii, 124, no. 1514;
Calder 1965, 89

633. Clothie
HU19505071   HU15SE 2
18.6m x 12m x 0.7m
RCAHMS 1946, iii, 151, no. 1657

634. Crawton
HU21485771   HU25NW 7
Crescentic, 16m(l) x 1.4m(h)

635. Dale Voe
HU457 456   HU44NE 4.1
DES (1978), 20

636. Dale Voe
HU457 456   HU44NE 4.2
DES (1978), 20

637. Dalsetter
HU40071579   HU41NW 6.1
0.6m(h)
RCAHMS 1946, iii, 42,
no. 1161; Calder 1965, 82

638. Dalsetter
HU40071585   HU41NW 6.2
Crescentic, 2m(h)
RCAHMS 1946, iii, 43,
no.1170; Calder 1965, 82

639. Dalsetter
HU40151604   HU41NW 6.3
1.2m(h)
RCAHMS 1946, iii, 43,
no. 1171; Calder 1965, 82

640. Danwall
HU43863686   HU43NW 8
Crescentic, 1.3m(h)
RCAHMS 1946, iii, 72, no. 1251;
Calder 1965, 83

641. Dutch Loch, Papa Stour
HU16076095   HU16SE 30
Allen 1980, 21

642. Easter Dale, West Burra
HU382 358   HU33NE 17
Crescentic, 5m(l) x 4m(b)
Possible
Hedges 1984, M113

643. Eillams Wells
HU32719148   HU39SW 5
Crescentic, 16.5m x 13m x 1.9m

644. Engamoor#
HU25945721   HU25NE 17
RCAHMS 1946, iii, 111, no. 1451

645. Exnaboe
HU40451185   HU41SW 5.1
Circular, 12.2m x 1.5m(h)
RCAHMS 1946, iii, 42, no. 1162;
Calder 1965, 82

646. Exnaboe
HU40471186   HU41SW 5.2
8.8m x 7.6m x 0.6m
RCAHMS 1946, iii, 42, no. 1162;
Calder 1965, 82

647. Forratwatt
HU24554944   HU24NW 3
1.4m(h)
RCAHMS 1946, iii, 150, no. 1634

648. Gardins
HU43727696   HU47NW 4
1.5m(h)
RCAHMS 1946, iii, 11, no. 1124;
Calder 1965, 82

649. Gardins
HU43777690   HU47NW 5
Crescentic, 1.5m(h)
RCAHMS 1946, iii, 12, no. 1125;
Calder 1965, 82

650. Glenlea
HU43053016   HU43SW 4.1
0.9m(h)
RCAHMS 1946, iii, 42, no. 1164;
Calder 1965, 82

651. Glenlea
HU43023017   HU43SW 4.2
Crescentic, 0.5m(h)
RCAHMS 1946, iii, 42, no. 1164;
Calder 1965, 82

652. Green Knowe
HU19564954   HU14NE 3
Crescentic, 13m(l) x 2m(h)
RCAHMS 1946, iii, 151, no. 1659

653. Green Knowe, Breibister
HU22014960   HU24NW 8
1.2m(h)
RCAHMS 1946, iii, 151, no. 1643

654. Griesta
HU41464438   HU44SW 7.1
1.5m(h)
RCAHMS 1946, iii, 124, no. 1518

655. Griesta
HU41554435   HU44SW 7.2

Crescentic, 1.5m(h)
RCAHMS 1946, iii, 124, no. 1518

656. Grunasound, West Burra
HU37403343   HU33SE 15
Crescentic, 2m(h)
RCAHMS 1946, iii, 76, no. 1274;
Hedges 1984, M107

657. Grunnavoe
HU25144866   HU24NE 20.1
1.5m(h)
RCAHMS 1946, iii, 150, no. 1632

658. Grunnavoe
HU25144865   HU24NE 20.2
Crescentic, 1.7m(h)
RCAHMS 1946, iii, 150, no. 1632

659. Grunna Water
HU45795486   HU45SE 21
Crescentic, 15m x 7m x 1.3m

660. Gruting
HU27874929   HU24NE 16
1.5m(h)
RCAHMS 1946, iii, 111, no. 1458

661. Gruting
HU27674912   HU24NE 17
Crescentic, 1.2m(h)
RCAHMS 1946, iii, 111, no. 1458

662. Gruting
HU27 49   HU24NE 18
RCAHMS 1946, iii, 111, no. 1458

663. Gruting
HU282 491   HU24NE 22
Circular, 12m x 1.5m(h)
DES (1978), 20

664. Gulver Knowe, West Burra
HU37893455   HU33SE 4
Crescentic, 19.5m x 16m x 3m
RCAHMS 1946, iii, 76, no. 1273;
Hedges 1984, M109

665. Hamnavoe
HU24048045   HU28SW 6
Crescentic, 1m(h)
RCAHMS 1946, iii, 97, no. 1374;
Calder 1965, 84

666. Head of Voe, Vaila
HU22414691   HU24NW 21
Crescentic, 13m x 8m x 1.8m
RCAHMS 1946, iii, 157, no. 1709

667. Heglibister
HU39085158   HU35SE 2
Circular, 9.1m x 0.9m(h)
RCAHMS 1946, iii, 123, no. 1512

668. Hestaford
HU27615081   HU25SE 11
1.5m(h)
RCAHMS 1946, iii, 111, no. 1459

669. Hevdigarth
HU201 491   HU24NW 15
RCAHMS 1946, iii, 151, no. 1650

670. Hockland
HU30145137   HU35SW 2.1
Crescentic, 2m(h)
DES (1957), 34

671. Hockland
HU30155133   HU35SW 2.2
Circular, 1.7m(h)
DES (1957), 34

672. Houbie
HU45514800   HU44NE 2
Circular, 11m x 1m(h)
RCAHMS 1946, iii, 124, no. 1516;
Calder 1965, 85

673. Houll
HU22404941   HU24NW 7
Crescentic, 1.3m(h)
RCAHMS 1946, iii, 150, no. 1642

674. Isbister
HU373 910   HU39SE 8
Fojut 1985

675. Kebister
HU45934567   HU44NE 7.1
DES (1987), 37

676. Kebister
HU45934567   HU44NE 7.2
DES (1987), 37

677. Kebister
HU45934567   HU44NE 7.3
DES (1987), 37

678. Kebister
HU45934567   HU44NE 7.4
DES (1987), 37

679. Kebister
HU45934567   HU44NE 7.5
DES (1987), 37

680. Kebister
HU45934567   HU44NE 7.6
DES (1987), 37

681. Kebister
HU45744543   HU44NE 8
DES (1987), 37

682. Knowe of Bakkasetter
HU37701550   HU31NE 1
1m(h)
RCAHMS 1946, iii, 43, no. 1172

683. Knowe of Willil
HU41122105   HU42SW 4
2m(h)

684. Knowe of Willol
HU41091812   HU41NW 7
Crescentic, 2m(h)
RCAHMS 1946, iii, 42, no. 1167;
Calder 1965, 82

685. Lainwall Knowe, Setter
HU20545050   HU25SW 17
Crescentic, 17m(l) x 1.7m(h)
RCAHMS 1946, iii, 151, no. 1654

686. Lamba Wick, Vementry
HU304 606   HU36SW 3
Circular, 5m
DES (1987), 36

687. Links of Quendale
HU38491286   HU31SE 5
Oval, 18m x 11m x 2m
RCAHMS 1946, iii, 42, no. 1163

688. Little Brownie's Knowe
HU17375669   HU15NE 7
1.3m(h)
RCAHMS 1946, iii, 150, no. 1627

689. Little Heogan, Papa Stour
HU18235985   HU15NE 11
2m(h)
RCAHMS 1946, iii, 155, no. 1700

690. Little Hoo Field, Papa Stour
HU18356129   HU16SE 7
20m x 18m x 2m
RCAHMS 1946, iii, 155, no. 1697

691. Littlure
HU20444784   HU24NW 13
Crescentic, 12m x 5.5m x 1m
RCAHMS 1946, iii, 151, no. 1648

692. Loch of Asta
HU41194109   HU44SW 8
Triangular, 12m x 2m(h)
RCAHMS 1946, iii, 124, no. 1519

693. Loch of Bardister
HU23635017   HU25SW 11
1m(h)
RCAHMS 1946, iii, 150, no. 1638

694. Loch of Breckon
HU21427802   HU27NW 7
Crescentic, 18m x 10m x 1.2m
RCAHMS 1946, iii, 97, no. 1373

695. Loch of Forratwatt
HU24454953   HU24NW 4.1
Crescentic, 0.6m(h)
RCAHMS 1946, iii, 150, no. 1635

696. Loch of Forratwatt
HU24484955   HU24NW 4.2
0.6m(h)
RCAHMS 1946, iii, 150, no. 1635

697. Loch of Garths
HU48436026   HU46SE 3
Crescentic, 15m x 6m x 1.3m
RCAHMS 1946, iii, 81, no. 1293

698. Loch of Grunnavoe
HU24974888   HU24NW 26
1.2m(h)
RCAHMS 1946, iii, 150, no. 1631;
Calder 1965, 85

699. Loch of Huesbreck
HU388 138   HU31SE 17
Crescentic, 16.7m(l) x 8.8m(b)
Calder 1965, 79

700. Loch of Kirkabister
HU49355821   HU45NE 18
Crescentic, 18m x 11m x 1.3m
RCAHMS 1946, iii, 81, no. 1294;
Calder 1965, 84

701. Loch of Kirkigarth
HU24024943   HU24NW 5
1m(h)
RCAHMS 1946, iii, 150, no. 1636

702. Loch of Kirkigarth
HU237 496   HU24NW 6
RCAHMS 1946, iii, 150, no. 1637

703. Loch of Niddister
HU27897558   HU27NE 12
Crescentic, 17m x 14m x 1.7m
RCAHMS 1946, iii, 97, no. 1372

704. Loch of Watsness
HU17795052   HU15SE 7
Crescentic, 8m(l) x 0.6m(h)

705. The Loch that Ebbs and Flows,
Papa Stour
HU16386142   HU16SE 15.1
20m x 16m x 2m

706. The Loch that Ebbs and Flows,
Papa Stour
HU16546129   HU16SE 15.2
Crescentic, 17m x 13m x 1.5m

707. Lower Loch of Setter
HU36819247   HU39SE 3
Circular, 16m x 1m(h)
RCAHMS 1946, iii, 97, no. 1370

708. Lower Loch of Setter
HU37049229   HU39SE 6

709. Midfield, Mousa
HU45842436   HU42SE 2
Crescentic, 1m(h)
RCAHMS 1946, iii, 55, no. 1207

710. Minn, West Burra
HU36203042   HU33SE 42
Crescentic, 13.5m x 11m x 2.5m
Hedges 1984, M103

711. Muckle Brownie's Knowe
HU17165639   HU15NE 6
Crescentic, 20m(l) x 2m(h)
RCAHMS 1946, iii, 150, no. 1626

712. Ness of Gruting
HU27684845   HU24NE 13
Crescentic, 15m(l) x 12m(b)
Calder 1958, 373, 375;
Winham 1980, vol. 2, 482

713. Noonsbrough
HU29575727   HU25NE 18.1
Crescentic, 1.6m(h)
RCAHMS 1946, iii, 111, no. 1452

714. Noonsbrough
HU29575727   HU25NE 18.2
Oval, 0.9m(h)
RCAHMS 1946, iii, 111, no. 1452

715. Noral Knowe
HU23685144   HU25SW 12
Crescentic, 1.7m(h)
RCAHMS 1946, iii, 150, no. 1639

716. Northbanks, Papa Stour
HU18326114   HU16SE 13
Crescentic, 13.5m x 13m x 1m

717. Orbister
HU31227675   HU37NW 5
9.1m x 7.3m x 0.9m
Calder 1965, 80

718. Papil, West Burra
HU36773155   HU33SE 41
Crescentic, 12m x 8m x 2m
Hedges 1984, M103

719. Punds
HU40211161   HU41SW 6
RCAHMS 1946, iii, 43, No. 1177;
Calder 1965, 83

720. Quildrin Knowe, Upper Dale
HU19365279   HU15SE 4
Crescentic, 1.4m(h)
RCAHMS 1946, iii, 151, no. 1661;
RCAHMS 1946, i, pl. 10, fig. 28

721. Sand House
HU34504727   HU34NW 5
10m x 8.5m x 0.9m
RCAHMS 1946, iii, 111, no. 1455

722. Sand of Meal, West Burra
HU374 354   HU33NE 12
Fojut 1985, 83

723. Scarfataing, Trondra
HU40153855   HU43NW 2
Oval, 7m x 4m x 0.7m
RCAHMS 1946, iii, 125, no. 1532;
Calder 1965, 85

724. Scarvister
HU20124855   HU24NW 14
Crescentic, 6.5m x 3.5m x 1m
RCAHMS 1946, iii, 151, no. 1648

725. Sefster
HU29975046   HU25SE 19
Circular, 24.4m x 2.7m(h)
RCAHMS 1946, iii, 110, no. 1448;
Calder 1965, 84

726. Sefster
HU30195020   HU35SW 15
Crescentic, 12m x 10m x 1m
RCAHMS 1946, iii, 111, no. 1457;
Calder 1965, 84

727. Setter, Papa Stour
HU17296026   HU16SE 9
1.5m(h)
RCAHMS 1946, iii, 155, no. 1699

728. Setter, West Burra
HU37993626   HU33NE 18
Crescentic, 6.5m x 4.5m x 1m
Hedges 1984, M113c

729. Skelberry
HU39301633   HU31NE 8.1
3m(h)
RCAHMS 1946, iii, 43, no. 1169

730. Skelberry
HU39311636   HU31NE 8.2
1.5m(h)
RCAHMS 1946, iii, 43, no. 1169

731. Skelberry
HU39311638   HU31NE 8.3
1m(h)
RCAHMS 1946, iii, 43, no. 1169

732. Skelberry
HU39371640   HU31NE 8.4
1m(h)
RCAHMS 1946, iii, 43, no. 1169

733. Skelberry
HU36548691   HU38NE 10
Crescentic, 19m x 15m x 2.1m

734. Skellister
HU46705470   HU45SE 20
7.6m x 4.5m x 0.9m
Calder 1965, 80

735. Sotersta
HU262 446   HU24SE 11
Elongated, 8m x 2.5m x 0.9m
DES (1981), 27

736. Sotersta
HU26094462   HU24SE 13
Possible

737. Sotra Water, Papa Stour
HU17285990   HU15NE 9
21.5m x 19m x 1.1m
RCAHMS 1946, iii, 155, no. 1693

738. Sotra Water, Papa Stour
HU17245990   HU15NE 17
0.5m(h)

739. South Ayre, Trondra
HU40043816   HU43NW 3
Oval, 5m x 2.5m x 0.4m
RCAHMS 1946, iii, 125, no. 1533;
Calder 1965, 85

740. South-Hill
HU35825034   HU35SE 5
1.3m(h)
Name Book (Shetland),1878, no. 2,
105; RCAHMS 1946, iii, 111,
no. 1454

741. Southvoe
HU39821475   HU31SE 6
RCAHMS 1946, iii, 43, no. 1173

742. Southvoe
HU39981444   HU31SE 7
Possible
RCAHMS 1946, iii, 43, no. 1174

743. Stanesland
HU21504884   HU24NW 11
Crescentic, 1.4m(h)
RCAHMS 1946, iii, 151, no. 1646

744. Stany Altar, Hevdigarth
HU20214911   HU24NW 18
3.8m x 2.4m x 0.5m
Name Book (Shetland), 1878,
no. 21, 198; RCAHMS 1946,
iii, 153, no. 1679

745. Staura Cottage
HU46663961   HU43NE 5
Crescentic, 1.5m(h)
DES (1972), 38; Whittle 1979, 167

746. Sunnybank, West Burra
HU37583379   HU33SE 3
15.5m x 7.3m x 1.5m
RCAHMS 1946, iii, 76, no. 1270;
Calder 1965, 83; Hedges and Hedges
1978; Whittle 1979, 170–1

747. Sweenister
HU42664611   HU44NW 4
Crescentic, 1.5m(h)
RCAHMS 1946, iii, 124, no. 1517

748. Swinister
HU17845112   HU15SE 6.1
2m(h)

749. Swinister
HU17845112   HU15SE 6.2
0.7m(h)

750. Swinister
HU42182442   HU42SW 2
Crescentic, 2m(h)
RCAHMS 1946, iii, 42, no. 1166;
Calder 1965, 82

751. Swinister
HU336 806   HU38SW 10
Crescentic, 14m(l)
DES (1978), 20

752. Symbister, East Burra
HU37062975   HU32NE 1.1
5m x 4m x 0.6m
RCAHMS 1946, iii, 76, no. 1275

753. Symbister, East Burra
HU37142984   HU32NE 1.2
8m x 7m x 0.5m
RCAHMS 1946, iii, 76, no. 1275

754. Symbister, East Burra
HU37172982   HU32NE 1.3
20m x 14m x 2.2m
RCAHMS 1946, iii, 76, no. 1275

755. Taingi Geo
HU40271436   HU41SW 7.1
RCAHMS 1946, iii, 43, nos 1175–6

756. Taingi Geo
HU40301436   HU41SW 7.2
RCAHMS 1946, iii, 43, no. 1180

757. Taingi Geo
HU40311439   HU41SW 7.3
RCAHMS 1946, iii, 43, no. 1180

758. Taingi Geo
HU403 143   HU41SW 7.4
RCAHMS 1946, iii, 43, no. 1175

759. Taingi Geo
HU403 143   HU41SW 7.5
RCAHMS 1946, iii, 43, no. 1175

760. Taingi Geo
HU403 143   HU41SW 7.6
RCAHMS 1946, iii, 43, no. 1176

761. Taingi Geo
HU403 143   HU41SW 7.7
RCAHMS 1946, iii, 43, no. 1176

762. Tang Wick
HU23357751   HU27NW 8
16m x 9.7m x 1.5m
Calder 1965, 80

763. Trowie Loch
HU47255378   HU45SE 6
Circular, 27.5m
Calder 1965, 80, no. 5

764. Tully Knowe, Skarpigarth
HU19834970   HU14NE 2
Crescentic, 12m(l) x 1.2m(h)
RCAHMS 1946, iii, 151, no. 1658

765. Tuni Garth
HU20625112   HU25SW 19.1
RCAHMS 1946, iii, 151, no. 1656

766. Tuni Garth
HU20645114   HU25SW 19.2
RCAHMS 1946, iii, 151, no. 1656

767. Turness
HU46985500   HU45NE 3
0.9m(h)
Calder 1965, 80

768. Utnabrake
HU40904017   HU44SW 9
Circular, 17m x 2m(h)
RCAHMS 1946, iii, 124, no. 1520

769. Vaila House, Vaila
HU22704685   HU24NW 22.1
7m x 4m x 1m
RCAHMS 1946, iii, 157, no. 1711

770. Vaila House, Vaila
HU22704685   HU24NW 22.2
RCAHMS 1946, iii, 157, no. 1711

771. Vaila House, Vaila
HU226 469   HU24NW 23.1
RCAHMS 1946, iii, 157, no. 1710

772. Vaila House, Vaila
HU226 469   HU24NW 23.2
RCAHMS 1946, iii, 157, no. 1710

773. Vatster
HU42764860   HU44NW 3
14m x 13m x 1.5m
RCAHMS 1946, iii, 124, no. 1515

774. Voe of Clousta
HU30915729   HU35NW 9
1m(h)
RCAHMS 1946, iii, 111, no. 1453

775. Voe of North House, East Burra
HU38003166   HU33SE 6
Crescentic, 14m x 12m x 0.8m
RCAHMS 1946, iii, 74, no. 1264;
Calder 1965, 83

776. Wadbister
HU39244659   HU34NE 13
Crescentic, 1m(h)

777. Wats Ness
HU17735089   HU15SE 3
Crescentic, 14m(l) x 0.8m(h)
RCAHMS 1946, iii, 151, no. 1660

778. Weisdale
HU39565345   HU35SE 1
Crescentic
RCAHMS 1946, iii, 123, no. 1511

779. West Burra Firth
HU25755766   HU25NE 16.1
Crescentic, 1.7m(h)
RCAHMS 1946, iii, 111, no. 1450;
Calder 1965, 84

780. West Burra Firth
HU25755766   HU25NE 16.2
Oval, 0.9m(h)
RCAHMS 1946, iii, 111, no. 1450;
Calder 1965, 84

781. Westerwick
HU28414277   HU24SE 1
RCAHMS 1946, iii, 111, no. 1456;
Moar 1949, ; Calder 1965, 84

782. West Lunna Voe
HU48406977   HU46NE 1.1
1m(h)
RCAHMS 1946, iii, 81, no. 1291

783. West Lunna Voe
HU48426979   HU46NE 1.2
Crescentic, 1.6m(h)
RCAHMS 1946, iii, 81, no. 1291

784. West Lunna Voe
HU48456946   HU46NE 2
2.5m(h)
RCAHMS 1946, iii, 81, no. 1292

785. Whirlie, Papa Stour
HU17115941   HU15NE 10
14m x 8m x 1.5m
RCAHMS 1946, iii, 155, no. 1694

786. Whirlie, Papa Stour
HU170 593   HU15NE 12
RCAHMS 1946, iii, 155, no. 1701

787. Whirwill Knowe
HU21015069   HU25SW 18
20m x 18m x 2m
RCAHMS 1946, iii, 151, no. 1655

788. Whitesness
HU25144755   HU24NE 14
1.4m(h)
RCAHMS 1946, iii, 150, no. 1633

789. Wick
HU441 393   HU43NW 7
RCAHMS 1946, iii, 72, no. 1250;
Calder 1965, 83

790. Willa Pund
HU22025679   HU25NW 6
18m x 12m x 1.8m
RCAHMS 1946, iii, 150, no. 1628;
Calder 1965, 85

791. Will Houll#
HU43732887   HU42NW 7
RCAHMS 1946, iii, 42, no. 1165

792. Will Houll
HU44442991   HU42NW 11
13m x 10m x 1.6m

Unst

793. Haroldswick#
HP637 126   HP61SW 15
Unknown number
Possible
Edmonston 1873, 286; RCAHMS
1946, iii, 139, 141–2,
nos 1568, 1585

794. Mailand#
HP60680148   HP60SW 11
Circular, 11m x 0.5m(h)
RCAHMS 1946, iii, 139, no. 1570;
Calder 1965, 85

795. Murrister#
HP609 914   HP60SW 10
RCAHMS 1946, iii, 139, no. 1570;
Calder 1965, 85

796. North House, Underhoull
HP57980422   HP50SE 14
Crescentic, 12m x 6m x 1m
RCAHMS 1946, iii, 139, no. 1571

797. Underhoull
HP57670432   HP50SE 20
Circular, 21.5m
RCAHMS 1946, iii, 140, no. 1575

Whalsay

798. East Loch of Skaw
HU59326655   HU56NE 10
RCAHMS 1946, iii, 86, no. 1327;
Calder 1965, 84

799. Huxter
HU56196222   HU56SE 5.1
RCAHMS 1946, iii, 87, no. 1330;
Calder 1965, 84

800. Huxter
HU56196222　　HU56SE 6.2
RCAHMS 1946, iii, 87, no. 1330;
Calder 1965, 84

801. Infants Gairdie, Brough
HU55296475　　HU56SE 6
Crescentic, 1.5m(h)
RCAHMS 1946, iii, 86, no. 1325;
Calder 1965, 84

802. Isbister#
HU58　64　　HU56SE 8
RCAHMS 1946, iii, 87, no. 1329;
Calder 1965, 84

803. Knowe of Willerhoull, Isbister
HU57896402　　HU56SE 7
RCAHMS 1946, iii, 86, no. 1328

804. Loch of Sandwick
HU53856170　　HU56SW 3
Crescentic, 16m x 13m x 3m
RCAHMS 1946, iii, 87, no. 1332

805. Mutter Knowe
HU58666633　　HU56NE 11
RCAHMS 1946, iii, 86, no. 1326;
Calder 1965, 84

806. Oo Knowe
HU56586556　　HU56NE 9
Crescentic
RCAHMS 1946, iii, 86, no. 1324

807. Sandwick, Whalsay
HU53906161　　HU56SW 2
10m x 6.5m x 1.2m
RCAHMS 1946, iii, 86–7,
nos 1322, 1336;
DES (1956), 26; Calder 1965,
77, nos 11–12

808. Whirlie#
HU54526160　　HU56SW 4
RCAHMS 1946, iii, 87, no. 1331

Yell

809. Brocken Burn#
HU48　93　　HU49SE 5
Unknown number
Irvine 1887, 218; RCAHMS 1946,
iii, 165, no. 1728; Calder 1965, 86

810. Harpadale
HP52450472　　HP50SW 9
RCAHMS 1946, iii, 168, no. 1751

811. Houbs of Setter
HU49109147　　HU49SE 8

812. Loch of Birriesgirt
HU44089114　　HU49SW 2
Circular, 5.5m

813. Roseville, Burravoe
HU51658002　　HU58SW 3
2m(h)
RCAHMS 1946, iii, 165, no. 1729

STRATHCLYDE REGION

Argyll and Bute District

814. Allt Nan Creamh
NR67282982　　NR62NE 30
Crescentic, 8m x 7.5m x 0.6m

815. Beachmeanach
NR69394246　　NR64SE 32
Crescentic, 10m x 9m x 1m

816. Borraichill Mor, Bridgend, Islay
NR30906521　　NR36NW 6

817. Borraichill Mor, Bridgend, Islay
NR307 652　　NR36NW 7
Crescentic
DES (1981), 29

818. Borraichill Mor, Bridgend, Islay
NR31646452　　NR36SW 19
Crescentic, 11m x 9m x 1.3m

819. Borraichill Mor, Bridgend, Islay
NR31896452　　NR36SW 20
Circular, 7m x 1.2m(h)

820. Mecknoch

NS045 588　　NS05NW 16
Oval, 10m x 7m x 1.4m
DES (1987), 41-2; DES (1988), 23

Cumnock and Doon District

821. Whitefield
NS70403069　　NS73SW 6
Oval, 7m x 6m x 0.8m
Possible

Cunninghame District

822. Glaister Farm
NR927 350　　NR93NW 11
Lehane (this volume)

823. Glaister Farm
NR928 349　　NR93SW 74
Lehane (this volume)

824. Glaister Farm
NR928 349　　NR93SW 75
Lehane (this volume)

825. Machrie North 1, Arran
NR89963438　　NR83SE 30
Crescentic, 10m x 1.7m x 0.7m
Possible

826. Machrie North, Arran
NR89933433　　NR83SE 32
Crescentic, 12m(l) x 9m(b)
Lehane (this volume)

827. Machrie North, Arran
NR89813408　　NR83SE 33
Lehane (this volume)

828. Machrie North, Arran
NR91793368　　NR93SW 73
11.3m(l) x 9.9m(b)
Lehane (this volume)

829. Machrie North, Arran
NGR not available
1.2m(l) x 0.1m(h)
Lehane (this volume)

830. Machrie North, Arran
NR90023438　　NR93SW 77
Lehane (this volume)

TAYSIDE REGION

Perth and Kinross District

831. Ashintully
NO10416220　　NO16SW 99
Crescentic, 7.5m x 4.4m x 0.5m
RCAHMS 1990, no. 163

832. Burnside of Drimmie
NO17225236　　NO15SE 42
Crescentic, 8.1m x 0.5m(h)
RCAHMS 1990, no. 164

833. Craigton
NO12485843　　NO15NW 28
Crescentic, 8.5m x 5.6m x 0.5m
RCAHMS 1990, no. 165

834. Creag Bhreac
NO06986747　　NO06NE 30
6m x 4m x 0.7m
RCAHMS 1990, no. 166(1)

835. Creag Bhreac
NO07056745　　NO06NE 31
Circular, 4m x 0.5m(h)
RCAHMS 1990, no. 166(2)

836. Creag Dubh-Leitir, Glenfernate Lodge
NO05406511　　NO06NE 37
8.4m x 4.8m x 0.7m
RCAHMS 1990, no. 167

837. Drumderrach
NO27975076　　NO25SE 42
12.3m x 11.2m x 0.5m
RCAHMS 1990, no. 168

838. Dulater
NO09374813　　NO04NE 23
Crescentic, 6.7m x 5m x 0.5m
RCAHMS 1990, no. 169

839. Glenkilrie
NO12796234　　NO16SW 72
Crescentic, 11m x 0.8m(h)
RCAHMS 1990, no. 170

840. Heatheryhaugh
NO18905100　　NO15SE 39.1
Crescentic, 9.8m x 8m x 0.5m
RCAHMS 1990, no. 171

841. Heatheryhaugh
NO18905100　　NO15SE 39.2
Possible
RCAHMS 1990, no. 171

842. Hill of Alyth
NO22985024　　NO25SW 21
Oval, 4.5m x 3.5m x 0.6m
RCAHMS 1990, no. 172(1)

843. Hill of Alyth
NO22725066　　NO25SW 24
8m x 5.5m x 0.6m
RCAHMS 1990, no. 172(2)

844. Loch Benachally
NO07175097　　NO05SE 45
Crescentic, 10m x 10m x 0.9m
RCAHMS 1990, no. 173

845. Loch Charles, Woodhill
NO08805437　　NO05SE 60
9.2m x 5.6m x 0.6m
RCAHMS 1990, no. 174(1)

846. Loch Charles, Woodhill
NO09365398　　NO05SE 61
Crescentic, 7.5m x 5m x 0.6m
RCAHMS 1990, no. 174(2)

847. Pitcarmick
NO07415580　　NO05NE 125
Crescentic, 9m x 6.5m x 0.9m
RCAHMS 1990, no. 175(2)

848. Pitcarmick
NO08235556　　NO05NE 126
Crescentic, 8.5m x 5.3m x 0.5m
RCAHMS 1990, no. 175(1)

849. Rochallie
NO14235065　　NO15SW 29
Crescentic, 8.3m x 0.5m(h)
RCAHMS 1990, no. 176

850. Smyrna
NO18885330　　NO15SE 51
Crescentic, 9.7m x 4.9m x 0.5m
RCAHMS 1990, no. 177

851. Torr Lochaidh
NO14326430　　NO16SW 60
Crescentic, 7.5m x 4.5m x 0.5m
RCAHMS 1990, no. 178

852. Uchd na H-Anaile
NO08556610　　NO06NE 17
Crescentic, 9.3m x 6.5m x 1m
RCAHMS 1990, no. 179(1)

853. Uchd na H-Anaile
NO08516646　　NO06NE 18
Crescentic, 6.5m x 3.5m x 0.6m
RCAHMS 1990, no. 179(2)

854. Welton of Creuchies
NO19704979　　NO14NE 78
Crescentic, 8.7m x 0.7m(h)
RCAHMS 1990, no. 180(3)

855. Welton of Creuchies
NO20234938　　NO24NW 55
14.2m x 8.2m x 0.4m
RCAHMS 1990, no. 180(5)

856. Welton of Creuchies
NO20444988　　NO24NW 56
Crescentic, 9.2m x 8.2m x 0.4m
RCAHMS 1990, no. 180(2)

857. Welton of Creuchies
NO20564995　　NO24NW 57
Crescentic, 11.2m x 6.3m x 0.6m
RCAHMS 1990, no. 180(1)

858. Welton of Creuchies
NO20204943　　NO24NW 59
Crescentic, 10.5m x 0.6m(h)
Stat. Acct. vi (1793), 406;
RCAHMS 1990, no. 180(4)

BIBLIOGRAPHY

ALLEN, J.W. 1980 *A preliminary report of a survey of the archaeological monuments of Papa Stour, Shetland.* Unpublished report.

ANDERSON, J. 1873 Notice on the excavation of 'Kenny's Cairn', on the Hill of Bruan; Cairn Righ, near Yarhouse; The Warth Hill Cairn, Duncansby; and several smaller sepulchral cairns in Caithness. *PSAS* **ix** (1870–2), 292–6.

BAIN, G. 1893 *History of Nairnshire.* Nairn.

BATEY, C.E. 1984 *Caithness coastal survey 1980–82: Dunnet Head to Ousdale.* Durham University, Department of Archaeology Occasional Paper No. 3.

BLACK, G.F. 1891 Report on the archaeological examination of the Culbin Sands, Elginshire, obtained under the Victoria Jubilee gift of his excellency Dr R. H. Gunning. *PSAS* **xxv** (1890–1), 434–511.

CALDER, C.S.T. 1958 Report on the discovery of numerous Stone Age house-sites in Shetland. *PSAS* **lxxxix** (1955–6), 340–97.

CALDER, C.S.T. 1965 Cairns, Neolithic houses and burnt mounds in Shetland. *PSAS* **xcvi** (1962–3), 37–86.

CHALMERS, J.H. 1962 Notice of remains found under a cairn, surrounded by upright stones, on the farm of Burreldales, parish of Auchterless, Aberdeenshire, in a letter to the Secretary. *PSAS* **iv** (1860–2), 429–31.

CRAW, J.H. 1922 Early types of burial in Berwickshire. *HBNC* **xxiv** (1919–22), 153–94.

DES (date) *Discovery and excavation in Scotland.* Annual publication of Scottish Regional Group, Council for British Archaeology.

EDMONSON, T. 1873 Notes on some recent excavations in the Island of Unst, Shetland, and of the collection of stone vessels, implements etc., thus obtained for the Society's museum. *PSAS* **ix** (1870–2), 283–7.

FOJUT, N. 1985 Some thoughts on the Shetland Iron Age. In B. Smith (ed.), *Shetland archaeology — New work in Shetland in the 1970s*, 47–84. Lerwick.

GAJ Glasgow Archaeological Journal

HBNC History of the Berwickshire Naturalists' Club

HEDGES, J.W. 1974 The burnt mounds at Liddle Farm, Orkney. *Current Archaeology* **4** (1973–4), 251–3.

HEDGES, J.W. 1977 Excavation of two Orcadian Burnt Mounds at Liddle and Beaquoy. *PSAS* **106** (1974–5), 39–98.

HEDGES, J.W. 1984 Gordon Parry's West Burra survey, *GAJ* **11** (1984), 41–59.

HEDGES, J.W. and HEDGES, M.E. 1978 Summary report — Tougs, Burra Isle, Shetland. *PPS* **44** (d1978), 455.

HEDGES, J.W. 1979 The excavation of the Knowes of Quoyscottia, Orkney: a cemetery of the first millenium BC. *PSAS* **108** (1976–7), 130–65.

HENSHALL, A.S. *1963 The chambered tombs of Scotland.* Edinburgh.

HUNT, J. 1866 Report on explorations into the archaic anthropology of the islands of Unst, Bressay and the mainland of Zetland. *Memoirs of the Society of Antiquaries of London* **2** (1865–6), 300–2.

HUNTER, J.R. (ed.) 1984 *Fair Isle Survey: interim report.* Bradford University Schools of Archaeological Sciences and Physics, Occasional Paper No. 6.

HUNTER, J.R. (ed.) 1985 *Fair Isle survey: interim report.* Bradford University Schools of Archaeological Sciences and Physics, Occasional Paper no. 5.

HUNTER, J.R. (ed.) 1986 *Fair Isle survey: interim report.* Bradford University Schools of Archaeological Sciences and Physics, Occasional Paper No. 7.

HUNTER, J.R. (ed.) 1987 *Fair Isle survey: interim report.* Bradford University Schools of Archaeological Sciences and Physics, Occasional Paper No. 8.

IRVINE, J.T. 1887 Notes on some prehistoric burial-places and standing stones on the Island of Yell, Shetland. *PSAS* **xxii** (1886–7), 215–19.

LINTON, H. 1876 Notice of a collection of flint arrowheads and bronze and iron relics from the site of an ancient settlement recently discovered in the Culbin Sands, near Findhorn, Morayshire. *PSAS* **xi** (1874–6), 543–6.

LONGWORTH, I.A. 1963 An Early Iron Age vessel from Muckle Skerry. *PSAS* **xcvi** (1962–3), 354–5.

MARWICK, H. 1925 Antiquarian notes on Papa Westray. *POAS* **3** (1924–5), 31–47.

MARWICK, H. 1927 Antiquarian notes on Stronsay. *POAS* **5** (1926–7), 61–8.

MERCER, R.J. 1980 *Archaeological Field Survey in Northern Scotland, Vol. I, 1976–79.* University of Edinburgh, Department of Archaeology, Occasional Paper No. 4.

MERCER, R.J. 1981 *Archaeological Field Survey in Northern Scotland, Vol. II, 1980–81.* University of Edinburgh, Department of Archaeology, Occasional Paper No. 7.

MERCER, R.J. 1985 *Archaeological Field Survey in Northern Scotland, Vol. III, 1982–83.* University of Edinburgh, Department of Archaeology, Occasional Paper No. 11.

MERCER, R.J. (forthcoming) *Archaeological Field Survey in Northern Scotland, Vol. IV, 1984– .*

MILLER, R. 1967 Landuse by summer-shielings. *Scottish Studies* **11** (1967), 193–221.

MITCHELL, A. 1870 On some remarkable discoveries of rude stone implements. *PSAS* **vii** (1866–8), 118–34.

MOAR, P. 1949 Pottery from Westerwick, Shetland. *PSAS* **lxxxiii** (1948–9), 231.

MORRIS, R.W.B. 1981 *Prehistoric rock art of southern Scotland.* British Archaeological Reports, British Series 86, Oxford.

MORRISON, I. 1973 *The North Sea Earls.* London.

MORRISON, J. 1883 Archaeological finds in the east of Moray. *Transactions of the Inverness Scientific Society and Field Club* **II** (1880–3), 36–47.

NAME BOOK (county) Original Name Books of the Ordnance Survey.

NEIL, N.R.J. 1981 A Bronze Age burial mound at Holland, St Ola, Orkney, *GAJ* **8** (1981), 32–45.

NSA *The new statistical account of Scotland* (Edinburgh, 1845).

PETRIE, G. 1857 Description of antiquities in Orkney recently examined with illustrative drawings. *PSAS* **ii** (1854–7), 56–62.

PETRIE, G. 1868 Notice of a barrow containing cists, on the farm of Newbigging, near Kirkwall; and at Isbister, in the parish of Rendall, Orkney. *PSAS* **vi** (1864–6), 411–18.

PETRIE, G. 1890 Notice of the brochs or large round towers of Orkney with plans, sections and drawings, and tables of measurements of Orkney and Shetland brochs. *Archaeologia Scotica* **5** (1890), 71–94.

POAS Proceedings of the Orkney Antiquarian Society

PPS Proceedings of the Prehistoric Society

PSAS Proceedings of the Society of Antiquaries of Scotland

RCAHMS 1911a The Royal Commission on the Ancient and Historical Monuments and Constructions of Scotland. *Second report and inventory of monuments and constructions in the County of Sutherland.* Edinburgh.

RCAHMS 1911b The Royal Commission on the Ancient and Historical Monuments and Constructions of Scotland. *Third report and inventory of monuments and constructions in the County of Caithness.* Edinburgh.

RCAHMS 1915 The Royal Commission on the Ancient and Historical Monuments and Constructions of Scotland. *Sixth report and inventory of monuments and constructions in the County of Berwick.* Edinburgh.

RCAHMS 1946 The Royal Commission on the Ancient Monuments of Scotland. *Twelfth report with an inventory of the ancient monuments of Orkney and Shetland.* Edinburgh.

RCAHMS 1979 Archaeological Sites and Monuments Series 6. *Easter Ross, Ross and Cromarty District, Highland Region.*

RCAHMS 1980a Archaeological Sites and Monuments Series 10. *Berwickshire District, Borders Region.*

RCAHMS 1980b Archaeological Sites and Monuments Series 11. *Sanday and North Ronaldsay, Orkney Islands Area.*

RCAHMS 1982 Archaeological Sites and Monuments Series 16. *Rousay, Egilsay and Wyre, Orkney Islands Area.*

RCAHMS 1983 Archaeological Sites and Monuments Series 19. *Papa Westray and Westray, Orkney Islands Area.*

RCAHMS 1984a Archaeological Sites and Monuments Series 19. *North Kincardine, Kincardine and Deeside District, Grampian Region.*

RCAHMS 1984b Archaeological Sites and Monuments Series 23. *Eday and Stronsay, Orkney Islands Area.*

RCAHMS 1987 Archaeological Sites and Monuments Series 26. *East Rhins, Wigtown District, Dumfries and Galloway Region.*

RCAHMS 1988 Archaeological Sites and Monuments Series 28. *Midlothian (prehistoric to early historic), Midlothian District, Lothian Region.*

RCAHMS 1989 Archaeological Sites and Monuments Series 29. *Hoy and Waas, Orkney Islands Area.*

RCAHMS 1990 The Royal Commission on the Ancient and Historical Monuments of Scotland. *North-East Perth: an archaeological survey.*

RENFREW, A.C. 1979 *Investigations in Orkney.* Report of the Research Committee of the Society of Antiquaries of London, No. xxxviii. London.

RHIND, A.H. 1857 Notes of excavations of tumuli in Caithness made in the summer of 1856. *PSAS* **ii** (1854–7), 372–6.

RUSSELL-WHITE, C. and BARBER, J. 1987 Burnt mounds in the East Rhins of Galloway. Central Excavation Unit and Ancient Monuments Laboratory Branch Report 1987, Edinburgh, 55–61.

SIMPSON, J.Y. 1866 On ancient sculpturings of cups and concentric rings etc. *PSAS* **vi** (1864–6), appendix 40.

STAIR, THE EARL OF 1874 Note of a burnt cairn dug out in Culcaldie Moss, near Lochinch, Wigtownshire. *PSAS* **x** (1872–4), 700–1.

STAT. ACCT. *The statistical account of Scotland.* (Edinburgh, 1791–9).

STEEDMAN, K.A. 1980 The archaeology of the Deerness Peninsula, Orkney. BA dissertation, Department of Archaeology, University of Durham.

STUART, C. 1872 On British cists discovered at Frenchlaw and Edington Hill, Berwickshire. *HBNC* **vi** (1869–72), 349–50.

STUART, J. 1866 Notice of cairns recently examined on the estate of Rothie, Aberdeenshire. *PSAS* **vi** (1864–6), 217–18.

WHITTLE, A. 1979 Scord of Brouster. *Current Archaeology* **65** (1979), 167–70.

WINHAM, R.P. 1980 Site morphology, location and distribution: a survey of the settlement archaeology of Shetland, investigating man-environment interactions through time. M. Phil. thesis, University of Southampton.

APPENDIX 3

List of contributors to this volume

(In order of contribution)

D. POWER — Archaeological Survey of Co. Cork, c/o Dept. of Archaeology, University College Cork.

T. CONDIT — Sites and Monuments Record Office, Office of Public Works, Dublin.

F. MITCHELL — The Gardener's Cottage, Townley Hall, Drogheda, Co. Louth.

J. SHEEHAN — Dept. of Archaeology, University College Cork.

M. RYAN — National Museum of Ireland, Dublin.

C. WALSH — Planning Dept., Dublin Corporation.

S. CHERRY — National Museum of Ireland, Dublin 2.

A. BRINDLEY — Archaeological Survey of Ireland, Office of Public Works.

J. LANTING — Biologisch-Archaeologisch Institut, Groiningen, Holland.

J. BARBER — Archaeological Operations and Conservation (AOC), Scottish Development Dept., Fleming House, 28–31 Kinnaird Park, Newcraighall, Edinburgh.

C. RUSSELL-WHITE — AOC, Scottish Development Department.

S.P. HALLIDAY — Royal Commission on the Ancient and Historical Monuments of Scotland, 54 Melville St, Edinburgh.

D. LEHANE — AOC, Scottish Development Department.

A. HAGGERTY — AOC, Scottish Development Department.

C.E. LOWE — AOC, Scottish Development Department.

O. OWEN — AOC, Scottish Development Department.

M.A. HODDER — Planning Dept., Sandwell Metropolitan Council, West Bromwich, England.

M. NIXON — 'Greenwood', Blind Lane, Tamworth-in-Arden, Solihull, West Midlands.

R.S. KELLY — Gwynedd Archaeological Trust, College Rd, Bangor, Wales.

G. WILLIAMS — Dyfed Archaeological Trust, The Old Palace, Abergwili, Carmarthen, Dyfed.

T. LARSSON — Dept. of Archaeology, University of Umea, Umea, Sweden.

D. HURL — Archaeological Survey of Northern Ireland, 66 Balmoral Avenue, Belfast.

D. Ó DRISCEÓIL — 'Tosca', 52 Beaumont Drive, Ballintemple, Cork.

M.G.L. BAILLIE — Palaeoecology Laboratory, Queen's University, Belfast.

V. M. BUCKLEY — Archaeological Survey of Ireland, Office of Public Works, Dublin.

J. HUNTER — Dept. of Archaeological Sciences, University of Bradford, West Yorkshire.

S. DOCKRILL — Dept. of Archaeological Sciences, University of Bradford, West Yorkshire.

I. MÁTÉ — AOC, Scottish Development Department.

L. FERGUSON — Royal Commission on the Ancient and Historical Monuments of Scotland.